CLOSE TO THE WIND

To Noël

With best wishes
from

Michael Heseltine

The author

CLOSE TO THE WIND

by

MICHAEL TREVOR HASLAM

The Memoir Club

© Michael Trevor Haslam 2006

First published in 2006 by
The Memoir Club
Stanhope Old Hall
Stanhope
Weardale
County Durham

British Library Cataloguing in
Publication Data.
A catalogue record for this book
is available from the
British Library

ISBN: 1-84104-143-2

Typeset by TW Typesetting, Plymouth, Devon
Printed and bound by CPI Antony Rowe, Eastbourne

Dedication

*To Shirley, who has supported me
and my foibles through fifty years*

Contents

List of illustrations

Foreword

Shrinks – well they are all a bit eccentric, aren't they?

Perhaps Michael's eccentricity is his curiosity – curiosity reinforced by a dogged determination to explore any query or question which has caught his imagination. The reader will find many examples of strange and often amusing tales of investigations of some odd topic that has caught his interest. His is an endlessly inquisitive mind – that is to say, an ideal instrument for research.

I think it important whilst reading this Memoir to remember it was written for the most part in prison, in longhand and without the ability to refer to any reference media. It shows a prodigious memory for facts, details and dates. The book relates the development of a first-class career, taking us from a joyful childhood up through an idyllic university education to the various phases of his medical and psychiatric qualifications.

He has gradually moved to the forefront of experimental psychiatry, and his work has been praised by many psychiatric organisations throughout the world. This is the sure and steady progress of a consultant's career, passing through and coping with the endlessly changing systems and problems of the NHS. He describes a happy life, a happy marriage, a happy family, experiencing many of the joys of life: parenthood, sport, worldwide travel and the pleasures of the arts.

But no life passes without some misfortune. Especially there was the fearful illness of his son at age thirteen; in his early life the death of his father, and, more recently, the loss of his mother after a long period of devoted care. Then, not least, the final scorn poured out on him, at first by the media and then by the Law itself.

It is ironic to think that it was perhaps the avant-garde experiments in fields such as hypnotism, the Kirlian Photography, vaginismus, etc. which mystified the jury at the trial and left them with an unpleasant suspicion that all was not in the aid of science. Their sympathies probably lay with the patients rather than with the well-fed scientist.

The book gives Michael the opportunity, long denied, for him to state his case clearly and without distortion either by media or the process of a trial. He also has the chance to make a strong indictment of the Health Inquiry. He believes himself innocent. If he is not then who, but a madman, would sue the *Sunday Times* with a guilty conscience?

Another of his many virtues has been his loyalty to friends, always keeping in touch, and it was, as he says, a great source of comfort for him to have so many ready to support him in his hour of need.

But his staunchest support has come from his wife, Shirley, and his family. Their devout Christian upbringing has resulted in a close-knit unit strongly supporting the family honour. It is now hoped that with the aid of the Criminal Case Review Commission they will be successful in clearing his name in the not too distant future.

A long spell with hepatitis did, he says, give him time to finish his book *Psychiatry made Simple*. He had even more time at his disposal in prison to finish these Memoirs. Let us hope that in his future retirement his time will be his own and he will be able to regale us with more tales of the Curious.

Christopher Davy

Acknowledgements

The author would like to express his gratitude to his wife Shirley and to Michael, Fiona and Melanie for their support in the writing of this manuscript and for their loyalty during his troubles. He is grateful also to the Society of Clinical Psychiatrists, and to the many friends, colleagues and ex-patients who in various ways have offered support and solace and whom it would be invidious to name personally.

Thanks too are due to Christopher Davy, for agreeing to carry out the taxing duty of writing a foreword to this manuscript, and to the staff of the Memoir Club for their attentive assistance.

Author's notes

When asked to write one's biography, the first reaction is to feel flattered. Then one asks oneself why? Doubts as to the level of interest sweep over one — will it sell? But does that matter; is it not for self-satisfaction that one creates a record of one's life?

How to set it out? It would be too easy to begin to sound pompous. It must be readable. A catalogue of events, dry and baldly presented, would serve only as an inducement to sleep in the reader — useful for insomniacs but few else. Should it have humour? Yes, I think so. There is plenty to laugh at in most people's lives, not least mine. Pathos? There has been a good slice of that too. 'Forbid it Lord' too, 'that I should boast' — except where necessary!

Then one must set it out. There is a logic in tracing life in chronological order — a chapter on babyhood perhaps — the seven ages of man? Yet there are themes in life — interests, challenges — that run through over the years, which in piecing together a character, putting across the totality of one's personality, cannot be compartmentalized chronologically but needs must be picked out as something to be dwelt on across the decades of time.

At the time of writing I am in my early seventies. My father died at 51 at the end of the Second World War. In many ways I am like him. Yet my mother died when nearly 103. Hopefully I have her longevity genes, since I am enjoying life and hope for a couple of decades yet. But, 'Vain man, this very night thine soul may be required of thee!'

Seven chapters for seven decades — and perhaps an addendum for the sixth edition? No, there must be a mixing of these two concepts. Chronology must somehow sit easily with special interest groupings. One must see how the themes develop — and one must not bore with excessive length.

Middlemarch runs to some 800 pages but it was written at a time when evenings were long. There was no radio, no TV. Evening entertainment under the oil lamps of winter, apart from a singsong around the piano and a little crochet work, could be difficult without a good book. The collection of books called the Bible has some 1,500 pages or more. Yet, many successful, more modern books can be pithy and captivating, but be read in one weekend. Research suggests, other than for the extra-famous, the Churchills and Mandelas of this world, that some 75,000 words should suffice. Perhaps some fifteen short sharp chapters. There will have to be some statement of fact at the beginning to set the scene. Let us without more ado then, commence.

The family escutcheon

CHAPTER 1

In the beginning

WHO AM I, for Heaven's sake? Well, I was born, and still am, Michael Trevor Haslam, at Sister Pulleyn's nursing home in Burley, Leeds on 7 February 1934. My father put the welcome news in the newspapers on 8 February, because that is what he thought. But it was four minutes to midnight on the seventh, as Mother assured him, and she should know.

Why Trevor? Is there a Welsh connection? No. I guess I am the usual English genetic mixture: a dollop of Anglo-Saxon, a few smidgens of Norman-French (at eight smidgens to the dollop) and no doubt some smidgens of Celtic too. I had an Irish great-great-granny, who my uncle said smoked a clay pipe, and a grandmother who before marriage was a Kaye. I suppose they might have come from Scotland once upon a time but no Welsh. The name Haslam, in fact, derives from Hazleham, a territorial name from North Derbyshire. I like to think my ancestors shared a cave with Peverill of the Peak. So why Trevor? Well, my mother wanted Paul because she liked it. My father's side wanted Gerald as the second name, as my father was called Gerald. So my mother told the registrar Trevor, because she'd had a friend of that name when she was young!

What of the escutcheon? Any Dukes or Earls – or come to that any murderers? If one researches one's family tree, one does not always come up with what one wants to find! My father when young looked very like the Duke of Windsor but George V had never been about at the right time! Richard Arkwright, who invented the 'Spinning Jenny', was a distant cousin, and Percy had run away to sea and then became a postman.

Now Great-Uncle Elam Barley turned out to have been the illegitimate offspring of a girl with whom he was raised, by what actually were his grandparents, as brother and sister. Who the father was nobody said. He became a minister in the Congregational Church and wrote a book of sermons. There's exciting for you, as the Welsh would say. Then there was the daughter of a Lady Troutbeck some generations back who ran away with a lad called Peacock, the coachman, and eloped. Or so it was said. The parents disowned her and the page in the church records was said to have been torn out. Uncle Bertie tried to establish the connection, thinking there might be money in it, but he never got anywhere. Their grandson, the last of the Peacock line, lived in Ouseburn near York and died there at the age of twenty-three when he was run over by a horse and cart.

1

My progenitor: Gerald Haslam

My father Gerald came of a family of teachers and was actually born in Totton, 'the biggest village in England', near Southampton, in 1895. Later the family moved to Sheffield and grandfather, William Arthur, before my arrival ran a private school near Hunters Bar. My father had three sisters, two of whom, Winnie and Ethel, remained single, whilst Zoë married and produced two cousins for me, Jean and Zoë. More will be heard of Winnie. She had bad eyes. She inherited grandfather's house. She was engaged and her fiancé was killed in the First World War. Ethel, also a teacher, lived with her and was engaged to 'Uncle' Leonard. Winnie didn't like him. He had suffered gassing in the war and was badly affected in his chest. Ethel was the breadwinner and if she had married, in those days, would have lost her teaching job. So they stayed engaged for forty years and then he died. Father's mother, Miss Kaye, came from a family of watchmakers in Leeds. The Haslams had come from Manchester before father was born, an ancestor curiously having married a girl whose family contested the claim of Arkwright's to the 'Spinning Jenny'.

Mother was born Edna Beatrice Oldfield in Sheffield, of a Derbyshire family, her father a director of an insurance company and one of the first car owners in the city. They lived on Rustlings Road by the park. My mother was always called Nettie, and indeed it is on her gravestone in Crayke churchyard. It was her father's second marriage after his first wife died, and my grandmother was the young second wife – 'she's almost as young as his children, and she not buried this two year since!' They had three children, my mother the eldest, and two boys, Roger and Edgar, who both went into banking. There must have been some sporting genes in the Oldfields or Barleys, since Edgar played tennis for Yorkshire and later golf for the Abbeydale Club. My mother was also a very good tennis player at club level, as was my father, both playing for the Hallamshire Club where they met for the second time whilst my father was at Sheffield University, later to become a chartered accountant. During the war he had been in the Queen's Own Yorkshire Dragoons and had been injured and had first met my mother, who when in her teens had done some voluntary hospital visiting, and had talked with him there while he convalesced.

They married at St Augustine's Church at Hunters Bar in Sheffield and went to live in Moor Oaks Road. Mother before marriage had written children's stories and poems, many of which had been published (some genes from Elam Barley's stock, no doubt). To jump ahead, one of the most moving and poignant memories I have is of my son reading one of these poems at her funeral in Crayke Church in 2001:

'A whisper is blown by the breeze
A whisper that summer is near
A message from over the seas
A message that brings good cheer . . .'

For her hundredth birthday I collected up all her literary works that I could find and had them published privately for her as a birthday present. She was very chuffed.

So father progressed in accountancy; they played tennis and delayed a family until he got promotion and became the company secretary of a woollen manufacturers, Thomas Burnley & Sons of Gomersall, near Leeds, and they moved to live in West Park in Leeds. By then, of the four grandparents I might have had, only my mother's mother was alive, and I was born, with some difficulty, in 1934 when Mother was thirty-five. I was the only child. 'Never again,' said Mother! Though I do not recall it (and have never had hypnotherapy to recover birth trauma!), I was there.

Memories of one's very early life are fickle, fragmentary and often muddled with things one has been told. We lived in a newish house. Our immediate neighbours were John and Dolly Baker (of Baker-Bessamer Fame) whose son Anthony was a few months younger than me; we became lifelong friends. They say you rarely remember anything before about two or three years of age. When the Second World War started I would be about five. Our telephone number was 52809 and father's car, CWR 740! Those useless facts along with the declining of *mensa*, a table, have stayed with me for sixty years or more. Would that I could recall last year as clearly. I recall having to sit on my potty until I'd finished when on holiday at Sandsend, which may explain my later slightly obsessional traits! And having presumably had a tantrum in my pushchair, being scared out of my wits by a passing tram driver who shook the strap (which they had, for some reason) at me. I thought he might come and beat me with it!

I recall my father showing me a field mouse's nest under a flat stone step in our garden, and teaching me to skim stones by some lake, I suppose on an early holiday in the Lake District. It is strange how these little snippets come to mind. What else is stored in the brain, I wonder, waiting to be unearthed, or perhaps lying dormant forever? I recall that he, John Baker, and the Alcocks, had guns in two Shoots, one near Sutton Bank, and one at Rudston near Bridlington. On occasion we would all drive over, and, once, I was allowed a shot, which knocked me off my feet! Other close friends at that time were Tom Haigh who lived up the road, and the Hardcastle girls, Joyce and Mavis, who lived near the West Park parade of shops, and Tony Townend, whose older sister had to go into the Land Army when the war got going in earnest.

How did the war affect us, in the outskirts of Leeds? To a child of five rising six, it was the small practical things that one remembers. We all had gas masks. My very first was shaped like a clown's face, to make it less frightening to put on, but after a year I got a grown-up type, made of black rubber, with a transparent plastic type of eyepiece and a snout with special adaptors screwed on to it for particular types of poisonous gas, which one breathed through. We had to carry this everywhere with us and had gas mask practices at school.

I wore a small bracelet with my name and address and identity number on it – KGMP.114.3! It was silver in colour, on a chain. Everybody had one. I also had a liberty bodice! This one wore in the winter – not quite stitched into it like little Chinese children – but it was strong and warm since, apart from a fire in the grate and gas fires in the bedrooms, there was no central heating, and the winters of the forties were much severer than they are today. I also had a belt made out of some sort of early rubber, round my waist to cover my tummy button which had a bulge which I now know to have been a para-umbilical hernia. When I was four I had to go back to the nursing home to have it repaired and then I could go to school without this problem. The nurse in the operating theatre gave me some perfume to smell. 'Isn't it nice? Now try smelling this one.' I woke up in a bed sometime later and was sick on the sheets. Such is memory.

My first school was Far Headingley Kindergarten, run by a Miss Davies. We used to walk, my mother and I, from home to the school and back, and do this twice a day. We must have covered two miles! I had a little satchel and my gas mask in a case which later housed my first camera, and which I still have in a treasure box in the loft! We had a maid called Freda in those days, when having a servant was a normal 'middle class' thing to do, and girls often went 'into service'. Also, before I went to school there was a Miss Howchin who came and took me out for a couple of hours once a week whilst Mother 'got on', by going into Leeds shopping. On the last day that she came before I started school I ran away from her while we were out, and did not return until she'd gone. I suppose it was because I didn't want to say goodbye, but Mother was not amused!

The war caused a number of hardships but these were hardly noticed by a child. The Bakers had moved out to a bigger house in Horsforth, and we had moved to a house on Arncliffe Road, a nicer house but only some quarter of a mile from our old one. There was still a field directly over the fence from the back garden, but this was now Pickles Farm, not Rowson's. Bordering the road we had a metal railing on top of a low wall. One day men with acetylene blow-lamps came and cut them all off at the base and took them away. They were taken, said the men, to help make bombs for the war effort. There was rationing – of clothes, meat, butter and sugar, for which one had coupons. There were very few sweets, only water ices, few oranges and no fresh bananas until the end of the war.

As the war developed air raids became frequent. Most of our relatives lived in Sheffield and Sheffield suffered a severe blitz one night, much of the city centre being destroyed. My father, too old in this war for national service, had nevertheless been placed in the auxiliary mobile police force and at night was required to drive into Leeds if the sirens sounded, and report to his local police station. It had one advantage, an extra petrol ration, and we were able to drive over to Sheffield to see his sisters two days after the Sheffield Blitz. I remember that we drove into town and the whole of the 'Moor' was demolished. The skeleton of the two big shops, Walshes and Cockaynes, were standing stark on the skyline, burnt out. The Town Hall and much of the Cathedral had somehow escaped. Sheffield had relied on barrage balloons to protect itself from attack. The enemy planes had flown over them and tried to hit the steel works but missed, so the barrage balloons in that sense had been a success; but the city centre had gone. The aunts were getting water from a standpipe, and the electricity was off.

Auntie Winnie was my favourite, probably because when I was a baby my Mother had broken her leg going down a helter-skelter at the Woodhouse Feast, a big fair annually on the Leeds Hyde Park Moor, and she, Winnie, had come over to look after me, no doubt at a critical bonding age. She was to come and look after us again in 1946.

The Leeds Blitz, later, had been a less exciting affair for the city, rather less important to the enemy with its emphasis on wool. Nevertheless, one night the sirens went – Father drove off, and my mother, myself and Freda, the maid, gathered under the dining room table. Father had had the choice of an Anderson shelter in the garden, the cellar, or reinforcing the dining room with steel shutters and wooden joists and beams, and had chosen the last option. The bomb fell in the garden and made a ten-foot hole in the back lawn. It was what was known as a 'bread basket', a cluster of incendiary bombs that ought to have opened and scattered as it fell, but didn't. An incendiary landed in the roof but did not go off, and most of them simply landed still in their casing. It blew out the garage windows but did little other damage. Leeds was protected by a circle of rocket guns rather than barrage balloons, and we had one group sited nearby at the top of Butcher Hill, which made an incredible noise that night.

Butcher Hill led from West Park down to Kirkstall Abbey, and was where I learned my alphabet with Miss Howchin. For some reason the stones in the wall bordering the road had, at intervals, letters of the alphabet all the way from A to Z. We learnt them on the way down, had a little 'elevenses' picnic in the Kirkstall Abbey grounds by the River Aire, and I was tested on the way back! This would have been sixty years ago now, however, and the wall has gone.

My stay at Miss Davies's school, later called Richmond House, was to be broken briefly when the school evacuated out of Leeds and into the Dales for a couple of terms. In the matter of pupil numbers and finance it was a disaster since many of the families did not choose to let such young children go off to board. Unlike London, where mass evacuation of children had been almost compulsory, the citizens of Leeds did not perceive these to be such a high risk. I went briefly to Miss Nicholson's at Shire Oak. I missed Miss Davies's where by and large I had been happy, though not on my second day when I cried and Mavis Hardcastle held my hand, nor the third when I wet myself through not daring to ask to go to the loo, nor the last when Miss Thompson put me in a room by myself as a punishment for climbing on the wall bars in the little gym when a teacher wasn't present and then forgot me!

Eventually, at the age of eight, I moved to a prep school, a day school in Leeds called Moorlands under the headmastership of Stuart Woodhams. This school had also just returned from being evacuated for similar reasons, and it restarted in a house called Ashwood Villas near the Leeds girls' high school at Hyde Park. We used the girls' playing fields for games. The numbers were quite small when I arrived. It was much too far to walk from home and I caught the Number 1 tram from West Park, and returned home for lunch and back in the afternoon every day as I refused to eat school lunches! I was a faddy child and every mother's despair at tea parties where I did not like jelly nor trifle and would only eat brown bread sandwiches with marmalade inside! The only time I ever had a school lunch they had blue blancmange, which tasted of methylated spirits. I thought – never again! – but I tried to get back in the afternoon early enough to hear Mr Woodhams reading the Brigadier Gerrard stories to the school after lunch.

I stayed at Moorlands until I was 13 and then went to boarding school, but some big events were to happen in these years at prep school. I suppose I did well at Moorlands. I got to be Head Boy, and was awarded the John Dennison bowl, named after an old boy who had died, and awarded for the rather toe-wriggling boys' vote as to who was the 'most popular boy in the school'. I wonder if they still award it?

During the war some of the teaching was not brilliant since many staff had gone off to fight and indeed towards the end of the war a teacher called Mr Greer arrived and he had been 'behind the lines in France' in the resistance. He knew his French but could not keep discipline in the class and we must have made his life hell!

Halfway through my stay at the school, they moved to their old premises in Far Headingley, near St Chad's Church where Father, Mother and myself worshipped, walking there and back from home every Sunday. These premises were considerably nearer home, which meant I could cycle, but during the war there was a blackout strictly enforced by the ARP whereby there were no street lights, all house lighting had to be concealed by thick blackout curtains, and car headlights had shields fitted over them allowing only a slit light to show. Until this restriction was lifted, getting home on a winter's evening was a difficult task and Mother usually came to meet me.

It is during one's schooldays that one perhaps makes the firmest and most long-lasting of friends. Christopher Davy, later a respected married Leeds businessman, and very bright, made history at school by being the only boy ever to stick a compass in a master's hand (Mr Underwood) when he had a tantrum. Roger Moat, who later also went on to Sedbergh, blotted his copybook when he got there by telling with pride of his father's business as a builders and plumbers merchant, only to be christened 'Bog Harry' from then on, and Donald Adams after a shaky start became a successful prosecuting solicitor in Yorkshire. Then there was Michael Fenton, who also had great success in the legal world, but at the age of nine passed water on to me while we were both climbing a tree! In the holidays my main delight of a winter's evening was to work − or play − on my railway in a room in the attic which my father had set up with all-round shelving upon which we had a magnificent 0-gauge Hornby railway with six engines and some Bassett Lowke LMS dining cars with tables and seats and lighting inside.

The European war ended in 1945. I was eleven. I remember the celebrations in Leeds. Father drove us into town that evening. There were fireworks and great rejoicing. There were bonfires all over. There were bananas in the shops and the ice-cream man had real cream ices when he came round on his tricycle! The last time I had seen a bonfire was in 1939, I think. It had been raining and 'Uncle John' Baker, always somewhat of a daredevil, (he had jumped the Strid, dipped his fingers in a molten lead crucible to show one could if one wet one's finger, and was a hero figure) had poured a can of petrol on the bonfire and then shot a rocket into it. The explosion blew Roger, his eldest son, who was a bit close, off his feet!

With the end of the war some of the Moorlands teachers who had gone to war returned. One such was Mr Fleming who had played lacrosse for England. Before the war men's lacrosse was quite popular in Yorkshire and a number of schools, including Moorlands, had played. With the re-arrival of Mr Fleming, lacrosse restarted in the spring term. It was a game I thoroughly enjoyed and I went on to play for Leeds for a couple of seasons, and captained in due course the Cambridge Eagles XII against Oxford.

But Father's health had been strained by frequent night work in the police in addition to the day job at Gomersall. He, like most people, smoked, and he had gained some weight. Within six months of the end of the war he had a heart attack at the age of 50. He survived this cardiovascular incident but, as was customary, he had some weeks in bed. Anticoagulants had not been invented, nor the value of aspirin recognised. He got back to work for some six months but then was struck by a cerebral embolus (a dislodged clot from the heart lodging in the brain) and was once more laid low, with a mild hemiplegia, some loss of speech and quite marked confusion. He lived for some three months before a final heart attack. My mother, and the stalwart sister of Father's, Winifred Sofia, from Sheffield, who came over and lived with us for some months, nursed him. He never came downstairs again. He would get up and sit in a chair after a while, and wore a 'Joseph's' multi-coloured style of dressing gown (actually I think a bathing wrap). He often would call repetitively for 'John' who we thought was John Baker from next door, but I think now was actually myself with the wrong name. He would talk of plans to take me to London when he was well enough, and of teaching me to drive; and he tried to play cribbage with me, a game he had taught me and which he had learnt when in the army; but he could not remember the rules and I had to try to reteach him, though he never really grasped it. For a twelve-year old this was a distressing time, as indeed it must have been for his wife and sister.

We had other relatives in Leeds. There was Father's cousin on his mother's side, Teddy Moseley, who visited and sat with Father resolutely, and there were the great aunts Minnie, Nellie and Annie, three left of Father's mother's eight siblings. Annie lived at Hyde Park and Nellie and Minnie lived in West Park. None had married. As each died the money went to those who were left. The final one was Nellie, and her only surviving relatives were her three nephews, one my father, who had me, one uncle Teddy (childless), and one uncle Cyril in South Africa (childless), whom I had only seen once, when I charitably gave him chicken pox! And she left it all to Teddy! Mother was not amused.

Father died in March 1946 at the age of fifty-one. So, that was the end of having a father. The funeral and burial was at St Chad's and life had to go on for the rest. I tried to be the man of the house. When Christmas came I put up the Christmas lights and all went well until they fused and I could not make them go. Then my stoicism collapsed and I think I cried properly for the first time over my grief. Happily, Mother showed me how to fix them.

Mother did not find herself very well off. Father's pension was not enough. She decided she would have to take in lodgers to make ends meet, and we had a series. There were serious doubts whether she could afford to send me to Sedbergh School, where my name had been put down a few years before. The aunts thought we should return to Sheffield but Mother decided against it, though her two brothers and their families lived there, each with a little boy (Hedley, my cousin one year younger, and Robert, my other cousin, aged five).

One of my buddies at Moorlands preparatory school, however, Roger Moat, whom I have mentioned before, turned out to have a very generous father. Roger was also going to Sedbergh and his father offered to pay my first year's fees. I was entered for a scholarship to the school, which I sat, and although not reaching scholarship standard, was awarded entry and a fee reduction on my efforts. I was due to leave Moorlands in the summer of 1947, a year after my father's death, to go to Sedbergh in the October term. My other pals from Moorlands were scattered abroad, Christopher to Bootham School, Donald to Kingswood at Bath, and Tony Townend to Denstone.

There remained one event worth recording, and this was of Mr Greer, the French teacher, taking a school trip to France with eight of us in the summer holidays. In the meantime, unbeknownst to myself, Mother was being courted, as an attractive widow of forty-seven, by two suitors, a Mr Malcolm and a Mr Ringrose, the latter also widowed, his wife having died of cancer the year before. Both families already knew each other and Mr Ringrose had two children, Tom, then aged seventeen, and Stella, aged fifteen. Mr Ringrose won!

But returning to the French trip, we were to stay in a village called Cysoing, between Lille and the Belgian border. Mr Greer had been based there in the war and indeed had a fiancée in the little town. Only two years after the war, and the German occupation, Cysoing was in a poor way, many buildings yet to be rebuilt, and the swimming pool without a roof and with green algae covering the water surface. But the locals were very friendly. We were billeted between four families. Initially I was at the Rejkewaerts', Madame Rejkewaerts having been in the French Resistance herself, but I then moved to the Descatoires', who had two girls, José, my age, and Edith, aged ten. We spoke, or tried to speak, French. We ate artichokes on a picnic in the woods, stole pears from an orchard in Douai, and on the way back in the *camion*, when José was being teased by some of the boys, I rescued her and earned her eternal gratitude! We stayed friends over the years and our respective children exchanged visits. In Lille I was given a watch and bought for Mother some silk stockings, which I wore under my socks through customs. Perhaps this was an omen!

In September I was to go off to Sedbergh School. This would be the end of one and the beginning of a new era. Had I summed it up at the time, my life till then had been a mixture – of happiness and sadness, of minor triumphs at school, but a big sorrow at the loss of my father at home. I remembered friends, some of whom would move on with a new school. I remembered walks through the bluebell woods in spring, to the railway line running from Leeds to Harrogate to watch the trains; quiet days with Mother; the loss of Miss Howchin; the loss of Freda the maid; the loss of a house 'of our own'. What effect this was to have in the future, who knew?

The week before I went away to school, Mother had a chat with me. What did I think about her getting married again – to Mr Ringrose? My response must have surprised her. At first I laughed, perhaps through nervousness, but it seemed to a 13-year old rather hilarious that Mother, at her age, should have been courting! Then I had another thought. 'But what about my trains?'

'We've thought of that. You can have your own bedroom, a playroom next to it on the top floor, with a little bathroom, all for yourself. And it will give you a new brother and sister.' In fact it had all been arranged. They were to marry at the end of October.

CHAPTER 2

'Dura Virum Nutrix'

'THE STERN NURSE OF MEN'. This was Sedbergh's motto. The school had been founded as a grammar school in 1525 by Roger Lupton, a provost of Eton College and canon of Windsor, as a school in the north of England to establish learning, along with many chantry schools. It was promoted by Edward VI and had gone through triumphs and disasters in its over 400 years of history. The present headmaster was Bruce-Lockhart, international rugger player in his day and of a very talented family, under whose leadership Sedbergh was reaching new heights in learning, in music and Rugby football, carrying all before it. I can only say it 'made' me. It entered every aspect of my life for five years. Like clay to the potter, I grew and was shaped to success in life, learning to meet with triumph and disaster and treat those two impostors just the same!

Sedbergh is situated at the southern foot of the Howgill Fells. Winder stands proud immediately to the north, at some 1,500 feet high. To the east is Baugh Fell, a massive fell with its helm cloud which, with Wild Boar and Swarth fells, dominate the skyline. To the south lies Frost Row, and beyond it Middleton Fell and the Dee Valley with its settlement of Dent, home of Adam Sedgewick the geologist. To the west the land is softer, as the three rivers, Clough, Dee and Rawthey, come singing from the hills to join the Lune on its way to Lancaster and the sea. Beyond the Lune Valley are the Kendal fells; further still the town of Kendal itself and, beyond, the Lakeland mountains.

From the top of Winder, where on the first afternoon Simpson, the Head of House, took us, ten new boys in Evans House who had arrived the day before the rest of the school, one could see the fells of the Lake District and a little to the south the estuary of Morecambe Bay. To the north the Howgills spread before us, summit after summit as far as one could see. By the time I was eighteen I was to know these fells, if not like the back of my hand then near enough, and to love them.

It's the hills that have stood around us unchanged since our days began.
It's Cautley, Calf and Winder, that make the Sedbergh man

And women too now, indeed, since a little before the turn of this last century girls were admitted to Lupton House.

The school song, from which these lines come, finishes thus:

And when in days hereafter, in tamer lands you dwell –
Or in some fevered city far off from beck and fell,

11

The Howgill Fells, Sedbergh

As boyhood's days grow dimmer, the memory will not die,
Of Winder's clear-cut outline, against the evening sky.

That sums it all up.

The first term I was a little homesick, it being my first time away from home. I knew that I would not see the inside of our house again. In October Mother would be married, and would leave 15 Arncliffe Road for the last time and we would amalgamate with the Ringrose family at Westfield in a house into which I had never entered. It was to be an exciting new venture but it was another loss. New lamps for old, but scary. I believe for all my joys and successes in life, loss has been a dominant theme, and I have coped with this by building a wall of self-sufficiency – 'If you don't want me, I don't care. I can cope.' But perhaps to some degree it shuts one off from full emotion. I think it started when my mother broke her leg and was removed from me for a while. It was reinforced when my father died; by boarding school and by the house move. Not that I worked this out at the time.

At any event, when I got back to Leeds for Christmas 1947 it was to a new, and indeed finer, house. My stepfather had fixed trestles round the attic room for my trains. My bedroom furniture was all in place in the room next to it, the erstwhile housekeeper's room (she had left when mother had taken over). Stella, my new stepsister, was there to welcome me. So it was almost home from home. But of course it wasn't my home. Still, it all worked very well. Mother said years later that it had been a very happy time, married to Tom Ringrose. He was grateful to my mother. I got on well with him and with my stepsiblings, and it had of course solved mother's financial problems. We were taken on good holidays. He taught me later to drive and I was able to borrow his car. Living also in the house was mother's second husband's first wife's mother – my step great-grandmother-in-law, I suppose. Mrs Hopps was 84 and my stepfather had promised to look after her when his first wife was dying: an awkward situation for both my mother and her, and when my stepfather died, as he did in 1957 and Granny Hopps was still alive, more awkward still. But mother nursed her, as she had my father and my stepfather in his drawn-out terminal illness, until in 1964 she died a few months off her century, of pneumonia caused by a bad cold caught from our first daughter.

The whole family were taken to Craiglands Hydro for that Christmas of 1947 when we had a jolly time. My stepfather was a chemical engineer, who designed the Ringrose miners' lamp which measured methane, and a similar device for carbon dioxide levels in submarines, and an anaesthetic continuous flow monitor, known as the 'Ringrose-Rowling-Harboard carbon dioxide continuous flow monitor'. He ran a private company in Leeds known as 'International Gas Detectors', where he researched and invented new monitor devices.

I returned to Sedbergh in January, a sophisticated second-termer, to lord it over the three new boys! I joined the choir, and learned the piano. I played in the junior fives team and was tipped to do well in the junior three-mile fell race. Each house entered six runners and there were house trials to see who would make it. Big regret number one in life – for some reason I was scared to run in the big race, and held back in the trial deliberately, coming seventh. Aaagh!

The fells and fell running were a big part of Sedbergh life. If not playing rugger one would be up on the fells most days. We ran on the fells, explored caves in the fells, and swam naked in the tarns on the fells. In winter we skated on these tarns. We watched birds on the fells, studied their geology, and had our CCF field day amongst them.

We see the heather redden; we hear the curlew cry –
About us is the moorland; above the windswept sky.

We were free in those days, free to roam, and we explored every inch. A love of the fells has lasted me my lifetime, and at seventy I still climb them.

The great event in Sedbergh's life was the annual ten-mile fell race, the 'Wilson Run', founded at the end of the nineteenth century for the first five years as a paper chase, and then taking the form it has now, a gruelling course over swollen ghylls, up on to the heather of Baugh Fell, across Danny Bridge and back finally up the Garsdale road into town, finishing mercifully by the 'grubber', the tuck shop on Loftus Hill. Pumphrey had won in record time in 1899 in just over 1 hour 10 minutes. Grandage was close behind. Their times had never been beaten (until a chap called Sykes did it some ten years ago!). A contemporary and lifelong friend of mine, Giles Shaw, later to go on to be president of the Cambridge Union and enter politics, who was only 5 feet 4 inches, won it two years in a row and was a hero. Almost everyone who was anyone and over sixteen ran in it, and hundreds of old boys would make the pilgrimage back to watch the race, which had usually some eighty entrants. I would love to have won the 'Ten'. My best was 14th in a time of 1 hour 19 minutes. In the evening there was always a concert and it was inspiring to see some who had run now playing in the orchestra. At the end, the runners all went on stage in the order they had come in, and the concert always finished with everyone lustily singing 'The Long Run' (the school running song).

Strain and struggle, might and main; scorn defeat and laugh at pain.
Never shall you strive in vain in the Long Run.

Under Bruce-Lockhart, Sedbergh became a famous rugger school and a master who arrived to teach Physics and be in charge of rugger was a Mr Vaughan, very kind, but a bruiser of a man who stood no nonsense and had played for the Royal Navy. I recall at his first lesson for our set, the class 'naughty boy' was in his usual place in the back row, flicking ink-filled blotting paper pellets at all and sundry, as was his wont, while Mr Vaughan was writing on the blackboard. From the eye in the back of his head he must have seen him, for he said nothing but put his chalk down and walked to the back of the class, taking the boy by the hair and marching him to the front where he banged his head – not over gently – on the blackboard. He then marched him back and returned to get on with what he was writing. There was dead silence. He never had any more trouble and later as we grew older we were all good friends. But he had made his mark. And the rugger team was virtually unbeatable! Our main rivals were Loretto (Scotland v England), Uppingham (North v South) and Ampleforth (Catholic v Protestant) and in those days we usually beat the lot!

Of course today Mr Vaughan would have been suspended. There would have been an enquiry and no doubt he would have left, a great loss to the school. But in those days fair was fair. If you broke a rule – and we all knew what the rules were – you got the punishment, usually three strokes on the bottom with a 'bim stick' and it hurt! But that was the end of it. I only suffered the indignity once, and then administered it in my turn as a school prefect, but it was salutary! When I took up a consultant post in York much later in life, a Dr Foggitt, one of the first GPs to ring me to ask me to do a home visit on one of his patients, introduced himself: 'You may not remember me. You beat me for snowballing in the school precincts in 1952!' That is how true friendships are made!

My first spring term, in 1948, was a very cold winter, the snow lay on the fells for weeks, and Lilymere, a lake on the Kendal road, was frozen over and skatable for three weeks. We played ice hockey and could skate well by the end. They don't make winters like that any more! There was a superb toboggan course on the south western side of Winder, following the track which led up to the cairn and then sledging down the zigzag with a total run of some three hundred yards. It was as well not to take a wrong turning. Moxon ruptured his spleen when he did, and I in my last winter tore a three-inch long gash in my thigh. (Viewing by appointment!).

Caving was another, but summer, activity. There were the official caves for instance at Clapham and Ingleton, for official visits, but we knew of small caves at Danny Bridge, Dovecot and Gawthrop. Danny and Gawthrop demanded crawling along up a blind passage, but Dovecot could have been a show cave, with the Ghyll flowing through it, a cavernous top entrance, and emerging at the bottom end, some one hundred yards later, into a charming wooded valley. River bathing, too, was a summer 'extra half' pursuit, in Lord's Dub, and various stretches of deep quiet water on the River Lune and the Rawthey, where young Adonises, often naked, would frolic, and get bitten by the ever ready 'cleg', the horsefly!

The years of thirteen to eighteen are perhaps the greatest for forging lifelong friendships. There were Graham Burgess and Edward Vickerman, both to become headmasters; Bob Sykes, who captained Fixby Golf Club; Bill Whimster, who became a pathologist in London. He, Gordon McKay, and Bob Anderson, killed in a flying accident at nineteen, are now all dead and gone. Then there were the Birdsall family: James, who became an author; Tim, who became a well-known cartoonist and writer, featured on *That Was The Week That Was* and wrote a superb poem to win the Stirling English Verse Prize, but who died of leukaemia in his twenties; and in music, Jowett; and the Gwilts who went on to fame and fortune. The school produced bishops, judges and leaders of industry and Sedbergh was famed for its musical talent which in my day was led by Chris Cowan who went on to prestigious posts as an organist; and a number of boys got into the National Youth Orchestra. The Arts produced a school of watercolour led by Bruce-Lockhart and 'Chris' Christopherson and organised by Sandy Ingles. Boys also learned fly-fishing in the local trout streams and to tie their own flies in one of the optional arts and crafts classes.

At the chapel service on old boys' weekend the list of benefactors was read out. Posthumous Wharton always amused us, but there were many famous names. Viscount Brendan Bracken, who had paid for the refurbishing of the school library, had a strange story to tell. Born in Ireland, he had appeared at Sedbergh on his own and requested admission to the school of the then headmaster. He was almost at school-leaving age at the time but proved very able and paid his own fees. The headmaster, with intuitive foresight, agreed. Brendan stayed only one term, climbing the political ladder subsequently and becoming Churchill's right-hand man in the Second World War and eventually entering the House of Lords. He was a school governor in my day and always took a lot of interest in his short-lived old school. General Sir John Shea was another character. The school had very fine memorial cloisters, and a special memorial to the four old boys who had won the VC, which was unveiled during my stay.

I learned to play fives and squash at Sedbergh. Fives in particular was a favourite ball court game and the school at that time had some ten courts. It was a game I much enjoyed and was good at, winning the Ingmire Fives Cup and going on to play at Cambridge and to captain a Bart's Hospital team. Later in life I was to start a Winchester fives doubles tournament which rotated through the main Winchester fives-playing schools of Sedbergh, Bradfield, Malvern and Winchester College itself. There are three commonly played styles of fives: Eton Fives, with a complex open-backed court of buttresses and steps, Rugby Fives, with a plain court similar to a small squash court, and the Winchester style, with a single diagonal buttress on the left-hand wall. The game is played with a ball the size of a squash ball but of the consistency more of a tiny cricket ball, and hit with gloved hands rather than a racquet, the court having a stone floor and walls (or nowadays composition cement), up against the front wall as in squash. Sedbergh curiously, for historical reasons, due to the then headmaster, had the Winchester-style courts rather than the Eton-style, from whence we were in a sense founded.

So far this chapter has not mentioned work! Yes, we did indeed work and most of the boys mentioned above finished up at Cambridge. I took my school certificate, as it was, in 1954/55 and matriculated, as one had to, in English Language, English Literature, Maths and Advanced Maths, French, Latin and Physics and Chemistry. We then entered the Lower Sixth Form and chose subjects appropriate to probable career choices. I was aiming to do a natural sciences degree at Cambridge and go on to study medicine, and opted therefore for Organic Chemistry, Physics and Biology, which allowed for the making of the '1st MB' exam, which effectively, if passed, gained one entry to Cambridge with the completion of the first year of pre-clinical medical studies.

The system at Sedbergh insisted that in addition to one's classes for Higher Certificate (later to become A levels), each student must take two optional subjects, non-exam but to the equivalent of a school certificate grade, in subjects other than ones chosen for A level. Thus, taking sciences as I was, I had the choice of classical languages, modern languages, History and Geography or English Literature. A strong secondary interest and enthusiasm of mine being languages, I opted for German and Russian, the latter taught by a Mr Hammer who was noted for his tight braces and trousers some three inches too short! However, we worked through Moore & Struves, books I and II, the short story *Taman,* and one or two of Tolstoy's tales, such as *The Woodcutter and the Watersprite (Mujik i Vadianoi)*.

When I first entered Evans House, Len Taylor was housemaster and Evans was the senior of the seven houses, in rotation. We were good at fives, rugger and running, but usually bottom in the corps drill competition and the music competitions, commonly won by 'The School House'. Len Taylor was a bluff but kindly man whose wife acted as matron in my first year. In my last year, however, Len Taylor retired as housemaster and Ken Bishop came in his place, a tall, slightly austere man who ran the school CCF and was going to pull the 'rebel' Evans House into line. His first Head of House, a Taylor appointment and a Taylor man, caused slight problems. I was made Head of House for my last two terms and struck up a friendship lasting until his death, some three years ago.

I took my A levels and first MB at seventeen and, because of the Cambridge entry system at the time, would not be entering St John's College until October of 1952, still a year off. I had a pleasant last year, therefore, sitting an A level in zoology, doing the recently introduced General Paper, and learning German from Ken Bishop, my housemaster. I captained the house team at cricket, played in the school fourth eleven and in the house rugger team, and was a pirate in *The Pirates of Penzance*. A master at the school, Michael Thornley, used to put on a Gilbert & Sullivan operetta on alternate years. Sir Giles Shaw in his day was Sir Joseph Porter in *HMS Pinafore*, and Jock Slater, one time first Lord of the Admiralty, was Mabel! His voice of course at the time had not broken!

With the retirement of Bruce Lockhart, Michael Thornley became head-master and led the school very successfully for many years, on retirement becoming the Hon. Secretary of the Old Sedberghian Club, of which at the time and for many years after I was a committee member, and we became good friends.

On the final evening of the summer term we went to the school chapel for the end of term service. Sedbergh had also given me a sound basis of religious practice and belief.

> *Make this school as a field that the Lord hath blessed, that whatsoever things are pure, lovely and of good report, may here forever flourish and abound.*

In the evening light, Brian Wicks (another friend, later to be a lawyer) and I walked back across the cricket field towards Evans House, with Winder's clear-cut outline against an evening sky. Leaving Sedbergh would be another huge loss. I quote from Tim Birdsall's prize-winning poem which captures the spirit of this place so well. It is called *Sedbergh Revisited*.

> Let me sit here in the sunlight. Let me rest awhile and sigh
> Let me dream, and so remember how the years have hurried by;
> ★   ★   ★   ★   ★   ★
> We are vanished and forgotten in the mists of many years
> Dead the vital surging spirit; fled the hopes and dreams and fears
> But the heart can yet remember as the gentle shadows fall
> And softly in the stillness hear the voice of memory call
> Calling, calling in the sunshine, in the wind and in the rain
> Come you back – come back to Sedbergh!
> Come and find your youth again.

CHAPTER 3

Salad days

IN OCTOBER 1952 I entered St John's College Cambridge with a county exhibition, to read for a Natural Sciences degree, a BA, in Cambridge. My stepbrother, Tom, had preceded me there and was now at the Middlesex Hospital, also doing medicine. Tom was a rather serious-minded young man but had been very kind to me when I arrived at Westfield, helping me rebuild the railway and helping me at my entry in St John's. He went on after army service, and a spell of recall as a result of the Suez crisis, to specialise in radiotherapy and go first to the Mount Vernon Hospital, then to the Mount Sinai Hospital in New York as an associate professor, and finally settled in Canada becoming a consultant in Calgary.

My rooms in Park Place (in digs) during my first year were rather uninteresting. However, I joined the University Judo Club, and the University Lacrosse Club, the Scottish Dancing Society, Gilbert & Sullivan, and learned to play the chanter (the prelude to learning the bagpipes, a stage to which I never progressed). Well, you would, wouldn't you? I always was a strange lad – I started to learn Welsh as a hobby at Sedbergh! It is after all the second most commonly used language in the British Isles! Foolishly I did not take up fives. My reason was that Cambridge had Rugby Fives Courts, and Eton Fives Courts, but no Winchester Fives Court. Yet if I had chosen to adapt to the Rugby game, I might possibly have got a half-blue. Most of the players that year were old Sedberghians. A 'blue' is gained by playing for the University First Team against Oxford University. A half-blue is the same but in a minor sport – this was called a varsity match. My summer games were croquet, and a little tennis.

The subjects I was to study for the Natural Sciences Tripos were Anatomy, Physiology and Biochemistry. These subjects were necessary ones to choose if one wished to go on to medicine, and at that time the full six-year training could not be completed at Cambridge since there was no clinical school at Addenbrooke's Hospital. Most students went on to one of the London Medical Schools attached to the Great London Teaching Hospitals, sadly decimated by government policy in the last twenty-five years or so. Now, of course, there is a great shortage of doctors. Serves them right!

The anatomy school in Cambridge was centred about the dissection rooms. These were forbidding places at first sight, and indeed at first smell, since the stench of formalin, to preserve the bodies, filled one's nostrils. I do not recall

St John's College and the Bridge of Sighs, Cambridge

the exact number, but in this large space were some twenty to thirty cadavers, naked, of course, but for a sheet, pickled and waxy looking, and waiting for us to cut them up. We dissected, under supervision and with a dissection manual for each appropriate part, over a period of two years, doing a particular area of the body each term, which included a leg, an arm, the head and neck, the abdomen and pelvis, the chest, and the brain, working through the layout of the skin, muscles, blood vessels, nerves and bony structures and their inter-relationships in great detail. One soon got used to the bizarre scenario, and with working in pairs and some eight or so people working on each cadaver during the dissection classes, it became a social event and even occasionally, slightly, and 'unseemly-like', ribald! We were tested on each dissected section we had displayed, every two weeks or so.

Our other subjects, in particular Physiology, also had a lot of experimental work. Anatomy is a study of how the body is made up or put together. Physiology is a study of how it works. How do nerves control muscles? What is the function of blood? What happens if the spinal cord is severed? and so on. Quite a lot of the demonstrated experiments involved live animals, or semi-alive, and would have appalled an anti-vivisectionist, I do not doubt. It rather appalled me, but was necessary to qualify. We had to sign in for all these practical sessions, and as a consequence had a much more structured timetable than many faculties, where attendance at lectures was less compulsory, and far less frequent. It would have been difficult to have done a natural sciences degree, for example, and also to have been a top athlete in a major sport such as rowing or cricket. Of course, Cambridge was not just study and sport. There were a wealth of societies to suit every taste, from music to debate, art, religion, politics and dance. The danger was in joining too many and not becoming fully involved as a consequence in any. But in the first year one needed to experiment a little.

Still somewhat in my Scottish phase, I donned my kilt and went to the Scottish Dancing Society, and I joined the Home Rule Society, whose object was to produce a federation of Celtic nations, (Wales, Ireland, Scotland, Brittany, Cornwall and Man), and along with my co-editor, David Stephenson, I published a monthly newspaper, known as the *Celtic Times*, which had sub-editors for each linguistic sub-group and produced articles in these various languages – Welsh, Gaelic, Breton and Cornish, and of course in English too as the Lingua Franca. Most people could read only one of the Celtic languages, if they were lucky, but still, we tried! What has happened to it now I wonder? Four of these countries indeed now have some independence, the Isle of Man having one of the oldest parliaments in the world, though the Manx Gaelic language exists only now as an intellectual hobby, as does Cornish (a language similar to Welsh and Breton) and there is a small Cornish nationalist party 'Mebyon Kernow' – or 'Sons of Cornwall', that wins the odd local election. But of the society and the newspaper? Long gone, I fear, as have a lot of small societies of this kind at university.

My other main interest was music and I joined a choir known as the Granta Singers, which sang concerts, mainly in churches who needed money and where we gave our services free and the church pocketed the collection. We also, a group of us, started up a Gilbert & Sullivan Society, in St John's College to present concert versions of some of the thirteen operettas that Sullivan wrote with Gilbert. We had a good tenor in Geoff Reynolds, and baritone in Giles Shaw, and a bass in myself. We attracted a variety of sopranos and contraltos, such as Elizabeth Ann Willday, and Judy Lancaster. We were also fortunate in our pianist, a music scholar from the college. We did *Pirates*, *Pinafore*, both of which Giles knew well, *Ruddigore*, and *The Grand Duke*.

There were a lot of Old Sedberghians up at Cambridge at this time and we had an annual dinner in one of the colleges as a consequence. Some of us had gone straight from school to do our two-years' National Service before returning to university, and some of us, medics in particular, had got deferment and gone straight up to the university. I was one of the latter. The post-National Service group were twenty-one to twenty-two years old and quite a lot more sophisticated than the schoolboys, but found it less easy to settle back down into studying.

Of my particular school buddies, Graham Burgess had gone to do National Service in the Air Force and was flying in Canada. Bill Whimster was in Queen's College; Edward Vickerman was with me in St John's, as were Giles Shaw, Rodney Dodds, and indeed much of the University Fives Team.

Another interest was religion. I had been caught by R.A.K. (Richard) Haslam, an old Sedberghian two years ahead of me, and persuaded to join the Cambridge Inter-Collegiate Christian Union (CICCU) and to go with Richard (no relation) to various East End chapels on a Sunday where I would read the lesson whilst Richard preached the sermon! It was not really my scene, and the following year I switched to the more 'High Church' Student Christian Movement which met fortnightly for a discussion and prayer group. At the same time, Edward and I decided to go to a different church in inner Cambridge each Sunday morning, and reckoned it would take two years to complete this exercise. It was very interesting to make comparisons: the Presbyterian church with many of the hymns which we had sung at Sedbergh; the quiet white-washed simplicity of the Franciscan Church; the packed congregations in the High Roman Catholic Church; and the quiet peace of the Society of Friends. We managed our task, except for the Spiritualists, which made us nervous, and the Jewish Synagogue, where we felt we would be too unfamiliar with the rules!

The theatrical buzz of Cambridge life at this time was the Cambridge Footlights, and Jonathan Miller, a medical friend of mine, also in St John's, was a comedian of great talent in some of the sketches they produced. I remember his imitation of Nelson, whose words to Hardy, 'Kismet, Hardy', Hardy mistakes for 'kiss me'. Jonathan's expression as 'Hardy' bent down was superb. Another sketch was of King Arthur retrieving the sword from the lake, and he rowed himself across the stage on his bottom! Jonathan, of course, was to go on to leave medicine and make a career in theatre production in later years. Giles Shaw in the meantime was beginning to make his name in the Cambridge Union of which he was in due course to become president. Later he went into a career in politics, sadly dying in his late sixties before completely fulfilling his promise.

In sport in my first year I played some squash and tennis, but joined the University Lacrosse Club and played for the second team known as the 'Eagles'. I also began to build up my skills at the University Judo Club, and gained my first two 'Kyo' belts.

A feature of Cambridge social life at the end of the summer term is the May Ball. Most colleges have them, and some of the societies too. The Balls at King's, Trinity and St John's, however, were part of the social season, and girls were keen to get invited! In my first year I chose to go to the Medical Society May Ball, which was held at the Dorothy Restaurant in town. I chose to take a fellow singer, Judy Lancaster, and during the interval presumed to put my arm along the back of her chair. Here was my second big setback with the female sex, when Judy said, 'I'd rather you didn't do that!' I was as they say (some do anyway) gobsmacked – but was to learn that between my invitation and the date of the ball, she had become enamoured of someone else, and this interloper was actually at the ball with another woman. Heigh-ho!

The medics, along with a few other faculties, were required to return to Cambridge in midsummer (August mostly) for what was known as a 'Long Vac term' (long vacation). This allowed us between years one and two to dissect the thorax. It was also the chance to do a pharmacology course, but best of all, a chance to join the Long Vac Club. This splendid institution was a way for the Cambridge undergraduates and Ph.D.s who were 'up', to meet the foreign students, mostly doing language courses, who were over for the summer and were two-thirds female. That is to say two-thirds of the foreign students were female, not that we were overloaded with transsexuals! That year I met Ngo Chi Tran van Doc, from the Dutch East Indies, and we had a pleasant, though innocent, (for by and large I was still!) few weeks.

A final new skill for the long vac term was acquired from dancing lessons. For these I went to a lady in the Market Square who gave lessons and held one rather tightly, and I learned to tango! My first attempt at dancing had been in Leeds when I was five years old. My mother took me to some classes. At the first one I was required to be a butterfly and refused. I was not taken again! But it was necessary for a young man in the fifties to have ballroom dancing skills. So I had, in Leeds in my last year at school, classes with Miss Cooke-Yarborough at her academy, where my partner had been Philothea Robinson (Arthur's sister). I learned the skills of the quickstep, slow and quick waltz, foxtrot, reverse turns, the lot. But in Cambridge I wanted to learn the rumba, samba, and charleston, and did!

The summer holidays had taken us to the Ravenhall Hotel for two weeks – a great place in those days for teenagers. There were many of us and much to do; tennis, golf, swimming, riding, scrambles down to the sea, and dances in the evening. Ravenscar was a small village on a headland at the south end of Robin Hood's Bay, between Whitby and Scarborough. The evening sun picked out the bay, and to the north the picturesque and quaint village of Robin Hood's Bay itself, a three-mile walk along the beach. On the final Friday there was a fancy dress ball and my stepsister Stella insisted I went as Little Red Riding Hood, with a white tennis dress and her red Queen Margaret's school cape. The shoes rather spoilt what would surely otherwise have been a magnificent display!

Ravenscar was also, the summer after I left Sedbergh, the site of my last ever game of cricket. The holiday coincided with the Scarborough cricket test match and some of the team were wont to stay at the hotel, and arranged a match between the hotel and the village cricket club. Brian Close captained the hotel team. Under his captaincy I scored one run and the village team won!

A custom among the hardy younger people was to enter the open-air swimming pool at about 7.30 a.m. when the train to Scarborough whistled as it left Robin Hood's Bay station, and not to come out until it whistled as it came out of the tunnel to reach Ravenscar station. Brian was always in the pool, floating serenely in the centre when we arrived, and still there when we left. He chose to come to the fancy dress ball in his wife's bathing costume, which did not cover his modesty over well!

One tended to pair off for a holiday romance on such occasions. Of the three years that my stepfather took us, I recall Jill Riseam, Shirley Jackson, and finally Mariam Yanni. The last was a Lebanese girl, there with her parents and brother, who lived in Manchester, her father doing business with Beirut. They had initially been slightly outsiders but her beautiful black hair and olive skin attracted me mightily and on the first Saturday evening dance I danced with her much of the evening. These holiday romances rarely lasted many weeks after the end of the holiday, but Mariam and I got quite close, and at Christmas I was invited to stay with them for a few days. They were Maronite Christians. It was a nice weekend though the sparkle had gone a bit, and it all fizzled out.

In my second year at Cambridge I managed to get into college, and had a room at the top of the 'Wedding Cake' in New Court, over the river Cam on the Backs. St John's was joined by Roger Moat, hotfoot from the army and service in the Durham Light Infantry and the Black Watch, and a new circle of friends was formed, with Dick Ebberlie, Graham Sawley and others. I played some bridge with Edward Vickerman, Ron Steel, John Birchnell and Geoff Walker. Bill Whimster was in Queen's College, and we visited regularly. Roger Baker was in Corpus Christi.

The winter proved exceptionally cold. The river Cam froze over and we were for a couple of weeks able to skate the three miles up river to Grantchester for tea, where the clock still stood at ten to three since Rupert Brooke's time. And there was still honey for tea! Skating back we raced. Roger Moat took the centre of the river and was ahead. The river, however, flows fastest in the centre and the ice is thinnest. He disappeared with a cry through into the river, but happily was rapidly rescued.

I began to play squash more seriously and entered the Yorkshire tournament and played at the Abbeydale Club, in Sheffield, where my uncle had played golf. I also continued to play with the University Lacrosse Club, and played on the second team against Oxford the following spring term. Also the following year I fought regularly with the University Judo Club and was first reserve on the University team, with a 'yellow belt'. I did not get to black belt status, but had the rare opportunity to win my bout for London University against John Tooth, the Cambridge number six! This came about as one of the London team was ill and to make up numbers I was asked if I would care to fight as number six for London. I had practised regularly with John at the club and knew his tactics. He would move in and as he made contact would immediately go into a Tai Otoshi. There was a counter to this throw and I reckoned if I did the counter almost before he started, on the assumption that that was what he would do, it might work. The gamble came off and John was flat on his back. I managed to hang on for the rest of the bout and emerged the winner. Sadly I was not picked for the Oxford match so did not get my half-blue.

The May exams at the end of the second year were when the Tripos exam was sat in anatomy and physiology and the half subject of biochemistry. I did adequately in the two latter but only got a 'third' in anatomy and needed to do some swotting in this for the 'second MB', which was the pre-clinical element of the eventual medical degree (MB, B.Chir.) that would be awarded at the end of the sixth year. Apart from studying for exams there were two skills to be perfected, croquet and punting. Most of the riverside colleges had some punts of their own, or they could be hired at the downstream end of the backs, canalised in effect between the weir and a lock. At the upper end opposite the Mill pub beyond Queen's College and Queen's Bridge, punts could be hired to punt on the backs, or from above the weir, to punt up to Grantchester. In Cambridge one punted standing on the raised platforms at the rear of the boat. Oxford were said to punt from the other end, on the Isis. There was no varsity punting race! Where the river bottom was firm, the punt pole was dropped in parallel to the side of the punt on the right, if right-handed, and then pushed to move the craft forward. In muddy patches one could get stuck. There were two options, either to let go of the pole and float away into the sunset, or hang on to it, in which case the punt sailed away without one, and one got rather wet in the river, both to loud guffaws from watchers on the bank or bridges. The trick to avoid such an embarrassment lay in the shape of the bottom of the pole which had two prongs. If the pole were twisted as it was withdrawn, the prongs loosened it and allowed it to be pulled out. My only risky moment came when I lifted the pole too near a bridge at Grantchester and did not get it down in time and the pole jammed between the bridge arch and the bottom of the river. Those watching rushed across the bridge in the hope of seeing us shoot out either puntless or punterless, or both. By an amazing fluke, however, the pole had bowed before I let go, and it sprung forward somehow and I was able to catch it again as it fell. We cruised out from under the arch serenely and off downstream, no doubt to the disappointment of the assembled company!

The boat races, apart of course from the varsity boat race on the Thames, were held on the Cam downstream below the weir and lock beyond Magdalen College. The river was not wide enough for boats to row side-by-side, so the college races, known as the 'bumps' were a staggered start end to end and the boat which managed to bump the one in front, moved up a place for the next race so that eventually one became the 'head of the river'. Sedbergh, not being a rowing school, rarely produced an oarsman of any great prestige. Croquet was another thing. We played of an evening usually after we dined in the splendid College hall where we saw the coats of arms of our forebears, including that of Roger Lupton, the founder of Sedbergh School, and listened to the Latin grace read by a scholar before we dined.

Oculi omnium in tes sperant, Domine, et tu das illis cibum in tempore – etc.etc.etc. (or something like that!)

We played our croquet on the lawn of the Backs, outside New Court. This was proper association croquet, none of your 'golf croquet' stuff, but four-ball breaks and advanced non-handicap rules. It was the start of a lifelong interest.

It was in January 1954 that our Student Christian Movement decided to discuss the thirty-nine articles of the Anglican Church. Our group was made up of male students from St John's College, and girls from Homerton College doing the teacher training diplomas. It was a religious group, but also a good way of boy-meets-girl. I had on a fawn, camel-hair waistcoat with brass buttons, and I shared a prayer book with Thirza Burney. My eyes were more taken by another girl present whose name I later discovered to be Shirley Jefferies. I decided to ask her out, and a couple of days later cycled out to Homerton College, having invited her to come to supper and a film with me, in a pre-written note which I proposed to deliver, if possible, in person.

I enquired at reception if she were available, and a junior student was sent off to check. After a brief interval Shirley appeared and eyed me quizzically. I handed her the note to read, which was a little unfair, and watched as she read it. Her response was to ask were it not Thirza Burney that I had been seeking and perhaps got the name wrong! I assured her this was not the case, and she graciously accepted. We decided to meet at the cinema since the film started at 6 p.m. and to eat later. The Arts Cinema tended to put on specialist films, often foreign films with sub-titles, classics of their kind, but unlikely to get onto a routine commercial screen. The film we saw was a Swedish film, *Hon dansade i sommar*. The English sub-title was *One Summer of Happiness*, but a better translation would be 'She danced through summer'. It was a beautifully made film, with splendid scenic shots, and featured a nude bathing scene on a beach, very risqué in 1954!

We returned to my room for coffee after eating in a local café, and I am told I showed her my photo album, including shots of previous girlfriends! Later I saw her to the bus stop to get the bus back to Homerton College and am also told I got my diary and presumptuously asked when we should see each other next! Anyhow, we arranged it for the following week and at the time of writing these memoirs, we have celebrated our 45th Wedding Anniversary. There was a while to go, however, before marriage!

At that time my old friend Roger Moat was also enamoured of a Homertonian, one Sheila Jillard, who was a friend of Shirley's, and Roger and I decided to invite them to coffee in my rooms. I realised not long before that

I had no coffee pot suitable for four people, and nipped out to buy one at the market. It was green, and very fine. The girls decided to make the coffee, but it was not revealed till later that when they came to pour the pan of coffee into this jug, it was still full of packing straw!

That summer term was indeed a summer of happiness. We walked to Grantchester for tea, watched the bumps on the river, and fell in love. Shirley and Sheila joined the Gilbert & Sullivan Group, we all went punting together, and at the end of term attended the St John's May Ball and punted on the river at dawn!

During that year's long vacation term I did a pharmacology course, necessary before entering a clinical medical school, and also a course at the old schools in Scientific Russian, designed for those who wanted to read scientific papers in Russian – an increasingly useful skill in view of the output from that country and the difficulty of getting translations. It was also a useful refresher course in the language itself. The Long Vac Club was again in full flow, and this time I met a group of Italian students, Clelia Vaciago, Fanni, Carla, Georgio, Franca and Maurice. Clelia and I spent some time together and the 'gang' became friends, with whom we have continued contact over the years, and our respective children have had holiday exchanges.

The autumn term saw a few changes. I obtained rooms in Third Court, directly overlooking the river and the Bridge of Sighs at the rear and the courtyard of Third Court to the front. I shared with Roger Lemaitre, a geologist whose family came from the Channel Isles. Sadly Roger Moat had had to go down from the university without getting his degree, due to the untimely death of his father and the need for Roger to enter the family business forthwith. This term also marked the arrival back from Canada of my 'best buddy', Graham Burgess, who entered Queen's College to read Classics.

In the third year of the Tripos one read for part II of the BA natural sciences degree. The anatomy and physiology courses were completed and the other half subject had to be chosen. I decided to do morphology (or comparative anatomy) and spent the year studying and dissecting such creatures as the codfish, pigeon, tortoise and rat, examples of each of the different phyla of the animal kingdom. Judo slipped a little in importance as I concentrated on lacrosse training, and had the reward of being elected to captain the Cambridge Eagles against Oxford in the spring term. I was elected to membership of the Sixteen Club, which was the university lacrosse club, and I was pleased with that honour.

It was Shirley's last year at Homerton too, the course in those days being a two-year one, and she would be getting a junior teaching post the following September. I meanwhile was negotiating a place at Bart's (St Bartholomew's Hospital), one of the top London clinical schools and was fortunate to get a place, subject to qualifying with the Second MB prior to taking up my place.

In the early spring, Graham Burgess had met a German girl, Ingrid Rolle, who was working as a secretary in Cambridge and whom he met at a tea dance at the 'Dot', the Dorothy Café. Six of us became close friends, Ingrid and Graham, Shirley and myself, and Tony Buckland and his girlfriend Diane, Tony being in Jesus College, but a flying buddy of Graham's whom he had met in Canada.

Ingrid deserves a paragraph at this juncture. Her father, Latvian in origin, had been conscripted into the German army whilst Ingrid and her mother had remained in Germany. In due course her father was captured and became a prisoner of war in Britain. The Russians overran the part of Germany where they lived. At the end of the war her father decided to stay in England and work in farming. He managed to get his wife and daughter over after a lot of hassle, and here she was.

Graham joined the Cambridge University flying club, which at that time had a fleet of Tiger Moths, open cockpit two-seater (one behind the other) biplanes. I was taken up by Graham. We looped the loop somewhere north of Cambridge, and for a short time I took the controls. I guess there are not many people around these days who have looped the loop in a Tiger Moth!

On 7 February 1955 I celebrated my 21st birthday anniversary and we had a big party in our rooms. Many old Sedberghians came, including Giles Shaw, now president of the Cambridge Union, who gave me two cigars. (I was not a smoker but kept them and had one at a subsequent party, which made me sick, and one on the *Dunera* when she was a troopship, in the Bay of Biscay in 1961, which made me sick!) Jonathan Miller, then developing his early medical career, Timothy Birdsall, then developing his cartooning career, Gerald Vinestock and a number of other figures later to do quite well were all there. Roger Lemaitre's girlfriend had to be helped out, having had a little too much of the vodka-laced punch, and a good time was had by all!

Roger Lemaitre obtained a Shell Scholarship and during his part II Geology was one of a group who surveyed Gough Island in the South Atlantic near Tristan de Cunha. Subsequently he went to work in Australia and I lost track of him until at a reunion, fifty years from matriculation, he turned up and proved now, with his second wife, to be running a large sheep ranch in Tasmania!

At the final St John's May Ball in 1955, Shirley and I danced the night away until on a clear moonlit night at about 4 a.m. we took a punt and punted up, past festivities in other colleges, to a shady area beyond the Mill where I 'sort of' proposed, and Shirley 'sort of' said 'We'll see', having been warned evidently, by the Homerton director of studies, that girls should **never** accept proposals there and then in a punt in the middle of the night from slightly intoxicated male undergraduates! How wise! But a previous punting expedition had made up my mind. We had one afternoon headed up a small creek in the same area where we had moored for a while – I forget what for! When it came to be time to go we discovered that there was no longer water in the creek. Unbeknownst to us, it happened to be the outflow from the swimming pool, which coincidentally was being drained at the time we approached, the task now being completed. At any event we were stuck on the mud 'good and proper'. So Shirley offed with her shoes and stockings and, getting in the mud with me, helped me push the punt off and back to the main stream. 'That's the girl for me,' I thought, and in due course it was so!

In the vacation between Cambridge and Bart's, two holidays proved very congenial. The first was Shirley and myself spending a week on the Norfolk Broads. All respectable-like, we had arranged to go as a four, with Ted Walker and his girlfriend going too, hiring two double-berth Whippet yachts and meeting up each evening when the two men would sleep in one boat, and the two girls in the other. Yes. This is how we got permission from the girls' parents. Sadly (?) our two friends had to pull out with only two or three weeks to go, and the whole thing looked as though it might have to be cancelled. We devised a fiendish plot, however, to take some photos of the four of us on the river banks of the Cam and to intersperse these with our holiday snaps on our return. Naive, maybe. A snag proved to be that the two films when developed were printed on very slightly different-sized paper. At any event we had a splendid week on the Broads in our Whippet, fairly innocent by modern standards, and duly showed our holiday snaps to Shirley's parents. I noticed Mr Jefferies turning some of the photos over slightly quizzically, but he said not a word, bless him!

The other trip was the theme of a later, as yet unpublished, manuscript entitled *Nina*. In 1954 the London taxi service was to re-equip and to modernise its fleet. These old coupé-style taxis were sold off at £50 a time. A great many students purchased these vehicles. They did not go much over 50 mph but they could turn on a sixpence and go up the side of a house. A syndicate of five of us including myself, Dick Ebberlie, Roger Moat and two others, put £10 each into the pot, and bought one. She was called Nina, and this was painted on the side. At the beginning of the Long Vacation, Dick and his two friends, Graham Sawley and another whose name I forget, took Nina over to France and drove her down to Rome and the Italian peninsula, returning eventually to Paris. Roger and I flew to Paris and picked her up and we made off, via France, Switzerland, Liechtenstein and Austria to the Yugoslavian border. Our adventures on the way are another story. We could not get over the first pass we tried, but eventually, after much boiling, succeeded in getting over the Passo Predil and down to Tolmin where we were fêted by an ex-partisan bank manager. We spoke a mixture of German and Russian and English and got by. We reached the caves at Postojna and made a lifelong friend of a student working as a guide there, Matija Vilhar. We reached the sea at Rijeka (Fiume) to witness the arrival of the Turkish president to that then communist state under Tito. We entered after passing the island of Krk into what was then Trieste zone B, contested between Italy and Yugoslavia, and had a barbecue and sing-song in a multi-national campsite in the hills at Opatije. We found at breakfast we had been sold a dozen bad eggs!

We drove around the top of the Adriatic and reached Venice in the dark, camping in one of the few slots left, to find in the morning we had camped on an ants' nest. Fortunately the ants were too busy devouring our half-eaten watermelon to notice two sleeping humans. All over the continent we kept meeting other students in other taxis! In Piacenza we met up with Clelia, Fanni and Carla, from the last year's Long Vac Club days, and above Nice we towed a broken down Mercedes home over the mountains and received a free lunch in thanks. But eventually we returned to England, bearded and scruffy, our tyres worn through, our battery no longer charging, and after a couple of nights at Shirley's home at Farley Green in Surrey, sleeping in their caravan and getting our first bath for a month, we made it home to Leeds, and the end of another adventure.

CHAPTER 4

Round the fountain

Having scraped through my final exams at Cambridge – I got 3rd class honours – I started at Bart's that October. My pal Befecadu Ijjigu, who had once brought Princess Sybil of Ethiopia to coffee in my rooms, had got a 'special'. This meant his degree was borderline and was awarded as a non-honours degree. He wisely wrote home to his father in Addis Ababa and said that not only had he passed his Cambridge BA degree but had been awarded a 'special', and his father sent him a sizeable monetary gift for doing so well! At Bart's we entered the world of clinical medicine. For three years we would be studying medicine, surgery, pathology, and obstetrics and gynaecology, and would at the end have to pass exams in all these.

Again my first year was spent in 'digs' out at Sydenham Hill, a cold, rather bleak, long, thin room, the digs shared with Bill Whimster who was now at Guy's Hospital, south of the river. We had to go in by train to Blackfriars, and the possibility of becoming fully involved with the Bart's college hall activities, and sport, was similarly a problem.

Our work was divided into two systems. One was that of formal lectures on the various topics we were studying. The other was to be 'ward clerks' on a ward at the hospital, where we were attached to a particular consultant team and were required to take a history and examine each new patient who came in, and to write it up to present at the next ward round. There was also practical learning at these sessions, such as how to interpret heart sounds heard through a stethoscope, how to take blood, and how to examine the body systematically. We also had some training in nursing procedures, such as how properly to make a bed! During the first year we spent six months on a medical team, and six months on a surgical team, I with Dr Cullinan and Dr Black (medical) for the first six months, and Mr Badenoch and Mr Corbett (surgical) the second.

Meanwhile my unofficial fiancée, Shirley, had obtained a probationary teaching post at Carshalton, not all that far away. She lived at home near Guildford and drove up and back with her father, a headmaster of a school near Croydon. We were thus enabled to meet up reasonably regularly, and I went down to stay with her family in Farley Green some weekends. I also joined the Bart's choir, known as the Rahere Choir, who again performed sacred music often in local churches. I joined a south London lacrosse club and played for Purley for that winter season. In my second year I was able to get into the

31

The Priory Church of St Bartholomew the Great

college hall at Charterhouse Square, which was five minutes' walk from the hospital, the other side of Smithfield meat market.

St Bartholomew's Hospital was founded in 1123 by Rahere following a pilgrimage he had made to Rome, and was a priory hospital originally associated with the Priory Church of St Bartholomew the Great, in Smithfield Square, a beautiful church, much of which had been destroyed at the time of Henry VIII, but the chancel, now the main part of the church, remained as a parish church, the building being largely Norman.

Charterhouse Square held an eight-storey hostel for residential students, and also the pre-clinical school for students who were doing their complete medical training as part of London University. These students had only done the first and second MB courses and not the extra year required for the Oxford and Cambridge Natural Sciences degree and so there was a little bit of rivalry between the two groups. I made new friends in the hostel, while retaining Bill

Whimster who went on to be a professor of pathology in London but sadly dropped dead of a heart attack while giving a lecture to students, some five years ago.

My new 'buddies' were Cedric Davies, a Welsh-speaking Welshman (he knew English as well) who went on to public health in Wales; Michael Cawley, who became a rheumatologist on the South Coast; Anna Warriner, who married Clive Upjohn, a paediatrician; and Brian Richards who, apart from becoming a consultant surgeon in York, got his BTA 'diploma' (been to America), not to study medicine but as a jazz clarinettist. Cedric inspired me to learn some more Welsh.

It is interesting which languages we study in school and to what end we perceive their value. There was in the past good reason for learning the classical languages, principally Latin and Greek, but for the high fliers, also Hebrew or Sanskrit. The logic was to enable the 'educated classes' to read the classics, and the languages of religion, in their original, and also, as education broadened in the last century, for the brighter to get a grounding in the vocabulary, grammar and origins of our own English language and the modern languages of Europe – French, Spanish and Italian in particular, and also Romanian from Latin. Latin of course, before Norman French, had been the Lingua Franca of Europe – if that is not a mixed metaphor! English, from Anglo Saxon with a lot of Norman French and input from the Celtic languages is very rich in vocabulary, but it might almost be as logical to learn Icelandic to see the early roots of our language as it would be Latin.

Another reason for studying a modern language is its usefulness in the world of travel and commerce. This is the logic for learning French and, as a second language, German. Nowadays Spanish or Russian is also offered, both much more widely spoken than French or German. French is the language of France where a hundred years ago most people went if travelling aboard, but it is not that widely spoken outside of France, Belgium and France's ex-colonies. German is hardly spoken beyond Germany, Austria and Switzerland, but it is a language in which a lot of scientific publications are written. Spanish is very widely spoken, and by almost the whole of the Central and South American continents. The most widely spoken languages are Russian, the two main Chinese languages of Mandarin and Cantonese, and Arabic. But where would one find the teachers? More simply, an international language such as Esperanto might be a good idea – except that it has never taken off.

Welsh, however, is the second most widely spoken language in the British Isles. Most Welsh speakers learn English but, to the English, Welsh is largely a closed book. Why? Welsh is a member of the six still extant Celtic language groups – divided into the three Gaelic languages of Scotland, Ireland, and the little used Manx, and the southern group of Welsh, Breton and Cornish, the latter now only an enthusiast's hobby. So, being eccentric, I enjoyed learning Welsh!

I digress. In the second year we learned a number of other areas of medicine including pathology (the study of abnormal changes in tissue), pharmacology, and obstetrics and gynaecology. We also spent three-month slots part-time in the casualty department acting as 'dresser'; in dermatology (skins), the 'Special Clinic' (VD), paediatrics and orthopaedics (bones), and psychiatry.

The casualty department at Bart's produced a lot of injuries from the Smithfield meat market. The meat porters were familiar with our clinic and liked the dressers. We always got an excellent steak and chips at the porters' café over the road from the hospital. Then we got the usual problems of the time from the relatively small number of local residents still living in the city after the war. We had leg ulcers that wouldn't heal to clean and dress. We used red lotion, tulle gras and often packed deep ulcers with granulated sugar to clean them up if infected. Then there were the hydroceles to drain – old men with scrotums swollen to the size of a coconut, or even a football, in one case that I recall.

The city in 1955 was still largely a wasteland of bomb damage stretching from Charterhouse to the Bank. A few blocks of high-rise had been built, and one church stood out relatively untouched in the ruins, but most of the city had yet to be redeveloped. The Bart's hostel in Charterhouse Square was one such high-rise new building. I was on the seventh floor, said to be the nearest to heaven, not because it was the top storey; there was one above it reserved for female students. The college had tennis courts, squash courts and in the summer an excellent croquet lawn. At the hospital itself next to the old nurses' residency we discovered a fives court of Rugby style, disused for some years, which we cleared out of rubbish and put into use again, forming a team and playing in the London Colleges' League. I also played in the hospital tennis and squash teams in the London Hospitals' League.

The hospital was built round a fine tree-lined inner courtyard. There was a chapel with its own parish, known as Bart's the Less, a famous Great Hall filled with expensive classical paintings which also served as an examination hall, and in the centre the famous ornamental fountain where people would gather in a sunny lunch hour, and where on the annual open day, drinks and refreshments would be served.

One of our fellow students, a man called Mitchell, was a wag. He had a splendid lustful growl, and on the night of the Bart's Ball in college hall he played a high volume repetitive tape recording of this growl from his window, and dropped water-filled condom 'bombs' from the sixth floor onto unsuspecting revellers below. He had a habit of leaving a small set of upper dentures in a glass overnight in the communal washrooms and on the next founder's day a victim got his own back. Mitchell could not find his teeth that morning, and they were perceived on the arrival of important guests, to be hanging from the finger of a cupid in the middle of the fountain.

In our third year we did a further six months on the medical and surgical wards at a more responsible level. I was not entirely sure at this stage that a career in medicine, using this term in a general sense, was entirely for me. I enjoyed learning the skills; I found some of the subjects interesting, for example assisting at operations, but I found paediatrics quite stressful. Many of the women students loved working on the children's wards, but I found having to inflict pain on a child, for example doing lumbar punctures on young children with tubercular meningitis or even having to put a drip up, emotionally hard, and seeing young children with cancer of an eyeball, or dying of leukaemia, was horrid.

I discovered I did **not** like getting up in the night, an inevitable part of surgical and obstetric practice, and indeed the life of a GP in those days on call day and night. But I did get turned on by psychiatry – the small amount that we did. Our tuition in this sub-specialty was carried out by a Dr Strauss. There was at that time no professorship in psychiatry at Bart's and he only had three beds on the general ward. Most of his beds were out at Goodmayes Hospital (where we went to have the more acute psychotic work displayed for us and overcame our embarrassment at taking histories from people who might talk or behave bizarrely at times). I found this area fascinating, and Dr Strauss's very wide general knowledge inspiring.

Obstetrics was a problem at Bart's at that time. As the residential population of the Bart's city catchment area was so low, there were not that many women having babies, and it was necessary for much of our practical work to go elsewhere. I spent part of my practice at Carshalton Hospital, but made efforts to get to the Rotunda Hospital in Dublin for the rest, since that hospital at the time had a very high reputation and, Dublin ladies tending to have a high birth rate, gave one plenty of experience. To that end, in the early summer of 1958 I found myself flying into Dublin airport to spend some weeks living and working at the Rotunda at the top of O'Connell Street under the tutorship of Mr Thompson, the Master. We were part of Trinity College, Dublin and were in Dublin to deliver babies. The labour ward where we started by observing twenty deliveries and delivering under supervision was always very busy. It was also often bedlam. I recall a young Irish lady having this conversation with the large midwife, who was assisting her delivery:

'Oh, oh, mother of God, will you save me from the pain?'

'Will you shut your hollering, woman, and push when I tell you?'

'Ah sure, I'll never survive it!'

'Will you bloody push?'

The normal baby was delivered without more ado, though the conversation continued in similar vein!

When we had completed our labour ward experience and had had the first week of lectures, we were paired up, two students (without midwife or doctor) on the rota list for home deliveries. We did not see 'primips' (women with no previous pregnancy) nor 'grand multips' (over five), but went to the rest. When the family got in touch with the hospital, those at the top of the list were sent out to the house, by taxi, and had to stay there until delivery was completed. If anything untoward looked like happening, such as an unexpected difficult presentation, a post-partum haemorrhage, or retained placenta, we were to call the duty doctor, who would come out in an ambulance to assess and deal with it.

These simple tasks were not always easy. The new estate at Drumcondra had all its street names in Irish Gaelic. We had the address in English. The taxi driver didn't know the Irish for 'Miller Street' – it turned out to be 'Sraid a' mhuillin'. Often the houses had no phone and the call-box might not be working. Usually, however, there was a gaggle of female friends and relations gathered around the bed who were very willing to help. Sometimes we got there to find the baby had already been delivered.

The houses and flats in the inner slums were none too clean. Fleas were rife. I recall one house where on turning back the sheet to examine the woman's abdomen, I saw a tummy covered in flea bites, and one cheeky fellow actually sitting on the mons Veneris looking at me. While waiting, sitting on the sofa, I caught three with my own hands that were inclined to join me, and drowned them in the sink. One got adept at flea catching. There were two common kinds of flea in Dublin, the European black flea, whose maximum jump was around twelve inches, and a more vigorous American flea, red in colour and with a greater jumping capacity. When going to bed at night one, if sensible, armed oneself with a wet bar of soap, and flung back the sheets. Any flea sitting there could then be zapped with the wet soap if one was quick, and then rinsed away under the tap. The small non-biting ants that inhabited the towels when they came back from the laundry in the residency were presumably living in the airing cupboard. The cockroaches in the bathroom usually scuttled away when one switched the light on, but sometimes got trapped in the bath. They were friendly little fellows, and harmless scavengers, but amazingly quick and difficult therefore to catch. Well, it was 1958!

I was paired with Margaret Hanlon, an attractive redhead from Glasgow, also like myself doing an obstetrics elective in Dublin. Once a home delivery was successfully completed and we had checked back in at the Rotunda, we went to the bottom of the list, which usually meant some forty-eight hours free. We often congregated at the Elite Café, an all-night café opposite the hospital in O'Connell Street, or in Murphy's pub over the road. The Elite served ham and eggs all night and was useful if one had been on the district for some hours and got back very late. One of our fellow students, from Belfast, was thrown out for playing 'The Protestant Boy' on his mouth organ, but mostly all were welcome. Margaret and I would go to the cinema, and on one occasion down to the meeting of the waters in the Vale of Avoca, to Glendalough, and to Poulaphouca on our days off.

The residency had a squash court and a croquet lawn also for relaxation, and we had many parties. There was a party fortnightly to greet the new arrivals, a party fortnightly for the leavers, and usually a party in the middle for good measure. *Island in the Sun* with Harry Belafonte was on at the cinema, and a rebel song, 'The Rising of the Moon', was Top of the Pops, with 'Scarlet Ribbons' and 'Come back to Bally James Dough' second and third!

It was a fascinating elective. I delivered some forty babies, saw a retained placenta removed on the kitchen table under chloroform, and even used forceps under supervision. These days, of course, nothing like that would happen, and a trained midwife always goes out with the students. The insects are gone, and Dublin is buzzing. Sic transit Gloria Swanson! Back at Bart's there were the final ward allocations and we became busy with revision. There was still time, however, to visit Burnham-on-Crouch for some sailing on the estuary at the Bart's Yacht Club. The college had a small boathouse and a couple of 12-foot yachts (fireflies), and we entered the regatta with occasional success.

Dr Black, on whose team I was at the time, was on the Court of Electors of the Society of Apothecaries. The Society was one of the London Livery Companies, a Guild which had originally derived from the Guild of Pepperers & Spicers, through the Grocers, and getting its own charter in the sixteenth century when it catered for those who were to become, at a later stage, the modern pharmacists and general practitioners. It was led by Gideon de Laune in this battle.

The City of London has numerous guilds and livery companies, some of which go back to the eleventh century. In olden days they regulated trade in the city and maintained standards. Admission was by patrimony through one's father, through apprenticeship, or in some cases by purchase or given as an honour. Other cities such as York, Chester and Coventry also had guilds. Many disappeared in the last century as a consequence of changes in local government, but others survived. During their history, the Society of Apothecaries had its battles with the Royal College of Physicians over rights to practise and prescribe, as did the Barber-Surgeons Guild with the Royal College of Surgeons. The Apothecaries, however, still are one of the bodies who have a right to award a licence to practise in medicine and surgery and they have a superb medieval hall in Blackfriars, some ten minutes' walk from Bart's. Dr Black asked me if I would be interested in joining, and subsequently I did.

The other major event that occurred during my time at Bart's is that Shirley and I got engaged. I purchased the ring, a diamond cluster, at a jeweller's in the area of St Bartholomew's Fair and asked her father for her hand, one weekend at Farley Green. To celebrate we purchased a car together from a fellow Bart's student. We called her 'Myfanwy'. She was a maroon 1934 open-top two-seater Morris Minor. She started by cranking and had a simple engine with a top speed of about 45 mph. She was not as beautiful as my fiancée but was nevertheless in her own way a beautiful little car. One weekend it took us to Cornwall and back to hear a service in the old Cornish language at a small church on the Lizard, as part of the Cornish Gorsedd celebrations, a round-trip of over 400 miles.

As a Cambridge medical student, I was to take my degree exams in Cambridge itself for the bachelor's degree in medicine and surgery (MB, B.Chir.) and Dr Black suggested I sit the Society of Apothecaries exam as a practice run up to the university finals, and a slightly easier exam, for the licence in medicine and surgery of the Society of Apothecaries (LMSSA). This I did in the late spring of 1958 and passed it. I then sat the Cambridge exam and failed the surgery paper. This was a dilemma, and my stepfather was worried, wondering if I would leave it at that and knowing that with only an LMSSA I could not expect to get far in a medical career. Also, the National Service Board – still in existence – wrote to me pointing out that I would be called up in early 1960, giving me time to do my house jobs! I was annoyed by failing surgery, and by my stepfather's prognostications, and this I suppose started me as a qualification collector, eventually finishing up, if one counted a BA as well as an MA, and a membership as well as a fellowship, with forty-seven letters after my name! I think I have at the time of writing finished, though I have not included an NVQ in 'Performing Manufacturing Operations' obtained when I was seventy!

So, I had to resit the Cambridge Surgical Exam six months later. I decided as another string to my bow to sit the 'Conjoint Board Exam in Medicine and Surgery' awarded as a double diploma MRCS LRCP by the Royal Colleges of Physicians & Surgeons in London and to try for the lot at once – i.e. exams in Medicine, Surgery, Pathology, Obstetrics and Gynaecology. This I passed in the autumn of 1958.

In the meantime I had spent a happy summer revising my surgery and since the London Bart's students took their exams later in the year, was able to develop with Cedric Davies the art of 'blogging' to its ultimate. Blogging was I suppose the equivalent of the aristocratic lifestyle of a young man in the nineteenth century. We rose late, but in time to have a bath before breakfast. After breakfast and reading the paper we would go over to the hospital and attend suitable lectures or study in the library for an hour or two. We would return for lunch before, in suitable weather, playing croquet on the college lawn. We got rather good and won a magnum of champagne in the Bart's Hospital croquet tournament. In the evening we would perhaps have a game of tennis, or go into town, and so to bed. A pleasant life, to be shattered once real work began! I resat surgery in Cambridge in the spring of 1959 and passed it. I now had therefore a BA, MB, B.Chir, MRCS, LRCP, and LMSSA, and was the most qualified person in the college! It had not done me a lot of good in one sense, however, since I had missed out on a Bart's house job and had

had to get gainful employment before I sat my final exam, since otherwise I would not have qualified for entering National Service as a medical officer the following year. One had to complete a year of pre-registration house jobs before becoming a fully-fledged doctor allowed to practise. I got a post in Harrogate.

CHAPTER 5

Doctor in the house

M Y FIRST SIX MONTHS at Harrogate were as house surgeon to a Mr Gordon
Bailey at Harrogate General Hospital, but also included covering the
ENT (Ear, Nose, & Throat) surgeons' beds, and one night a week on a casualty
rota. My registrar was Terry O'Donovan, a Rhodesian who went on to become
a heart surgeon and was with Professor Christian Barnard in South Africa when
the first heart transplant was performed.

Specialists in surgery call themselves 'Mr' for reasons of inverted snobbery.
In the days of the Barber-Surgeon's Company those who specialised as
surgeons, but were not physicians (one did not have to qualify in both in those
days; today one does) were not therefore technically 'doctors'. Now, everyone
qualifies in general medicine as well, but those who finish up in surgery revert
to being called Mr. Not that most doctors are doctors in the degree sense at all.
The majority are 'bachelors' (even the ladies) since the qualifying degree is
Bachelor of Medicine & Surgery (MB, ChB., or B.Chir., which is the posh title
– Bachelor of Chirurgery). One only becomes a doctor so far as the university
is concerned if obtaining the highest degree awarded, a doctorate, which may
be in medicine, or law or divinity or philosophy, or science, or letters.

I had a busy job. I was underpaid at £500 a year, was on call all hours of
the day and night, got little sleep, and was woken when on casualty call by
people turning up for the most fatuous reasons, which could have perfectly well
been dealt with by their GP or the practice nurse. I decided that, interesting
though it was, assisting at operations and doing my own varicose veins, the odd
appendix under supervision, and running the minor ops clinic (removing warts
and pimples and stitching up cuts) surgery as a career was not for me. Nor
would obstetrics and gynaecology be, since women mostly seemed to have their
babies in the night and I did not like getting up at night.

Shirley and I decided that we had waited long enough being engaged and
that we would get married on 2 May, halfway through my surgical house job,
and take my fortnight's leave for the honeymoon. Though I say it myself 'wot
shouldn't', the wedding was utterly splendid. We decided to marry at the Priory
Church of St Bartholomew the Great, West Smithfield in London. London was
convenient for the majority of local guests, and I was on the parish register of
Bart's the Great from my student days. We were in our fairly high church phase
and decided to have a full nuptial mass. The vicar was Neville Wallbank and
the organist Paul Steinitz. A choirgirl sang 'I know that my redeemer liveth'

40

Married – 2 May 1959

while the register was being signed. Shirley had two young bridesmaids, Caroline Power and Rosemary Killick, and my best man was Graham Burgess. Cedric Davies made a tape recording of the service for us.

My stepfather had by this time died, after a rather lingering illness, from heart failure and chronic bronchitis. Mother was able to come and my aunts from Sheffield, Shirley's parents and her brother Roger, who with her two cousins, Chester and Harvey White, and my cousin Hedley, made up the ushers. We then repaired to the Society of Apothecaries for our reception in their superb medieval banqueting hall, with drinks in the inner courtyard beforehand. There were some 120 guests, and some good speeches.

I had borrowed mother's car for the honeymoon, and after changing out of our morning suit and wedding dress, we left the revellers and headed off south out of London for, so far as Shirley was concerned, a secret destination, spending the first night at the Dover Stage Hotel. Mother had a classic Morris Minor of 1956 vintage, which did us proud throughout the 2,000 miles or so of our trip. Our second night we spent in Luxembourg, and crossing the Moselle by ferry (no bridge then) we completed the 400-mile drive on the next day to reach the Gasthaus Löwen in Vaduz, Liechtenstein, just in time for dinner. It was dark when we arrived. The hotel was in traditional alpine style, wooden framed, antique Austrian-type furnishings, and a big feather bed. When we awoke the next morning we drew the curtains. Above us was the Prince's fairy castle on a crag overlooking the 'capital' of Vaduz. A quaint main street ran down towards the shops. Mountains were all around us, and to the west the garden sloped down towards the Rhine and the Swiss border. We looked down from our window to the road outside – and there was a Wallace Arnold charabanc from Leeds!

In Liechtenstein we explored. We walked in the hidden valley of the Malbuntal, Malbun being reached by a hair-raising road climbing up the mountain past the castle, and then through a tunnel to appear in the next valley west, past the little community and church at Steg, with the peaks of the Dreischwestern to our left, and on up a valley running west-east from the Austrian border, to the little village of Malbun and its one hotel. (No longer. Prince Charles popularised skiing in the Malbuntal and it is now a well-known skiing centre). We explored the Saminatal, and met a lone walker coming down the mountainside towards us. He proved to be a Hungarian refugee, crossing the borders through wild mountain passes at night, and heading for Switzerland. We spoke, both in our limited German, and walked back down with him to the valley.

We dined at the Vaduzerhoff and started the dancing. We drove one day round to the Austrian pass at Arlberg, crossed to Italy and came back round to the southern end of Liechtenstein, passing the Red House, and to Vaduz again. We had our passports stamped at the tourist office 'Quick', run by Baron von Falzfein, and walked by the Rhine. After a week we headed back, to spend our last night at the Ritz in Paris. We dined there and drank of the wine. It was in the days before credit cards and easily transferable cheques. We had traveller's cheques but when we came to pay the bill I was ten francs short in French money. They magnanimously let me off!

Back to work in Harrogate I had to live in at the hospital. Shirley stayed with my mother in Leeds and got a teaching job in my old kindergarten at Richmond House, Far Headingley. I would arrive one weekend a fortnight, shattered and not in the mood for high romance! It was not a terribly good start but we had to make the best of it. Shirley had brought her dog, Storm, getting on in life and not to be left. We still had Myfanwy, and Shirley would come over to Harrogate the weekends I was on call. Graham Burgess had obtained a teaching post at Grosvenor House School in Harrogate and there was therefore a little group of old friends.

After completing my surgical six months, I took the six-month medical post available with a general physician, Dr Reah, and the paediatrician, Dr Prosser, again a joint post, but with less pressure and fewer night calls. I had hoped to do a third six months by obtaining a senior house officer post in Psychiatry in Leeds or York, but received my call-up papers and was required to attend at Mitchett in March of 1960, my job in Harrogate being due to end in February, which gave us a week or so together before I went off into Her Majesty's services.

I had, whilst at Sedbergh, reached the rank of 'Under Officer' in the school corps. We had passed the Certificate A and Certificate B exams and I had led a parade. In my last year I had been in the school CCF band as a bugler. The army therefore was not entirely unfamiliar. At Mitchett we were issued with kit, and given, as qualified doctors, the rank of lieutenant. Nevertheless we were required to do six weeks' basic training, in marching and drill skills, in map reading and other military necessities. We also had a week's lectures on army hygiene and tropical medicine and were about to go for our final two weeks when, because of the shortage of doctors in the army at that time, we received notice of our posting.

We had been asked where our interest and specialisation lay, and I had put down psychiatry. I was, surprisingly, posted to Netley Hospital at Southampton, the headquarters of army psychiatry, and settled into the mess. It was of course too good to be true and within the week was moved out to become the medical officer of the 17th Port Regiment based at Marchwood, on the other side of Southampton Water. Netley Hospital was a huge and imposing building, built to house wounded soldiers in the First and Second World Wars. It was, by 1960, largely empty and little went on apart from psychiatry, which was round the back in two wings, P Wing for psychotic patients, and some prefab accommodation for clinics, medical staff offices, patients with psycho-neurotic conditions, and so on.

I was fortunate in that, although the GDMO for the Royal Engineers, I was able on weekday afternoons to travel round the top of Southampton Water, through Southampton, to Netley to work part-time in the units there. The Commandant at the time was Brigadier McGhie, and Peter Abrahams, later to become head of army psychiatry but at that time an ex-medical student colleague of mine, shared some of my duties.

At that time, Netley Hospital was still using the deep insulin coma technique for the treatment of schizophrenia, and modified insulin therapy for people with anorexia nervosa. When first used, it was pioneer treatment at the end of the war and preceded electroplexy (ECT) in the treatment of psychotic states. Its history is interesting. In pre-treatment days when there was really nothing but sedation, with such medication as paraldehyde, to calm the more severe psychotic illnesses of melancholia, mania and schizophrenia, it had been noticed that certain individuals who had concomitantly suffered from epilepsy, sometimes after an epileptic fit, showed a temporary but dramatic improvement in their psychotic state. Why? It led Meduna to the idea that the deliberate induction of a seizure discharge in the brain might be an effective way of treating such conditions. How? It was known that camphor could induce such fits. Give the patient camphor in a sufficient dose to induce a fit, under controlled conditions and see. This was done, and surprisingly perhaps, proved quite successful in some long-term, otherwise untreatable, crazy people, but it was hazardous. The fits were unpredictable in strength and duration, and injury or even death could occasionally occur.

It was also noted that people suffering from hypoglycaemia, the opposite of diabetes, when the blood sugar becomes abnormally low, could produce fits. With the introduction of insulin to treat diabetes, a means of deliberately lowering the blood sugar to seizure levels was available, more controllable and thus safer than camphor. The patient, in the morning before breakfast, would receive an injection of a measured dose of insulin, in bed, and be carefully observed. This, in diabetic terms, was an overdose of insulin, and in half an hour to an hour produced a hypoglycaemic attack when the patient began to sweat, be tremulous and confused, lapsing into an unconscious state and then having an epileptiform type of convulsion. This could then be terminated by giving a glucose drink if the patient were able to swallow, or an injection of glucose if not. The dose of insulin could be varied to suit the individual, and termination was usually straightforward. People would have a course of ten to twenty such treatments, perhaps three times a week. Recovery from the psychotic episode was reasonably effective though about one-third relapsed. This was a dramatic breakthrough in the treatment of what in past times would have been called 'madness'. But the treatment was still not without risk. The epileptiform fit was not modified and still rather unpredictable in onset, so a nurse had to watch each patient individually over the course of perhaps two hours, and occasionally the hypoglycaemia could not be reversed, so that deaths could still occasionally occur. Better perhaps than a lifetime in an old-fashioned 'lunatic asylum', nevertheless.

At about the time that I started at Netley a new and much safer treatment was coming in, using an electrical stimulus to induce the epileptiform discharge. This could be literally switched on and off and was found to be particularly effective in treating the serious psychotic depression of melancholia, and in attacks of manic-depressive psychosis. This was of course a decade before anti-depressants became readily available. To begin with such treatment was used 'straight', the patient being conscious before the electrodes were placed on either side of the forehead and the current briefly switched on. The epileptiform seizure followed immediately afterwards, and staff knew exactly when it would occur and were therefore prepared. A later modification came with the development of rapid-acting anaesthetics and muscle relaxants, which improved the safety and acceptability of the treatment considerably.

But to talk more of Netley is unnecessary. Suffice to say that while in the army for my two-year National Service, I was able to take Part I of the diploma in psychological medicine awarded by the Royal College and to do some useful work helping the psychologist, Tom Brown, in administering psychological testing, including the famous Rorschach 'ink blot' test, popular at the time.

On the other side of Southampton Water lay Marchwood, curiously the next village down from Totton, where my father had been in 1896. I was housed in the mess until Shirley, still in Leeds, and I could find accommodation. There was no married accommodation available on camp. Shirley came down and spent a couple of days searching, and came up with a teaching post in Portswood and, at the eleventh hour, a bed-sitting room also in Portswood in a house owned by an elderly, and rather pernickety, spinster! Still, it was a roof over our heads. I moved out of the mess. We decided we needed another car and came across a Triumph Roadster, a red sports car with 'dicky' seats in the back and a let-down roof, run by a Standard Vanguard engine, a superb car with a gear lever (preceding the automatic) on the steering wheel. It and we looked very fine. Poor Myfanwy was sold. We called the new car Willoughby Fortescue, which somehow seemed appropriate.

I was in effect the general practitioner for the regiment and some families. The 17th Port Regiment's function was to train soldiers to run a port, to load and unload cargo from ships, load on and off a train, work the cranes, do shallow water driving repairs to jetties and landing craft, sail a craft and drive a train. The shallow water diving school was a particular interest for me. A few of the divers, who went down not more than some thirty feet, nevertheless developed a red eardrum. This was not an infection, nor was there any perforation. It did allow me, however, to write my second published work, and the first in a professional journal, (the real first being an article on my experiences on my Dublin elective, in the Bart's journal), the *Journal of Otorhinolaryngology*, (Ear, Nose, and Throat!) entitled, 'Diver's Ear'. I also had the opportunity to experience a decompression chamber.

We eventually got a quarter after the Colonel, who was speaking in Southampton that evening, asked if he could change at our house. The landlady kept switching the landing light off so that when he came out to go to the bathroom, and back, he was again plunged into darkness! The gas geyser in the bathroom was also faulty. We got a quarter at Marchwood within the month.

I was made up to Captain in my second year. We had a batman called Crocker who was very good to Shirley when in due course she became pregnant with our first child. In the medical centre I had a Corporal Hazlegrove, who surprised us one day by taking an overdose of Dexedrine and phenobarbitone, a cunning move that got him into hospital but did not kill him since the stimulant and sedative to some extent balanced each other out. The reason later became clear, when we discovered he had been buying agricultural equipment on hire purchase and selling it on illegally, and forging signatures. It was discovered he had been in the army and discharged dishonourably once before under another name! History inevitably repeated itself!

Captain Haslam, RAMC

We kept the house, a very pleasant three-bedroomed detached house in a close, until I completed my service. Sadly and unwittingly, not long before we left, we wrecked it. We had gone on Christmas leave and not turned off the stopcock in the rising main. There was a very sharp cold spell while we were away. Neighbours had broken in to see why water was pouring out of the back door. The metal connection to the cold water tank in the roof had actually split and come out. The water overflowed the tank and filled the loft, eventually bringing down the bedroom ceiling. The water then filled the bedroom and brought down the kitchen ceiling which, when full, exited through the back door. I was not court-martialled, since it had not been put in standing orders to turn off stopcocks! The adjutant was censured and I, by complete coincidence, was made up to acting major. The reason for this was that one Major Tullett, medical officer on the troopship *Dunera* had in some way blotted his copybook and been taken off the job, when the ship reached Southampton. There were three troopships operating out of Southampton at that time, the *Oxfordshire*, *Dunera*, and *Delwara*. A new medical officer was required at short notice for the *Dunera* and I was given the job. One week's embarkation leave and then off I went, made up to major and in charge of all the troops and families going out to Aden. I had a colleague, a drunken Irish ship's doctor

(Merchant Navy) who was in charge of the crew. I became a rare bird, since I was one of the ship's officers, an army officer attached to the Merchant Navy. I had two QA (Queen Alexander) nursing officers with me.

Shirley and I had a slightly tearful parting and I sailed away into the sunset. Crossing the Bay of Biscay it was quite rough. I ran my morning clinic and had to minister to the needs of the seasick passengers while intermittently vomiting myself! However, our lunch-time and evening social activities soon sorted this out. At lunch-time I quickly had to learn how to mix gin and daiquiri, to make 'pink gins' in the right proportions, and to ensure the drinks were doubles! Two double gins was standard pre-lunch fare, and all the available ships officers met by rota in our various cabins. My cabin steward soon put me right. In the evening we met again, when double whisky was the tipple. In the evenings there was a bridge four that I was invited to join and my bridge rapidly improved and seasickness rapidly vanished.

On the whole my clinics were not busy, indeed dentistry formed quite a part due to toothache. By the time we got to Gibraltar I was a hardened seaman. I discovered I was required to lecture the troops on hygiene (how to avoid the clap and the pox) and on tropical medicine, and such topics as sun stroke, dehydration and salt depletion. I wondered at my cheek, but the army health manuals told one exactly what to say!

A few days later and we were moored in Valletta where some troops were disembarked. One of the army officers offered me a day tour of the island, which allowed me to boast that I knew Malta well (even better than Sweden where I once went for a coffee!), then on towards Cyprus, skirting the island of Crete and getting a flu epidemic on board, which caused us to be refused landing rights at Famagusta, then on to the Suez Canal. We passed through the canal in convoy, a Russian ship ahead of us. There was a pause halfway in the Salt Lake, and then on out into the Red Sea. I liked to stand in the evening on the foredeck and see the stars, and sometimes flying fish in schools leaping ahead of the ship. It became much hotter and we changed into tropical kit. Eventually we docked at Aden where I had a week or so relatively free, as all the troops and families disembarked and we waited for those returning to the UK to embark.

Aden was in those days a British enclave, a colony, and had a sizeable garrison. The town centre was quite attractive. The place, however, had virtually no natural fresh water and relied on ships to bring water in. If one ventured into town one was quickly surrounded by little urchins, some Somali, some Yemeni, some Arab, and some Ethiopian who sought 'baksheesh'. One was not left alone unless one gave some money. Then the crowd doubled quickly and one was left even less alone! But the shops were duty free.

Up on the hillside above the town was a large shanty town where migrant workers lived in shacks made out of bits of wood, cardboard and material. Most of them, however, had aerials and one could hear music coming from them! The way to escape was to go down to the officers' club a mile or so out of town at the beach. The sand out of the shade was so hot one could not walk on it barefoot. The sun shone, the sea was beautifully warm and there was a shark net to protect bathers.

On the return voyage I had as a patient a baby with an irreducible hernia. I had no experience of what to do. My Irish colleague gave an ethyl-chloride anaesthetic and I was able to reduce the hernia. I worried, though, that the bit of bowel might become gangrenous. I strapped up the offending region and insisted, I think unnecessarily, with hindsight, and unpopularly with both the family and the captain, on the child being taken off the ship at the next port.

Our voyage – my only one – was also the last voyage of the *Dunera* as a troopship and I had the opportunity to broadcast on the BBC World Service on the life of a ship's MO to the Middle East Land Forces. On the last night but one of the voyage we were again crossing the Bay of Biscay and had a final party. I smoked the second of the cigars I had been given on my 21st birthday by Giles Shaw, and was sick again!

CHAPTER 6

The day job

WHEN I LEFT the army we had to move from Marchwood and find
employment. I decided to get a post in psychiatry and scanned the
jobs section of the *British Medical Journal* for vacancies. A trainee post was
advertised in Leeds, one in York, and one in Huddersfield. I applied and some
three weeks after moving temporarily into my mother's flat, I got an interview
for York. Mother had been living in the Ringrose house still, after my
stepfather's death, while Mrs Hopps lived on. She had seen Stella married at St
Chad's Church in Leeds to a vet, Robert Lapraik, from Edinburgh. Tom (the
son) was now working as a radiotherapist at the Mount Sinai Hospital in New
York.

I got the York job, based at Naburn Hospital on the Selby side, to the lee of
the sewage works. The hospital was one of the county mental hospitals, with
some 400 beds. Adjacent was Fulford Hospital, for maternity and gynaecology,
and we were given a maisonette to the rear of Naburn Hospital, accessed from
and attached to the hospital, but also out into nice landscaped grounds. Naburn
took the NHS clientele from York and Selby, whilst its sister hospital, Bootham
Park, an ex-private hospital now in the NHS, took the more select snob end
of the patient market! York, also for historical reasons, had the Retreat, a private
psychiatric hospital, a Quaker foundation, founded by Samuel Tuke as an
alternative to the 'shocking abuses' at Bootham Park in the eighteenth century!
On the north-west, Thirsk, side of York, was Clifton Hospital, the old North
Riding of Yorkshire county asylum which took admissions from Whitby,
Thirsk, Scarborough, Northallerton, Harrogate, Ripon, Knaresborough and
Wetherby. There were also two hospitals for mental handicap/mental defi-
ciency/subnormality/learning disability. But what's in a name? Stigma is a
product of ignorance of the condition and not the name of a building or the
group name for the conditions from which people suffer. No one can say that
most of the residents were not dis-eased. So, York was a centre for psychiatry
and was associated with Leeds University, whence it took students, and in
which there was held a two-year course for the diploma in psychological
medicine. Having already got Part I, I joined the second year of the course.

Shirley was by now heavy with child and duly gave birth to our firstborn on
the 3 June 1962 – not without a struggle! The child was named Fiona Dunstan,
the second name being my wife's side's family name, and Fiona was christened
in the Naburn Hospital Chapel.

One of the less selfless reasons for taking up psychiatry was my detestation of getting up in the night and my belief (unfounded) that a junior doctor in psychiatry would not need to get up too often. With hindsight, most admissions in psychiatry are emergencies, and quite often at night! Furthermore, in a four-hundred-bed hospital, and the only doctor on call in residence from 5.30 p.m. to 8.30 a.m., there are always things cropping up. Someone cuts himself and needs stitching; someone has an epileptic fit; an old lady falls out of bed – has she broken her leg?; someone may be developing appendicitis, and so on and so on. At least there was a rota of five of us, so allowing for holidays and illness, one night a week and one weekend a month one was busy. The other nights one could sleep peacefully – except that Fiona, bless her, never slept fully through the night until she was about three years old, though easily beaten by our third born, Melanie, in due course, who only slept through twice until she was five!

The medical superintendent for whom I worked at Naburn was a Dr Hugh Warren, a kind man though fairly punctilious. He lived in the superintendent's house in the grounds. He was to live to see the closure of Naburn Hospital, part of the general demolition of in-patient psychiatry, before very sadly dying of late onset Huntington's Chorea, his widow seeing their daughter die of a juvenile from of the disease in her middle teens, a particularly horrid, fatal and untreatable illness.

At this time I joined, on the recommendation of Arthur Bowen, the medical superintendent of Bootham Park, an organisation called the Society of Clinical Psychiatrists. I also became a member of the Royal Medico-Psychological Association on passing Part II of my diploma in psychological medicine. The Society of Clinical Psychiatrists had been formed originally to combat the excessive power, as it was then seen, of the medical superintendent in the county mental hospital and was a group for the advancement of consultants in the mental health service. When the Royal Medico-Psychological Association was considering the possibility of creating a Royal College of Psychiatrists, the Society of Clinical Psychiatrists under the chairmanship of Dr Howells was active in promoting this venture and a group of us canvassed towards this end. Dr Howells had aspirations to become the first president of the newly formed college, but that honour went to Professor (later Sir) Martin Roth, who was at that time the Professor of the major teaching centre outside of the Maudesley, in Newcastle upon Tyne. Sir Martin later went on to be Professor of the first chair of psychiatry at Cambridge University. Royal assent was in due course given for the formation of the college and I became one of its founder members, in 1972. That is further on in our story, however. Meantime, in York, I had determined that it would be a sensible career move to sit for the higher qualification in medicine, the membership of the Royal College of Physicians, which at that time most doctors who wished to become consultants in a medical speciality took, the surgical aspirants taking a similar qualification for the Royal College of Surgeons. I therefore began reading up and extending my knowledge of general medicine.

At that time the royal colleges acted individually. There were four colleges of physicians in the British Isles, one in London, one in Edinburgh, one in Dublin and one in Glasgow, which latter had a combined college of physicians and surgeons and awarded in their examination an MRCPS (G), (member of the Royal College of Physicians & Surgeons of Glasgow). The London college exam was allegedly the most difficult and registrars in London teaching hospitals in general medical specialities were competing. For a provincial trainee in a non-general post, such as dermatology, paediatrics, psychiatry etc., it was doubly difficult. By contrast the Edinburgh exam offered two papers, one in general medicine and one in certain special subjects, of which psychiatry was one. Every candidate therefore had to sit the general paper, and every candidate also had to choose from one of a range of specialist options. For those in specialist subjects this clearly gave some advantage. Edinburgh also offered a three-month crammer revision course of high repute, to assist aspiring applicants.

We stayed, Shirley, Fiona and I, some two and a half years in York during which time I had completed the diploma in psychological medicine and been upgraded to registrar status on the training ladder. The next stage was to decide on either a clinical career in a hospital, or a university post as lecturer in a professorial unit such as Leeds, Sheffield or Newcastle, or further afield. I was undecided, being inclined to the lecturer-researcher life with the teaching element involved, but financially this would have meant staying in the same grade for a further two years, whereas in a clinical post I could aspire to a senior registrar post straight away. I applied for and was offered a lectureship in Leeds, but at the same time was offered a senior registrar training post – rotational – under Professor Roth in Newcastle upon Tyne, which seemed to promise the best of both worlds, so opted for the latter. In the meantime I had taken my Masters degree (Master of Arts, in natural sciences) at Cambridge.

Oxford and Cambridge have what many feel to be a strange system for the BA/MA process. The MA is not a research degree or attained by examination as in most other universities and colleges, but is a senior degree obtainable five years after the acquisition of the bachelor's degree, simply by paying the appropriate fee and showing continuing academic progress in one's field, whatever that might be. Nevertheless the senior degree was awarded with due ceremony at the Senate House in Cambridge and one acquired certain privileges in college thereby.

The surgeons and physicians had similar inconsistencies. The physicians' primary licence was the LRCP (Licence of the Royal College of Physicians), whereas the surgeons' first exam led to a membership of the Royal College of Surgeons (MRCS). The physicians went on to a higher exam (MRCP) to attain membership, a higher qualification required for consultancy, whereas the surgeons' higher exam was to the fellowship, by examination, FRCS. The physicians' fellowship FRCP was awarded to senior physicians on career merit and did not require a further written examination.

So, on arriving in Newcastle-upon-Tyne, I had acquired the Apothecaries qualification (LMSSA) by examination, and the Royal Colleges LRCP and MRCS by examination, being thereby a member of the London 'Royal College of Surgeons of England'. I had the natural sciences BA (Cambridge does not have a B.Sc. degree) promoted to MA, and the basic medical and surgical degrees of MB, B.Chir. and a diploma in psychological medicine, DPM. Eat your heart out, stepfather!

In Newcastle we acquired a prestigious address and had address cards printed – 4 Asylum Row, Gosforth! The bungalow was part of the St Nicholas Hospital residential accommodation and had been the women's fever ward – suitably converted, since fever units had gone out of business. We were next to a cabbage field, quite pleasant except that the hospital farm having been disposed of by government decree (hospital farms were out; made slaves of the inmates etc.; not politically correct) the cabbages were no longer gathered to feed the hospital patients or staff, but left to rot, which for a few weeks in the year produced a somewhat pungent aroma!

Gosforth was a pleasant suburb of Newcastle, and the hospital had been the county mental hospital for the city. I was to be working, however, with Sir Martin Roth and his team at the Royal Victoria Infirmary in the city, where the university, medical school and the department of psychiatry were sited, and I was initially attached to a specialist unit for the treatment of neuroses. My immediate 'boss' was a Dr Kay who later obtained a professorship in the Antipodes. The senior registrars had various research and lectureship duties and also attended training sessions of their own under the senior staff in the different aspects of the speciality of psychiatry. A Dr Cobb gave us training in analytical psychotherapy and we would, over two years, rotate through various sub-specialities of general adult psychiatry, psychiatry of old age (psychogeriatrics), child psychiatry, drug and alcohol problems, and psychotherapy, which to psychiatry was as cutting with the knife was to a trainee surgeon, a basic skill that all should achieve.

The second rotation was with Dr Ken Davison at the district general hospital unit at Newcastle General Hospital; always over full, always with pressure on beds, with patients having to be discharged or transferred before they were really ready, and a lot of liaison psychiatry on general wards to advise on the management of patients with delirious states, confusion after operations, and organic psychoses from a variety of causes. The range of problems made it a very interesting rotation and to be in the midst of the general hospital with colleagues from all other specialities was a bonus. Curiously, the professorial unit at Newcastle General was one of the last wards in the unit to have a usable 'pad', though I never saw it used other than as a quiet place for nurses to drink a coffee! Padded cells, like straitjackets and other methods of managing the uncontrollably violent, were largely of a past age. But the alternative of clinical restraint with more modern medication was fairly new. I have twice seen the need for the 'pad'. Once was in a woman in her late thirties with Huntington's Chorea who went suddenly and completely berserk on the ward at St Nicholas Hospital, running repeatedly against what was luckily a partition wall and butting it with her head, and was not to be calmed even by large doses of Largactil, so was placed there for her own safety until the spasm blew itself out. The other was a very large woman of West African extraction, a nurse herself, who developed an unusual condition of acute mania, known as 'African Periodic Psychosis', as described by Lambo, and was apprehended by police and brought in to St Nicholas's, originally thought to be drunk; she had been marching down the middle of Gosforth High Street, stopping traffic, undressing and singing at the top of her voice. She was completely uncontrollable and was put in the padded room for everybody else's safety! It appeared that she had come over from Lancashire to see her fiancé, who was a white male nurse of small stature working locally. This lady, who being a nurse knew about such things, and had a hairgrip still on her person, had jammed the door lock with it on the inside! When I, who had the misfortune to be duty doctor that evening, was doing the evening round, I found the nurses trying to get the door open. They eventually succeeded and the inmate flung herself out and seized me, twisting my white sweater up round my neck until I was dangling from the end of it and going rather blue! She then foolishly kicked a nurse of small stature but who turned out to be a jujitsu exponent of some skill and who, to our amazement, got the woman back in her room and reshut the door with no trouble!

As happens with this condition, in some three days she was completely back to normal and apologised to the others and me and presented me on leaving with a white sweater she had knitted for me in the ten days or so she had stayed in! As a sequel to the story, the couple did indeed marry in Newcastle, some six months later, and I was invited and attended the wedding and reception. The couple were to go to Scotland for a honeymoon and to spend the first night at an hotel in Morpeth en route. I happened to be on duty that evening and at about 1 a.m. was woken by a phone call from the proprietor of the hotel. It appeared that a large West African lady, as it turned out disappointed by her husband's efforts, had gone berserk and smashed up the bedroom. She was in police custody now and could she be brought in to us? She reappeared with some eight policemen who, after removing the handcuffs, handed her over to the two female nurses, as is their wont, and sped away! Happily, she quickly settled down again and a week later they continued their honeymoon and sent us a card from the Highlands. We heard no more!

Towards the end of 1964, Shirley was heavy again with our to-be-second-born. By unfortunate timing, but unchangeable, I was due to start the three-month crammer course in April 1965 in Edinburgh and the baby, Michael Patrick Gerald as he came to be christened, was born on 22 February. He was to be Patrick Gerald – Gerald after my father and Patrick because we liked it – but Shirley, post partum and at the eleventh hour, decided Patrick was not to be the first name and Michael, my name, it should be. This caused some subsequent problems – Michael senior/Michael junior; the grandparents called him Michael-Patrick and this stuck until, at about twelve, he jettisoned the hyphen for himself! So when he was only a few weeks old I had to disappear on the train. It was unfortunate and Fiona missed me a lot and became frightened of trains, steam engines as they were then. Happily, however, she was a perfect little mother and Michael was her little living doll. I was home alternate weekends for the twelve weeks and found the course extremely useful. I had 'digs' in Bruntsfield Gardens and would walk up each day to the medical school, where the course was held, across the park. Edinburgh is a beautiful city and I was able in the three months to get to know it quite well. We had some step-cousins who lived at the top of the Royal Mile, who entertained me from time to time, and I studied hard in the evenings all the aspects of general medicine. The psychiatry part of the exam should, I felt, be fairly easy for me.

I took the exam later that year but suspected I was borderline on the general medical paper. The oral – viva – exam rather confirmed it.

'What is your speciality?'

'Psychiatry, Sir'.

'Hmm. There is a worm that, if it gets into the brain, can cause epilepsy and brain damage. Do you know it?'

'Cysticercosis, I believe'.

'Yes. Now, tell me the life cycle of that parasitic worm'.

I struggled through. I had to confess to myself I had not revised worms particularly well!

'Right – now tell me the life cycle of the roundworm?

. . . . the tapeworm?

. . . . pinworm?'

etc. etc. – the whole viva on the life cycle of worms!

I was referred back for six months, having failed general medicine. The exam pass rate was some 30 per cent. Rather than wait six months I decided to have a crack at the Glasgow exams, and wrote to enter. Happily, I passed this, and was able to stick membership of the Royal College of Physicians and Surgeons of Glasgow on to my qualifications, which meant in about a year I could start looking for consultant posts.

My last year of senior registrar training was with Dr Child, the medical superintendent of St Nicholas Hospital. This was a hospital similar to Naburn, but with nearly a thousand beds. It had been the Coxlodge Asylum before the NHS was invented, but now had good staffing, student attachment with the department in Newcastle medical school, rotation of trainees, and was generally 'buzzing'. A new admission short-stay unit had been formed, the Collingwood Clinic, and there were wards for the elderly and an adolescent facility. We had out-patient clinics and day centres in various parts of our catchment area, and research projects were encouraged.

These were exciting times in psychiatry. Forty years before, most patients had nothing much available in the way of treatment, and length of stay could be considerable. One either recovered or didn't. The first real cure came curiously with the treatment of long-term syphilis. This type of venereal disease could lie dormant for many years but the bacterium (treponema pallidum) that caused the condition gradually developed in the body, often attacking the central nervous system, brain or spine, or lodging in heart muscles or other parts of the body, producing slow or 'cold' abscesses, known as a 'gumma'. If it affected the spine, the nerves became damaged, giving a typical type of gait, a condition known as tabes, but, if mainly affecting the brain, it caused a gradual dementia whose old name (GPI) was 'general paralysis of the insane'. At one time, 10 to 20 per cent of psychiatric hospital cases were caused by the long-term effects of syphilis, particularly galling since there was prejudice (due to the sexual nature of its causation **and** the mental illness symptoms), and it might develop in the fifties, twenty years or more after a lapse of moral purity in one's youth, or even worse a moral lapse in one's partner who passed it on unwittingly to the innocent victim. It was known as the 'great deceiver' because of the varied ways in which the illness might present, and the unexpected 'respectable' middle-aged people who might get it. There was no cure in those days.

Then it was noticed that individuals who had had a high fever for some other coincidental reason, say in a typhoid or typhus epidemic, and survived, seemed sometimes to make a recovery. This led to the thought that if a high fever could be induced deliberately by some means, it might work as a treatment. What was the safest way to do this? Hey! – why not give them malaria? This was known to be caused by being bitten by an infected mosquito and could be treated with quinine. Thus developed 'malaria treatment', and a mosquito farm was set up at Horton Hospital in the UK where mosquitoes infected with benign tertian malaria could be bred, and individuals with this type of syphilis deliberately infected by mosquito bites. The patient then, hopefully, developed a type of malaria which was not normally fatal but did give a pyrexia of over 106° F for some days, and the malaria could then be treated with quinine. Would this kill off the treponema, which didn't like to get too hot? Yes! And at last psychiatry had a physical cause and an effective physical treatment for a sizeable chunk of their workload. It worked quite well, but was difficult to manage. In later years heavy metals such as antimony were found to work, and then with the advent of penicillin, syphilis ceased to be a scourge, but this malaria treatment had been a major breakthrough in psychiatric care and by the time I was in training it was rare to see a case, though occasionally still they would pop up. With the successful treatment of syphilis, there started the age of sexual freedom, egged on by the advent of the contraceptive pill. Everyone went whoopee – until AIDS.

Dr Child encouraged his senior registrars to engage in research, as did Martin Roth, and after completing my MRCP exams I looked to a project that might lead to an MD thesis for a Cambridge doctorate. The diagnosis of psychiatric illness in adolescents was fraught with problems. They had passed the conditions of childhood, autism, behavioural problems of maturing, such as bed-wetting, childhood phobias and the like, and were not yet established in the classical psychotic illnesses of adulthood, such as melancholia, the various types of schizophrenia, and manic-depressive illness. Often provisional diagnoses turned out to be wrong and predicting outcome was notoriously unreliable. My work in the adolescent unit had fired my interest in this group, and I began to formulate an idea that I might collect up all the adolescents admitted to psychiatric units over a year in Newcastle and do a three-year follow-up, trying to define the initial condition, and seeing what might influence prognosis. Firstly, I had to get the available literature on the subject and digest it, and secondly to apply to Cambridge to enrol in an MD thesis project by having the topic accepted and being allocated a tutor. This was in due course agreed, and I was allocated a Dr Hayhoe at the University of Cambridge who would supervise me. I needed a sufficient number to allow of statistical significance in my results, and decided to acquire a control group of adolescents matched for age and sex and from the same catchment area, but who had no history of psychiatric problems. We eventually decided on the local casualty department as a source, and collected up an equal number of young people who had turned up in casualty with cuts, sports injuries and the like, and would volunteer for a questionnaire standardised interview. We made fifty the cut-off point in numbers for the project. By the time I left Newcastle I had all the numbers I required, and the initial follow-up survey. The three-year follow-up and the writing up of the results remained to be done.

Our three-and-a-half year stay in Newcastle was a happy time for both Shirley and myself, though living in the hospital property with two young children was somewhat socially isolating for Shirley, and I was at a career stage when I was out a lot, and working for higher qualifications. I joined the local squash club. We felt the need with the arrival of the second child to jettison the Triumph Roadster, and Willoughby Fortescue was sadly sold. We acquired a Vauxhall Estate instead, which proved a very useful and practical vehicle, and in which we explored the Cheviots, Bamburgh and the Northumberland Coast, and made occasional forays to Scotland. The beach at Seaton Sluice, though a strange name, was very pleasant and nearby. The female toilets my wife told me had the most evocatively vivid graffiti she had ever come across, but I was not privy to the ladies' privy.

Shirley, however, found herself pregnant again within nine months of Michael's birth, and our third born, Melanie Shirley, arrived in July of 1966, a further bundle of joy but making Shirley even busier. Grannies came up to assist, Shirley this time being confined at Wallsend in a very busy maternity unit. By 1967, I had completed my rotational training, spending some time in the psychiatry of mental handicap, or 'learning disability', and started to look around with a view to applying for a consultant post. I was now 33.

The genetics of mental handicap was most interesting. Down's Syndrome had been understood as a failure of proper cell division at conception, whereby one chromosome in the gene was incomplete and left a typical syndrome in the baby, previously known as 'Mongolism', though that term later was thought to be pejorative. But there were many other rarer inherited syndromes that could crop up. When attending the Leeds course while working in York we had had a number of visits to Whixley and Claypenny hospitals, near York, under the tutorship of a Dr Newcombe and had seen examples of 'gargoylism', 'cretinism' and others, and an 'idiot savant' who, though of very limited intellectual ability, if asked a question such as, 'My birthday was the 7 February 1934 – what day was that on?' would, after a very brief pause, reply 'Wednesday' and would always be right. There were children with Asperger's syndrome, made famous by the Dustin Hoffman film, and adults who behaved like children, rushing up to give one a hug as a child might, but being chronologically in their forties. This took a bit of getting used to. St Nicholas Hospital had one ward for adults with severe learning disability, which I looked after, but the main hospitals for such problems in the Newcastle area were at Prudhoe and Morpeth. These places were real communities, albeit institutional, and the social care within them, though paternalistic, was excellent. Most such people are now outside the walls in the 'caring community', who by and large don't, and would prefer them not in their street. I'm never quite sure why social workers dislike paternalism!

My efforts at obtaining a consultant post were slow, in that there were no prospects of immediate vacancies in Newcastle, (though in due course a number of my colleagues at that time went on to get professorships of their own, Tom Fahy getting the post in Galway having, wisely, swotted up his Irish Gaelic before the interview!). An interview I obtained for a hospital in Berkshire clashed with the Gaskell prize examination I had entered for at the Maudesley Hospital so that I could not attend, and thus got in the end neither! But a post in a newly opened District General Unit in Doncaster came up shortly after, and this post I did obtain, my first consultant post, at 33, sharing the job with a colleague, Dr Ted Howarth, who had already been in post there some six months.

CHAPTER 7

A fine fellow

I WAS REQUIRED to give three months' notice of leaving Newcastle, and we spent some time visiting the Doncaster area to look for suitable housing. A consultant post was a permanent post and a considerable increase in salary. I was to work at the new unit for eight sessions a week at Doncaster Royal Infirmary and two sessions at the long-stay hospital at Middlewood Hospital, Sheffield. We found a house at Tickhill, a charming market town some eight miles from Doncaster on the Sheffield side, and some ten miles from Worksop. The house was built in the thirties, had double bay windows at the front, a secure garden for the children, was detached, and called 'Moorlands'. The only snag was the kitchen, fashionable in the thirties, no doubt, but with walls completely covered in green glass tiles rather like a fish and chip shop! But it was spacious and had a good-sized utility room adjacent. The house had four bedrooms and a separate garage. The children were now aged five, two-and-a-half and one, and we needed to be thinking about schools.

Shirley, being a teacher by profession, explored the prospects of starting a playgroup which would be suitable for Michael, and Fiona was placed in St Mary's on our side of Doncaster, a preparatory school, and ideal. Looking further ahead we could see there would be problems, since for state education Tickhill was zoned into Edlington, at that time rather a rough, tough place with a poor reputation, and private schools were rather far away. Doncaster Grammar School was 'zoned' and we were outside the zone.

My post was a very busy one. A new unit had opened, there were only two consultants and we were therefore on alternate day and night call. We wished to encourage referrals from other parts of the hospital (Liaison Psychiatry), and we also wished to maintain a decent input into our two wards at Middlewood Hospital. We found they contained a total hotchpotch of patients of all ages, shapes and sizes, who had been collected up from the rest of the hospital – some 1,000 beds – and any that had come from the Doncaster catchment area were transferred into our sixty beds. We obviously had to try to sort this out.

I had many friends and relations in Sheffield, including my now elderly two maiden aunts, Winnie and Ethel. Sheffield was only a short journey away. We had therefore no shortage of potential social life, and my mother was in Leeds, only an hour away. There was, however, little time for such activity, especially with three young children. There was no time for sport either. At that time, psychiatry was in process of 'moving back' into general medicine. The alienist in the asylum was long past, and the ability to treat psychiatric problems increasingly in a general environment encouraged the start of the closure of mental hospitals, and the creation of short-stay units for new admissions in district units. We had three floors of mixed units, 'racetrack' style, and outpatient facilities in the general outpatient department. The downside was that the patients had no pleasant grounds to walk in to relax and recuperate, as was available in most psychiatric hospitals, and limited daily occupation in the shape of occupational therapy.

Happily in the second year, our staffing was able to be expanded at all levels, including a third consultant, and Middlewood got sorted out. We developed a psychogeriatric facility at Tickhill Road Hospital, a geriatric hospital in Doncaster, liaised with the consultant at St Catherine's, the mental handicap hospital in Doncaster, and started an outpatient clinic in Thorne.

I was invited to do some lecturing at the local technical college on 'preparing for retirement'. (I look back with wry amusement at my taking on this task. What did I know about it?!), and Shirley, becoming increasingly involved in the burgeoning playgroup scene, also started lecturing on playgroup development at the same 'Tech'.

In my spare time (!), I started to write up my thesis and to begin the three-year follow-up exercise on the adolescent group I had started to see in Newcastle-upon-Tyne. This meant a few trips up to the city again, which was nice in that it allowed me to see old friends. I also needed to visit Cambridge to see my tutor. I was now a 'Yeoman' in the Society of Apothecaries and was due to proceed to the Livery, a sort of equivalent of a membership of a college. This allowed us to attend some pleasant dinners at the Hall and the Royal College of Psychiatrists was also becoming a nearer reality. In the meantime, my father-in-law had retired and they had taken a house in Buckden, at the bottom of Langstrothdale. This was a perfect spot for the children to enjoy and we were grateful to be able to take them up there not infrequently at holiday time.

Tickhill had a castle, an attractive pond with ducks and geese, nice walks, and a beautiful church, and town centre. We were regular church attendees. It was also a tradition that we had kippers for breakfast on a Sunday morning. Not any old kipper, the reader must understand, but from Whitby on the East Cliff, and preferably from Fortunes, oak-smoked, the oak derived from old whisky casks and thus steeped in whisky! Craster Kippers are good, Loch Fyne are good, those from the Isle of Man are good – but Whitby is unmatched! So Michael, aged three-and-a-half, coming out of Tickhill Church one Sunday morning, and in the hearing of the vicar, asked innocently 'Daddy, why do we go to church on kipper day?'

When I was at boarding school, and through my Cambridge and Bart's days, my aunts in Sheffield sent me fortnightly a slab of parkin in an old-style metal cocoa tin. Not any old parkin, mind; parkin from a secret recipe made by Miss Middleton's shop at Banner Cross with medium oatmeal and golden syrup. They are long gone, but Thomas's in North Yorkshire now produce very similar. Perhaps they inherited the recipe. But under some new decree they now only sell it in October and early November. It has become seasonal! One has to stock up the deep freeze in the few weeks it is available. But don't thaw it out in the microwave! It turns it into gingerbread, which is **quite** different. I must have eaten a couple of hundredweight in my time. I joke that my brain is made of kipper and the rest of me is parkin. Perhaps it's true!

Sadly, the aunts were getting frail. Winnie in her last months had probably a slight stroke and became increasingly confused; Ethel who had developed a cancer of the breast but wouldn't have it operated on, in her eighties, had to look after Winnie, two years older. I did my best to help. I tried to get her into local hospital care but failed; I slept over for a few nights; eventually she was admitted to the geriatric wing at the Northern General, and gradually over a few weeks, slipped slowly away. She had been a second mother to me and I felt this loss deeply. Ethel went to live at my cousin's, her niece, called Zoë, in Cheshire, taking their little West Highland terrier with her and I only saw her once more. She died the following year. As an executor to their wills I had the task, with my cousin Jean, of clearing their house. Jean was a 'chuck it in the bin: nobody'll want it' type. I was a hoarder and returned home with a carload of their treasures!

By 1970 it was becoming apparent that we were going to have problems with schools. I was coincidentally at a Royal College of Psychiatrists meeting and bumped into Arthur Bowen, by now a friend, and still medical superintendent of Bootham Park Hospital in York. 'Do you know,' he asked, 'that there is a consultant job going at Clifton Hospital in York in a few months time? It's due to be advertised shortly. Interested?'

Shirley and I discussed it. We had wanted to get back to York if we could. Why not apply? I did so and got the job. We put our house on the market and started looking in York. Our Tickhill house sold quite quickly. Shirley and the children managed to rent a ground floor flat in a big house that was being divided, in Tickhill, until the end of the summer term at school. I had to go to start my York job in May and had to look for accommodation during the week. I rang the York University Lodging Bureau and, to my surprise, talked to the landlady I had had in Edinburgh, who had in the intervening years taken the job of Lodgings Officer in York! However, I got a room in the Clifton Hospital Residency which solved the immediate problem. We spent the weekends touring the York area, in particular the Harrogate side, since my Clifton catchment area was to be Harrogate, Wetherby and Knaresborough. Nothing came up for a while, but one Sunday afternoon we drove through Crayke and saw an infill plot for sale. Shirley recognised the village as the one

Dr Haslam, MD (Cantab)

she had seen and liked when we had gone for a recommended bumpy drive to hasten the slightly late arrival of Fiona, our firstborn. We started to make enquiries and in due course purchased the plot, and the builder who had acquired it built us a house.

I had used the time in the evenings at Clifton to get on with finishing writing up my thesis for the Cambridge MD. I had become interested in writing, perhaps inherited from my mother and my great-uncle. I had published a paper on the treatment of vaginismus in a medical journal, and one in the *Journal of Behaviour Research & Therapy* on the treatment of obsessional states. The thesis was sent in for consideration in October of 1970, and, after some recommended revision, was accepted, and the degree of Doctor of Medicine awarded to me after a viva on my work, in 1971. It was a proud moment when mother, Shirley and my children came to watch me receive it in the Cambridge Senate House in the summer of 1971.

Clifton Hospital was a pleasant place, the original central part a Listed Building which had had delightful mullioned windows, sadly removed to make the inside lighter. There were six consultants working from Clifton, and Jerry Quinn was medical superintendent. My colleague in Harrogate was Dr William Samuel Kerr, qualified in Belfast, and his wife Beryl Bromham (her maiden name) was my clinical assistant. I held outpatient clinics in Harrogate twice a week and once a week in the Health Centre in Wetherby. I became involved with the psychology department at York University, then run by Peter

Clifton Hospital

Venables, who was Professor of Psychology, and Kathleen Jones, Professor of Social Studies for whose department I did some lecturing, and became a member of the senior common room at Goodricke College. I also did some lecturing for the school of occupational therapy based on St John's College, York, a university college whose degrees were awarded through Leeds. We also started to develop contacts with the department of psychiatry at Leeds Medical School with a view to taking students and rotating our registrars who were taking the diploma in psychological medicine at Leeds through the department. I became clinical tutor for Clifton Hospital, which allowed me an Honorary Lectureship in the Leeds department.

At about this time the Royal College of Psychiatrists finally opened its doors in Belgrave Square in London, and I received a founder's membership of the College – MRC Psych. I also began to plan how my thesis might be published in book form and eventually got Butterworth's to publish the book, with the title *Psychiatric Illness in Adolescence*.

Meanwhile the house, after a few hiccoughs, had finally been built and finished in Crayke, and we had moved in, in time for the children to start school in York, Fiona, now eight, at York College for Girls Junior School, and Michael also. Melanie was, as yet, too young but went to a playgroup for a while. Meanwhile to 'help pay the mortgage', Shirley got a job teaching at Shipton Street School in York, running the nursery department. Melanie when old enough then attended that school in the mornings with Shirley.

Crayke is a most attractive village. It is built on a hill, a hilltop village indeed, which goes back to before the sixth century. St Cuthbert was granted a piece of land in Crayke by the Bishop of Durham, as a resting place between Lindisfarne and York, on condition he built a monastery and hospitium there. It is a village of two saints, for St Echa in the eighth century is also recorded as a man with a gift of prophecy, an anchorite who 'died peacefully in Crayke in 767 AD'. Cuthbert did indeed build a monastic church on the top of the hill, and the hospitium of St Mary de Pratis. It was probably destroyed in Viking or Norman times, but a castle keep was built adjacent to the church site in the twelfth century, and the church was rebuilt and dedicated to St Cuthbert. Echa may well have been abbot of the monastery at some stage a century or so after Cuthbert's death. During archaeological excavations a Saxon burial ground was found to the east of the present churchyard and down on the plain (de pratis) a large villa was found below the deer run where there was once a stream, possibly Roman originally, but on the track to York, perhaps the site of the hospitium. The castle is now a private dwellinghouse.

Our house was on the southern slope of the hill, a hillside full of springs. There had been a primitive Methodist chapel on the site, and an orchard, so the house was called Chapel Garth. We had an attractive view across the Forest of Galtres to York Minster in the distance and, far, far beyond, the tops of Ferrybridge power station could be seen. To the west were the first foothills of the Pennines, and joy, on a clear day, the top of the Emley Moor television

Chapel Garth, Crayke

mast, some forty-five miles away – the highest building genuinely in England, at 1,050 feet only 200 feet lower than the Empire State Building. Easingwold was the nearest market town, with an attractive market square and old Town Hall, now a printer's firm, and a weekly market. It had had a station, a small branch line off the main York to Newcastle line, but this had closed in 1957 with the Beeching cuts. Most of my career was to be spent at Crayke and working at Clifton Hospital, since I stayed until my 55th birthday in 1989. Shirley continued to teach at Shipton Street for some twenty years. The children grew up and spread their wings. Life went on congenially.

I began to get more involved in Royal College of Psychiatry affairs. I became chairman of the clinical tutors' committee and we hosted a number of annual meetings, a particularly memorable one being in Dundee when a copy of the *Beano* was signed by the full committee! I became an examiner for the college in the late 1970s, for the college membership exam for the MRC Psych, which was interesting work and took me to Edinburgh and Glasgow, as well as London, and on one occasion to Dublin. In 1979 I was elected to the fellowship of the Royal College of Physicians and Surgeons of Glasgow, and in 1980 was elected a Fellow of the Royal College of Psychiatrists, later becoming involved with the journal committee of the Royal College of Psychiatrists and being increasingly involved in research and publishing, and indeed writing in general as a hobby.

I had also developed my involvement with the Society of Apothecaries and, having become a liveryman, was able to receive the Freedom of the City of London. The Freemen and the Society, quite apart from their professional activities, organised many interesting social events. I got on to the Livery Committee of the Society and spent some four years helping to organise various functions, including an annual ball, and a garden party at the Chelsea Physic Garden. This garden had originally been a herbal garden for medicinal herbs which were supplied to Apothecaries for treatments. The Society, like most livery companies, had its barge on the Thames and regular visits were made from Blackfriars upriver to the Chelsea Garden pier to gather herbs and to train students. These days the role of medicinal herbs is much reduced but the Society, along with the Royal Horticultural Society and the University of London, combine to maintain the garden for teaching and research. Its position, adjacent to the River Thames, was a very pleasant spot for an outdoor event.

My other role on the committee had been to review and catalogue the Society's silver, of which they had a very impressive collection, it having been a tradition for the Master during his term of office to present a piece. The Society also had a valuable collection of portraits, including of Charles I, and Gideon de Laune, the founder. There was stained glass in the court rooms, and in the Great Hall were stained-glass coats of arms of the past Masters. The rooms were oak-panelled and most attractive.

Apart from providing a licence by examination to practise medicine and surgery, the Society also provided a number of postgraduate courses for diplomas in various topics, such as 'History of Medicine', and a Master's degree in midwifery. They also ran a course based on the London Hospital for a diploma in medical jurisprudence, which I decided to take. This involved a lot of forensic psychiatry, which I knew fairly well, but also forensic pathology, such as estimating times of death, causes of death, and examination of bullet wounds etc. There was also much medico-legal work – useful if doing reports or presenting evidence in court which was not infrequently a consultant psychiatrist's lot. In due course I took the exam and got the diploma – DMJ.

In the 1980s, the General Medical council was concerned about the standard of some overseas doctors who wished to come and practise in this country, and set up an examination in medicine and surgery and English Language, which doctors, who had qualified at home from a medical school which did not have reciprocal recognition with the UK, could be required to take. Examiners were drawn from the Royal College of Physicians, of Surgeons, and from the Society of Apothecaries, and I became one of the examiners for the General Medical Council for this exam, the 'Professional & Linguistic Assessment Board', through the Society. This was fun, and a pleasant social occasion. We rotated through various colleges who hosted us, including in London the Society of Apothecaries, the Royal Colleges of Surgeons, Physicians and Obstetricians and Gynaecologists, the Royal College of Physicians in Edinburgh, the Royal College of Surgeons in Edinburgh, and the Royal College of Physicians & Surgeons of Glasgow. Examining in the oral exam, the 'viva', was the most interesting. We worked in pairs, a surgeon and a physician together, I of course the latter. One started with easy questions to put the examinee at ease and then pushed them to their particular limits of knowledge. Occasionally we would get someone who knew more than we did, which was good. Luckily, we only had to think of the questions! I had a few basic ones to see if they knew emergency medicine, vital if, as often happens, they finished up as senior house officers in casualty, or geriatrics.

'A man, aged 50, comes in to casualty, from watching a football match, and with chest pain. You are casualty officer. You are taking a history, when he coughs, falls off the chair onto the floor and lies still. What would you do?'

'You are duty doctor. It is Saturday afternoon. A nurse rings from the ward and says a new admission has just had what she thinks is an epileptic fit. What do you do?'

'A woman comes into casualty. She has been stung by a bee. She is feeling weak and ill, and her face has swollen a bit. What are the problems you need to look for?'

One could quickly pick up those who had had to deal with these situations in practical terms and not just textbooks. The first man might have had a cardiac arrest and this leads to such questions as to how quickly he will develop brain damage if not resuscitated. Often in the second case the examinee would say, 'I would give diazepam', or some drug to control a fit. The trick in the question is that the nurse said she had just **had** a fit – it was over. What the doctor needed to do was to set in motion why she had had it; or if she had ever had one before. Likely as not it might be a withdrawal fit from stopping something she had been taking too much of, such as diazepam, or even alcohol, and had not mentioned to the admitting doctor. The third was a question about the risks of anaphylactic reactions to bee stings and what might be needed in the way of emergency treatment.

The pass rate of this not too difficult exam was only about 30 per cent. During most 'viva' exams I would have been killed off had I been the patient, perhaps 20 per cent of the time. Very sobering!

Another college enterprise that I became involved with was an accreditation exercise. The Royal College of Psychiatrists, having initiated a college membership exam, wished to improve training for junior specialists and decided that all hospitals and units that accepted trainees should be assessed for the quality and comprehensiveness of such training, and would be graded, and if necessary their role as trainers would be withdrawn. This was initially a major task. The UK was divided up into zones, and teams of consultants would make visits to the hospitals and units in the zone to which they were allocated, and provide a report. This would take a couple of years to complete, and thereafter, as appropriate, return visits would be made. I was paired with Ken Davison from Newcastle, and our zone was Scotland. We visited some fascinating institutions. The old asylums of Victorian times were often built with no expenses spared. They were castellated, with great baronial entrance halls, set in beautiful countryside, where the 'furiously and dangerously mad' could be contained. They still, some of them, practised segregation, not just of male and female patients, but also of staff – male nurses on male wards and female nurses on female wards, and never the twain should meet! Quite unsuitable for care in the 1970s and 1980s – but superb!

From the seventies, and ongoing, the Health Service has been plagued with reorganisation after reorganisation – scrapping this – bringing in that – deciding 'that' doesn't work – an ever-revolving wheel which has continuously distracted from good care. But through it all was a trend back from the institution to community care. Get the patients out! Where to? Back home to caring relatives – into hostels – onto the streets with statutory parting gifts of a cardboard box and some newspapers? No, that came later! Certainly the numbers at hospitals like Clifton were dropping, largely because, when a bed became empty, it was taken down! New district hospital units were proposed in Harrogate, Northallerton and Scarborough and the York hospitals looked like heading for gradual reduction and closure. Certainly the long-stay patients, mostly with chronic schizophrenia, were dwindling as treatments became more effective, and the number of children in 'sub-normality' hospitals was falling dramatically. Well, they would; mostly they had had patients with Down's Syndrome and one didn't get so many of these now. They were pithed when foetuses!

There were still some intriguing characters around, however. A lady, a Polish refugee, was paranoid but so kind, always making a coffee for the visiting doctors on the ward. She was a chain-smoker and ash would often drop into the cup, but one was duty bound to drink it! Then there was a salutary lesson which we showed the students. A woman had come in with an absurd tale. She had inherited a large sum of money. She had given some £10,000 to a man she had met in a café. He had absconded with it but later she had re-met him and they had married. They had gone on a honeymoon and soon after arrival he had gone to get cigarettes but had not returned. She heard a whirring in the ceiling and knew it was a flying saucer that had taken him. She had been depressed and, a year or so after all this, had come into our hospital. That morning she had seen this man, her 'husband', in the main corridor, but did not speak to him as she had gone to the hospital office. Give her more Largactil! The whole story proved to be true, apart, one assumed, from the flying saucer! The man **had** absconded with the joint cheque book; gone to Scarborough; lived it up on the 'stolen money', and then run out. In danger of exposure, he had in fact taken an overdose and been admitted by the Scarborough consultant to Clifton a few days before! The moral: do not assume the improbable to be delusional until you've checked!

Delusions and hallucinations are characteristic features, part of the psychotic disorder, seen in schizophrenia in most cases. A delusion can be defined as a false belief, unamenable to reasoned argument and outside of the individual's cultural and intellectual background. These provisos are necessary, else how do you explain superstititions (walking under a ladder; leprechauns under the bridge on the road to Castletown in the Isle of Man; UFOs or even religious beliefs of the more way-out kind – or even the orthodox kind come to that!) Delusions are different from misinterpretations, illusions, and primitive thinking, and it takes experience to pick them up.

Another project at which Clifton Hospital was in the forefront was in the treatment of people with marital and sexual problems. This had in the past been a rather taboo subject. Sexuality outside the norm, such as homosexuality, had indeed been illegal until 1967 between males, and penalties severe. Leo Abse's Act produced a more liberal and humane view of normal minority behaviour, and not before time. A number of research publications in the sixties produced two classic textbooks on the topic, by Kinsey, on human sexual response, and by Masters & Johnson in the USA, who did research into the physiology of sexual response, and devised a method of treatment, known as 'sensate focus', for such common problems as impotence, frigidity and premature ejaculation.

A couple, the Bancrofts, at that time from Oxford, had spent some months in the USA studying Masters & Johnson's methods and opened a clinic in Oxford to promote those ideas. Those of us who were already working in the area of psychosexual medicine – and I had published one or two papers on the treatment of impotence and related topics – were invited to a meeting in Oxford, and out of this was formed the 'Association of Sexual & Marital Therapists', to promote research and treatment into this important but neglected area.

A team at Clifton Hospital, including Dr Anne Pattie, the senior clinical psychologist at the hospital, myself, and a number of clinical assistants, was set up initially at Clifton for a few months, but subsequently two sessions a week were allocated by the health authority, and the clinic was run in the York District Hospital Outpatient Department. This area of work 'took off' and our PSD Clinic (Psychosexual Disorders) published much research and hosted in 1972 the second national conference on psychosexual problems, and I lectured internationally on these topics, as far afield as Taipei, Athens and Honolulu, to name-drop but three!

The first conference had been held in Bradford by Dr Hugo Milne, a well-known psychiatrist in the area but had had the embarrassment on the second day, devoted to what were then called 'sexual deviances', of being raided by the Bradford University 'Gay-Lib' student group who took over the meeting and totally disrupted it. Our conference, therefore, two years later, devoted one day, at the university, to marital and sexual problems, and the second day, held at the main hall at Clifton Hospital, to problems related to sexual and gender preferences. I ensured that our speakers were on the whole representatives of those 'minority groups', as well as therapists, so that the former were given a platform, for the first time, in a professional symposium, to state their points of view to professionals in the audience. I like to believe that this was a pivotal moment in understanding differences in these areas. We had a speaker from the Albany Trust, from Gay Rights organisations, from lesbian groups, and from the Beaumont Society representing people with cross-gender issues, transvestism, transexualism, and the like. Some speakers started nervously but received much applause at the end. The secretaries organising the day had to come to terms with which toilet the cross-dressed attendees used, and at a formal dinner in the Merchant Adventurers Hall the following evening the dresses of some of the cross-dressers outshone the 'real girls'! It was a first, and led the way to an increased understanding and tolerance between client and professional in this area. I was made a trustee of a transgender trust, the Beaumont Trust, (named after a well-known historical cross-dressing figure, the Chevalier de Beaumont in the last century) on the strength of it, and an honorary member of their society.

The Society of Clinical Psychiatrists meanwhile had, with the formation of the college, became more of a ginger group, putting forward ideas and challenging matters such as hospital closures, which the college might have had difficulty in raising. I had by now got on to the committee of the Society, a group of some 350 senior members of the psychiatric profession who met bi-monthly in London and the provinces, alternating, and later also at an annual overseas meeting. There was a research and fund-raising element whereby we raised money to fund small research projects by individual colleagues who could not get financial backing elsewhere, and we developed out of our newsletter a journal, which came out six times a year, and was called *The Journal of Clinical & Social Psychiatry*. I became secretary of the Society in the late eighties and chairman in the early nineties, with the retirement of Harry Jacobs.

Perhaps the biggest contribution we have made in recent years has been the debate on 'suspensions pending enquiries', a scandal costing the NHS millions of pounds a year whereby senior doctors have been suspended from their work by politically exact trust managers or health authority staff, often on what to a casual observer would appear fatuous, trivial reasons, sometimes for month after month, or even in some cases year after year, on full pay pending enquiries, unable to work, and costing the health service a fortune, only at the end of it in a number of cases to have the matter dropped. Indeed, more often than not the complaint has had no relevance to their clinical work yet their patients are suddenly deprived of support as a consequence. The society was the first to publish their report on this matter and has had a standing committee monitoring the situation, and offering support to those put in this invidious position. The Royal Colleges have been singularly ineffective in offering any help whatsoever to their fellows and members in trouble, tending indeed to try to distance themselves from the issues.

Clinical tutor work in York increasingly involved the training of both undergraduate and graduate trainees in association with Leeds University, and I became as a consequence an honorary lecturer at the University in Leeds. Later we were also to take students from the University of Grenada in the unit in York and as a consequence I became for a few years an associate professor of psychiatry, University of Grenada. I did not, however, get the opportunity of a visit to my 'alma mater'. Another interesting short-term project was to appear on Radio York as the radio psychiatrist – quite fun but not taken up for long. In 1980, however, a hiccough occurred which had both good and bad consequences. I caught Infectious Hepatitis (type A) (jaundice) as a consequence of attending a posh dinner at the Society of Apothecaries.

CHAPTER 8

A family man

THE SOCIETY OF APOTHECARIES held an annual ladies' night banquet – a posh affair – evening dress and medals. (I had my National Service Medal. A small thing but mine own!). My wife and I usually went. The speeches varied but the ambience was splendid. On this particular year we again enjoyed splendid fare, and 'good wine a' plenty'. The Society of Apothecaries had an excellent cellar. We returned to the Royal Society of Medicine, of which I was a member, and where we were staying. Shirley had had an excess of red wine and, luckily, was 'sick as a pig' later! I was all right. Some six weeks after I acquired a high fever and turned yellow. I was retired to bed and tests showed infectious Hepatitis A (the respectable sort. Hepatitis B was often acquired from naughty practices with naughty people!) and I was ill. I lost a lot of weight. I was exhausted, and I itched! A few weeks into my illness we received a letter from the Apothecaries:

'It has come to our notice that a number of our members and guests at the recent ladies' night dinner have developed jaundice. Should you notice any symptoms of this disease, would you be good enough to let us know?'

Huh!

Shirley also had the tests, very mildly positive. Good old vomiting! I missed my daughter's eighteenth party as a consequence. The outbreak, and it proved to be a big one with over eighty diners, and indeed two deaths, proved to be a fascinating exercise in forensic public health. One member of the waiting staff only got jaundice. Hepatitis A is a food and water-borne infection. What had she done? She had polished off the raspberry fool. Fool she was for doing so! Everyone who got it had had the raspberry fool. (They had wondered if it had been the loving cup, a communal drinking bowl of wine passed round as a toast at the end of the meal). Significantly a small wedding party in London on the same day had a number of cases, of the same strain.

So where did the raspberries come from? From a catering company in London. Who were their suppliers? Bejams. Where did Bejams get their raspberries from? From a supplier in Dundee who grew them. Who picked the raspberries? Itinerant workers from Glasgow, who lived in tented accommodation in the season. They gathered the raspberries in buckets, and were paid by weight. The raspberries were then deep-frozen, which killed most known germs, except hepatitis virus, which seemed to like the cold. A lot of senior doctors in private practice had lost a lot of money, being off work for around three months. Who was liable? The Society? The caterers? The suppliers? The growers? A Glaswegian with hepatitis?

Well, the lawyers got rich. I, on advice, waited to see. Something to do with hanging on to their coat tails, or some such expression. I was being paid so it was not a great loss. I got £1,000 compensation. And I gradually got better. I was not allowed back to work for three months but in the last few weeks felt well enough. I wandered around York, went to a spiritualist meeting where the medium saw a monk-like figure behind my shoulder and said I had the gift, and I found an advert for hair restoration in a magazine. I had gone rather more rapidly bald during my illness, and didn't like it. The firm was based in Manchester. I approached them and someone came to see me. The family were doubtful but I committed myself to a process known as hair fusion where the 'hairpiece' is bonded and woven into one's own natural hair. It is fixed and cannot fall off or be removed, except professionally. But of course every six weeks or so it needs reattachment (at a cost) by a specialist hairdresser, since one's own natural hair to which it is bonded grows out. They didn't really make that clear! The nearest was in Leeds. Anyway, I thought it looked rather good and improved me. Those who agreed praised my decision. I guess those who didn't on the whole kept silent! When I eventually got back to work, a young woman long-stay patient said, 'Ooh, a wig' and grabbed at it. It stayed in place, to her surprise, and that seemed to settle that! I was to keep it for twenty years, though when I say keep it, it is a little like the Irish woman's broom – been in the family for three generations and only needed three new heads and two new handles. The 'piece' did need replacing, at a cost, every couple of years or so. Such is the price of vanity!

We have reached a stage in these memoirs when a chronological approach ceases to be so useful and one must look at certain important aspects of one's life, which have a common theme but span the years. One such, and the first and most important, is marriage.

Shirley was of Surrey stock, living when we met at Farley Green, a pretty hamlet between Shere and Albury, in the midst of heathland and forest. Her father, Alfred Jefferies, a Norman-French name, I guess, had, owing to his father's premature death and a large family, been sent by his mother to King Edward's School, Whitley, where he did well, as a boarder, becoming head boy and going on to London University where he obtained his boxing 'purple' for the university. He had met Shirley's mother, Eileen Dunstan, of Celtic stock, part Cornish and part Welsh, as her father had been a teacher at King Edward's School. In the war Shirley's father had had, as headmaster of a school in London, to be involved in the traumatic task of evacuating children, leaving their parents for an unknown destination, a label tied to their coat, a little case of belongings, on a train to somewhere, perhaps, if their parents were killed in

Michael, Fiona and Melanie circa 1984

the London Blitz, not to see them again and to become orphans. Shirley and her younger brother Roger and their mother had been evacuated to South Wales until it seemed safe to return to rural Surrey later in the war (little realising what might be to come with the V1 and V2 rockets). Roger had gone as a boarder to Ottershaw School and later to the Merchant Navy Officer Training School, and was to become a first officer with 'Blue Funnel Line'. Shirley was to go to Homerton College, Cambridge, after Guildford High School. How and where we met and married has already been related. We had by now, at the time that this chapter has reached (1980), got three teenagers. Fiona was eighteen. She had, when we arrived in York, gone to York College for Girls and worked her way up through the school, to being a prefect, interested in tennis and gymnastics, and taking A levels in History, Geography and English to obtain entry to New College, Durham to do a B.Ed. for a teaching career. She had, in Crayke, a steady boyfriend, Andrew, who with his brother and father were farming a manorial farm in the Crayke locality, north of York.

Michael, our second child, born in 1965 and now fifteen, had entered the junior school at St Peter's School in York. He was down to go to Sedbergh, my old school, in 1978. However, in the winter of 1975 a flu-like viral infection had spread through York, a nasty bug which seemed to cause a mild encephalitis, laying low a professor of mathematics for some weeks with vertigo and weakness, and killing two young people of our acquaintance. Michael got it, and became dizzy and sick and could not sit up without vertigo causing him to lose his balance. It must have been very frightening for a 10-year old: bad enough for our friend, the maths professor. Michael gradually improved. We had a holiday booked on the Broads a few weeks later and we all went. We thought it would do him good. I suppose, initially, it did. He started to sit up and move around a bit, though was not venturesome enough to come for a sail in the dinghy that we towed behind our five-berth motor launch. Perhaps this was as well. When we got to Oulton Broad, I took Melanie out for a sail. I stepped the mast to find that it was the wrong one for the dinghy, having a square shape and the socket being round. It was a good practical example that you cannot put a square peg in a round hole. We sailed merrily away into the sunset but the first time I tried to go about, the wind took the mast and sail out altogether and we capsized! Luckily, Melanie was a good swimmer and had a life jacket on. However, a large yacht swept past us, she was plucked from the water and taken, as it turned out, back to our cruiser where she changed, and got warm. I, however, was left in the middle of Oulton Broad with an upturned dinghy! Eventually I managed to right it and paddle back, but the holiday, sadly, was a bit too much for Michael, who retired to bed with a return of vertigo when we got home. The condition did not improve. He could not and would not let his head become vertical, and became quite depressed and weepy. He would cry inconsolably perhaps for two hours in an evening, whatever one did. He was seen by a specialist paediatrician and admitted eventually to Great Ormond Street Children's Hospital in London. I feared he had a brain tumour and, as Shirley and he drove away in an ambulance heading for London, I wept. I hadn't done that, I guess, since I was a child too, and can count on one hand the times since. I thought I might never see him alive again.

He had some unpleasant tests in London – lumbar punctures, strobe lights, EEG and so on. Happily, nothing ghastly turned up. It seemed a mild encephalitis with a post-viral syndrome. Perhaps these days it would have been labelled ME. They thought it would gradually improve. He was, after some weeks, transferred back to York under the local paediatrician, a friend of ours. But there was little progress and it was suggested that he might go to a children's rehabilitation unit at Highlands, a unit at Burley in Wharfdale. This proved a horrible mistake. The staff lacked sympathy and understanding of the problem, and the final straw came when, having been put on a drug called chlorpromazine, known to cause photo-sensitivity, he was left out lying on a lilo, on his side, in the sun, and got first degree burns to his cheek. We took him home and we arranged some hydrotherapy. He had swum for St Olave's School team and enjoyed swimming, and we took him down to the local swimming pool attached to Easingwold School, where with much trepidation on the first occasion I lowered him into the water. He proceeded to swim (under water! Aaagh!) to the end of the pool, and obviously loved it. This was perhaps the start of real improvement. He was still unable to walk or sit up properly but had found something he could do and enjoy. That summer we took the family to Cornwall with our caravan and he swam with me in the sea, snorkelling in a beautiful bay full of fish and sea creatures.

He returned to school in the autumn in a wheelchair, and the headmaster, a very sensible man, allocated a couple of his friends as chariot bearers. By now he could sit up but still got very quickly tired. They pushed him round, as boys would, quite rapidly, and had fun. He would go to sleep in some of the lessons and, as the head said, he was the only boy who had been 'allowed to nod off' in his maths lesson in the whole of his career.

In the autumn half-term we went to Sandsend for a week in a holiday cottage, on the East Coast near Whitby, and he took his first steps. We were as excited as the day Fiona had taken her first steps at a year when staying with some friends in Wales. From then on he rapidly improved. By his thirteenth birthday he was playing rugger and swimming well. He went to Sedbergh to boarding school in 1978. With hindsight, however, it was too soon. Although he did well the term he was there, playing the violin in a little concert, it did, I think, bring back all the trauma of being away from home in hospital two years before. Why was he there? Well, for me to relive my youth, I suppose. So we did some quick negotiations in the Christmas holiday and for the spring term he entered the senior school at St Peter's, York, where indeed most of his St Olave's friends had gone.

A major aid to his recovery at age eleven I must attribute to a friend and colleague, Ian Martin, working in psychological medicine in Darlington, who came to see him and put him on a paediatric dose of amitryptiline for a few weeks, which made a dramatic difference, and to Tony Murphy from Fylingthorpe, husband of an old friend of ours, who wrote to him regularly with splendidly humorous and mad letters, which he came to look forward to with great enthusiasm. So all was now well in the Michael world. He played the violin, played rugger for his house, and rowed and swam for the school. He obtained good A levels and entered Edinburgh University to study Architecture in 1983, and later Bath, getting a B.Sc. and B.Arch.

Melanie, our third child, was also born in Newcastle, in July of 1966. She and Michael were much of an age really, only eighteen months separating them, and she was a quick developer, so they were good pals at junior school. Melanie also went to York College for Girls but obtained a sixth form scholarship to St Peter's School and went to Reading University to get a degree in Chartered Surveying. She also followed in my footsteps in becoming Secretary of Reading University Fives Club and going on to win a number of trophies in women's fives in the ensuing years.

An increasing interest in research developed as my career progressed. I suppose the article on Diver's Ear, and two small papers, one on the behavioural treatment of a woman with an obsessional state, and one on the treatment of vaginismus, started me off, I became involved in a number of drug trials commissioned by pharmaceutical companies, which took me to a number of overseas venues to present results and lecture. I was able to travel to Copenhagen, Tel Aviv and Athens, and Reykjavik, where I got booed for the second time for stating some unpopular views on the role of psychiatrists vis-à-vis psychologists!

The first occasion was a collective booing, at the 'Goodricke lecture' at York University, where Shirley and I were guests, since Professor Eysenck was the speaker and we were in his party. This would be about 1972, I guess, at a time when students were revolting, anarchy reigned somewhat, and the new science of sociology was promoting environment in contrast to genetics in terms of inheritance and acquired characteristics. Sadly the ignorant are often those who make the most noise, and students at that time cared little for discipline and authority, and indeed did not seem to care much for carefully conducted research, preferring mob behaviour. Eysenck had done some very interesting research on identical and non-identical twins and was to talk on the inheritability of intelligence which was a red rag to a bull to those who could not be bothered to listen and use reasoned argument. And these were university students! What hope for the rest?

The scene was set when the party entered the already packed lecture hall and we were all included in booing from the back. As Professor Eysenck began his lecture, a number noisily walked out. He was actually describing some other research, not his own, and quoting from it as a prelude to his own results, when a small group of students leapt forward and, in the minor affray that followed, the Professor's glasses were knocked off. These students were removed. Professor Eysenck, himself a Jewish refugee, was not phased by such Nazi-reminiscent behaviour and went on to give a very interesting talk.

Another interest that developed out of my clinical tutor work was that I became a tutor of an organisation called the 'Medical Correspondence College' and prepared a series of teaching aids for students taking exams in psychiatry. It occurred to me that the group of books in the Made Simple series, which had such titles as *Accounting Made Simple, Law . . . Psychology . . .* and so on, might find a *Psychiatry Made Simple* book of interest. I visited the publishers and suggested that the papers produced for the Medical Correspondence College would be the type of design which could form the basis of the manuscript. Eventually the publishers agreed. How I would have found the time to complete it had I not got hepatitis I do not know, but my convalescence from that allowed me to complete the book, which proved to be quite a good seller and ran to two editions and was translated into Polish!

Lecturing trips abroad gave me the travel bug – no, not Delhi Belly or Gyppy Tummy – but the desire to see the world. I was at a stage in my career when I was running on a high and getting known, and I received information on where conferences and meetings were being held in the coming twelve months or so. The NHS for some reason was quite well off in those days and grants were available for overseas travel on official business. There was a technique to this. Firstly, one must look down the list of conferences and decide where one might like to go the following year. One needed to have some research project on the go, the preliminary results of which could be presented. These conferences were always pleased to have overseas speakers, which added to the conference's prestige. One wrote therefore to the conference organisers, and offered to present a paper on the levels of rhubarb products in the blood of Welsh sufferers from Blog's disease or whatever, and usually received back a letter saying: 'We are very pleased to offer you the opportunity to present your paper on . . . at the Timbuktu International Conference on Psychiatry.' Armed with this letter one could approach the health authority and say: 'I have had the great honour of being invited to present a paper at this conference and would like to request a grant towards my expenses.' It usually worked. Of course if a drug company were sponsoring a lecture with research results on a product they were developing, this was not necessary, as they would fund the trip. In this way I was able to attend the World Psychiatric Association meetings over a period of a couple of decades, and of course one gets known and this leads to more invitations, perhaps to chair or organise symposia at such meetings. In this way I got to Mexico City, Honolulu in Hawaii, Kyoto in Japan, Vienna, and Athens again, to name but a few, and organised a symposium in Jerusalem.

Another passion that I was able to indulge with an increase of salary was that of cars! The NHS, in order to try to attract consultants to work full time for it, had to compensate in some way for the money that could be earned in private practice. They devised therefore a system of merit awards in four grades – C (the lowest, equivalent to about a third extra on one's salary), B, A and A+. One probably had to be a brain surgeon who cured the monarch of a tumour to get that! At any event I found myself the recipient of a C award – very welcome when educating three offspring in private schools, and university. We changed our Vauxhall for a Daimler 2½ litre, a lovely car which served us well over some years, but we changed it later for a 3½ litre Jaguar saloon, which was comfort personified and again took us on various holidays abroad, towing our touring vintage Sterling caravan as if it were not there!

I got on to the Livery Committee of the Society of Apothecaries, was an examiner on the Royal College of Psychiatrists Clinical Tutors Committee, became Chairman of the Society of Clinical Psychiatrists, and was made a Freeman of London. Life was good. They say the higher you fly the further you fall. We shall see.

We attended dinners and many receptions, travelled widely, and were presented to the Queen and Prince Philip, whilst attending a Freemen's reception in London. The art of attracting the Duke of Edinburgh's attention is to wear the wrong tie! I was an enthusiastic 'Old Sedberghian' and had got on to the OS Committee at the time Roger Baxter was headmaster. The school coat of arms at this time proved to have been for some 400 years the private grant of arms of the Lupton family, Roger Lupton, the reader will recall, being the founder. In the 1970s someone chose to draw the school's attention to the fact that this was technically not allowed. After much discussion with the Lord Lyon King of Arms, a modified coat of arms was devised, retaining the Lupton crest and motto, and surrounding the coat of arms with an additional – what is the word? – embrasure? Anyhow, Roger Baxter persuaded the Queen and Duke of Edinburgh to visit the school and to present the new coat of arms. As a committee member, I, and my wife, were invited. As the Royal couple walked down the line, the Duke spotted that I was not wearing an OS tie. I was in fact wearing the London Guild of Freemen's tie, which he identified and came across to ask me about it.

As it happened, at the Freemen's reception in London I was wearing an Old Sedberghian tie. This also he spotted! He stopped to chat to our group, but mistakenly believed us to be members of the Clockmakers' guild rather than the Apothecaries! It must be very difficult to think of what to say to all these people as one walks along the line.

'Do you know which clock tells the best time?' he asked. 'One that is stopped or one that is five minutes fast?'

Of course we 'did not know'.

'One that is stopped,' he replied, 'since that is right twice a day and the one that is five minutes fast is never right!'

The Queen was not so talkative, passing down the group of ladies on the other side of the line. My wife was almost at the end and the Queen paused there, since the Duke was busy chatting and had been left behind. 'Where is he?' she demanded rhetorically. 'He's always so slow!' – and passed on.

The Freemen and the Apothecaries between them laid on some very interesting functions and visits during the year. We got to many of the Guild Halls, to the College of Arms, to Twickenham, a concert at Windsor Castle, and a boat trip up the Thames to follow the 'Swan Upping' ceremony.

Meanwhile, back at the ranch there were more changes in the NHS. Naburn Hospital was heading for closure. Clifton was running down, and the residuum from Naburn was to be transferred to us. A unit had opened in Scarborough, and they were no longer admitting 'acute short-stay' to York. Thirsk was likely to be taken over by a new unit in Northallerton, and a unit in Harrogate was in the planning stage. It was proposed that the in-patient unit for the North York and Easingwold catchment areas should be moved to Bootham Park

Hospital which would become, with the closure of the County Hospital and the opening of a new District General Hospital on a site adjacent to Bootham Park, the acute short-stay hospital for psychiatry for the whole of York, Clifton to become simply the long-stay hospital for North Yorkshire.

At this time Dr Quinn, the medical superintendent at Clifton, was due to retire. With him went the post of medical superintendent. The hospital would now be run by a lay administrator and the York A and B management teams were scrapped. 'York District' was formed, later to become a Trust in yet another reorganisation. The teams were reorganised. I moved from Harrogate to take over Dr Quinn's catchment area and held clinics in York and Thirsk, and a new consultant, a Dr Rugg, was appointed to Harrogate. I only covered Thirsk for a couple of years pending the opening of the new psychiatric unit at the Friarage Hospital in Northallerton, after which I was given instead two sessions a week running the psychiatric input to the Special Unit for Epilepsy which was situated at Bootham Park.

At one point I had the privilege of having three juniors working for me, called Dr Beer, Dr Sida, and Dr Syn. Beer, cider and sin. Well, they went well together! Dr Syn, however, who was from Burma, became enamoured of an Englishman and they duly married. As her parents were in Burma and were not allowed exit visas by their home government to attend their daughter's wedding, she asked me if I would 'give her away'. I did so, at a pleasant Anglican ceremony. Did this make me a surrogate father? I wasn't sure.

One other event of significance occurred in the early eighties. A cottage became vacant just over the road from our house. Mother was now in her eighties and the flat that she was currently occupying, courtesy of Lord Wade, in Leeds, was to be sold as the Wades were retiring and going to live in Pateley Bridge. Mother had had it at a peppercorn rent. It was time for a move, to be nearer her only child. We purchased the cottage, which needed a lot of renovation, and in December mother, with some trepidation, moved in.

CHAPTER 9

'Each and every byway'

PSYCHIATRY IS RATHER different from many other medical and surgical specialities. In the past psychiatry was separated from general medicine by being in a different hospital. There were honorary consultant contracts, psychiatrists giving advice on the general wards, and surgeons coming to the psychiatric wards to assess patients who might need an operation for some reason, but by and large the alienist stayed in his asylum, and the surgeons felt a little nervous there. At the other end of the scale of psychiatric images held by the public was the bearded analyst with his couch, and preferably a central European accent, treating the worried well. Psychiatry, of course, was and is both, but increasingly it has become a community and outpatient speciality more like general practice, with in-patients forming a smaller part of the day's work.

Whilst surgeons need to learn the skills of cutting with the knife, psychiatrists need to learn the skill of psychotherapy, of empathising, talking through traumatic experiences and coping with what Freudians would call the transference phenomenon. Psychotherapy takes many forms. At the deep end is Freudian psychoanalysis, a separate training not usually available in the NHS and not necessarily requiring medical training. The training includes a personal analysis. Though Freud and other later analytical-style therapists such as Melanie Klein, Adler & Jung have contributed much to the understanding of mental processes, they were professionals of their time (Freud was a neurologist, in fact) and many of their ideas are now seen as rather fringe and outdated, and indeed a treatment for the neurotic rich. But Freud's ideas of the subconscious, repression, and defence mechanisms have remained as concepts understood by the public. Freud's ideas of transference were that an individual would transfer emotions, deep-seated and unrecognised, from childhood and early relationships, on to the therapist or indeed others, causing them to react in ways outwith their full control. These could be negative or positive, and the therapist might, from his or her own early history, experience counter transference for the patient; hence the need for therapists to have their own training analysis.

Running contrariwise, there developed a new skill, that of counselling. This derived to some extent out of feminist concepts; that people (including men) needed to talk, to let it all out, to relive their traumas, talk them through, feel some emotion, and (and this is the crucial bit) that doing that would 'do you good'. Now, family, friends and neighbours, the priest, the GP – these were the people in the past who provided such succour. Most women would probably say it produced some relief. Men perhaps would say, 'Where is the stiff upper lip? Being overemotional helps no one. Dressing up painful past events just prolongs them. Everyone has pain at times. One grows from it if one takes an attitude of fortitude!' Women might reply, 'Men would be better off if they let themselves "feel" a bit more.' Men would say, 'Women would do better if they got on with it and talked less.'

In reality, of course, there is truth in both. It is the way the sexes are and a terrible generalisation. There is a lot of gender overlap. It doesn't help to wallow in it. It doesn't help to bottle it up either. But does one need an army of professional, paid, undertrained counsellors from all sorts of backgrounds doing the job that has always been done voluntarily by kith and kin? Well, some people don't have close relations or relationships to which they can turn. It has, however, become a fashion out of which many make a lively living. So far as psychiatry was concerned, psychiatrists saw all these groups sometimes as allies, and sometimes simply knuckling in on their patch without the training to do it. A little knowledge is a dangerous thing! Drink deep, or touch not 'the Pierian Spring'. Firstly the profession of psychology, in the shape of the clinical psychologist in hospitals, tired and disillusioned from being the mental pathologist just doing IQ tests and the odd Rorschach inkblot tests, began to move into the treatment of psychiatric illness, in particular in the neuroses, with behavioural methods under various 'new' names. The psychiatrist, whose medical training allowed for diagnosis of medical conditions which might present with disorders of mood, thinking or behaviour (such as thyroid disease, delirium, anaemia and the like) were being pushed into the treatment of psychoses such as schizophrenia, and little else! The psychologist, who did not have medical training, did not have this diagnostic skill, nor the ability or licence, to treat with medication. Perhaps not surprisingly, then, they developed an ethos that medication was unhelpful!

Then the old concept of the almoner and the duly authorised officer, to become the mental welfare officer, transmutated into the generic social worker who perceived all ills from a sociological standpoint, came on the counselling scene. Then the registered mental nurse became a nurse therapist, and the old easy relationship between doctor and nurse was put under strain by nurses who wished to take over an increasing therapeutic role without bothering with a long medical and psychiatric training. Then there were a host of lay groups – marriage guidance, (now 'Relate'), bereavement counsellors, lay hypnotherapists, and a host of individuals who took on counselling work, with a three-month course perhaps, some good at it, some not, and in it for all sorts of personal reasons – who tended to discount the trained professionals and think they could do it better.

Well, it certainly altered the style of work we were trained for. As I said earlier, psychiatry wasn't like surgery. We got to know patients very well: often we were the lay priesthood. People came to depend on us. I have ex-patients who have kept in touch with me over a quarter of a century, perhaps by letter, perhaps by the occasional meeting up. To the patients we were friends, 'brothers', or 'sisters', parent figures, fantasy love objects. And they could be to us. People are individuals, even with mental illness, and should be treated humanely and humanly. But it is a long commitment. I do not believe that a professional counsellor who sees people for a fixed number of sessions, says 'thank you very much' and pockets the money, can take on this role. It may do some people some good, but the evidence of long-term benefit from studies carried out by researchers is not very convincing.

But I digress from the main theme of this homily! It shows, I think, that in the eighties, the job which I thought to do when I entered hospital work as a specialist in the sixties, was undergoing a great change, an erosion of that which had excited me, and the trivial round and common task were being replaced by an atmosphere of friction and competition. Perhaps it was an erosion of power. Perhaps it was simply the changes associated with one's own ageing, but life no longer, in its clinical professional form, grabbed me with enthusiasm on waking to a new day. Psychiatry as we knew it was in decline. We faced hassle and criticism at work. The 'multi-disciplinary team' was taking over. Instead of seeing patients in the ward with a nurse and one's junior, or having individual tête-à-têtes with patients who wished to confide, we, and the patient even more so, were faced with an army of individuals, all wishing to be in on the act. The patient entered the crowded office to face me, my junior, 'my' clinical assistant the nurse therapist, the social worker, the psychologist, a couple of students, and the occupational therapist. It was not actually what they wanted to do!

And at meetings, the consultant and his medical team would not be faced with equals in experience from these other disciplines. The nominated nurse would not be the sister. The social worker would not be a senior. They were too busy to bother with clinical matters and were in administrative posts. The psychologist could not be turning up to every consultants' get-together! Some psychiatrists turned to administrative posts themselves. Some simply voted with their feet and took early retirement. The new breed coming up knew no better and seemed happy just to be the pill-pusher cog in the multi-disciplinary team. The GPs were having a similar struggle but had more control. They were the employers! Perhaps losing the medical superintendent had not been a good thing after all!

My wife was teaching in York. We were earning well. Mrs Thatcher had agreed that all doctors, in their own time, could earn up to 10 per cent of their NHS earnings without losing paid NHS sessions. (Before that we could in our spare time run a taxi service, drive a bus, or whatever we liked, as long as it did not interfere with being owned twenty-four hours a day, seven days a week by the NHS, as long as we didn't see a private patient for payment!). The private psychiatric hospital, The Retreat, in York, took the bulk of private in-patient work, but outpatient private practice was relatively untapped locally outside of Leeds. I decided to set up a private practice, one-half day session a week, within the government parameters, based in York. Initially, I acquired a room at The Retreat.

I continued to pursue my research interests, being particularly interested in treatment methods such as abreaction and relaxation. An organisation had been set up the better to control the practice of hypnosis within medicine, an art within the NHS, sometimes seen as somewhat fringe but practised by psychiatrists, GPs and dentists increasingly. They were the 'British Society of Medical & Dental Hypnotists' and they awarded a certificate of competence to those who passed their written exam and showed evidence of skill in its practice. I had learnt some skills in this subject whilst in Newcastle as a trainee, and received some further training from a colleague in Hull, including being 'put under' myself on two occasions.

With regard to my own experience, I started a little sceptically and thought myself on the first occasion to have been fully aware throughout. My colleague said that after I 'woke', my left hand would feel numb for two minutes but the right would feel normal. He then 'woke me up' and asked how my hands felt. 'Perfectly normal,' I replied. He picked up a fold of skin between my thumb and forefinger and before I knew what was happening, shoved a needle right through it! It had to be admitted that it did not hurt nor did it bleed. 'What about that, then?' he asked. I suggested it was probably an area of skin not very sensitive, and the speed with which he had done it had reduced the feeling. 'Let me put one through the right hand then similarly.' Interestingly, I refused! He removed the needle. I became convinced! The second occasion I was hypnotised was a relaxation session, a technique used to deepen the trance state and to help people with stress problems. I 'woke' to hear myself saying, 'I want my daddy' and bursting into tears. This was very curious. My father had died when I was twelve. I had not been thinking of him particularly. But certainly I had never had the opportunity to grieve properly. I hardly recall him being mentioned after his death and I had not attended the funeral. I was now forty-eight. I used the technique in my private practice later, after acquiring the certificate, and indeed lectured on the use of hypnosis in psychiatry at one or two BSMDH meetings and demonstrated the technique in group situations.

My career path in the 1980s was that I was getting increasingly involved in speaking at meetings and travelling abroad. Both Shirley and I were enthusiastic and adventurous travellers, enjoying the less usual venues and exploring less popular spots. Our favourite, however, was always Venice. I have never been there to a meeting, but we have travelled to Venice many times and explored

The Venetian lagoon and Shirley

its every alley and waterway. We have usually stayed at the Cipriani, an hotel on Giudecca Island across the lagoon from the bottom of the Grand Canal and St Mark's Square, and with its own swimming pool, rarely found in the city. The view from the terrace, across the bay towards the Lido, with a lone gondolier reflected in the early sun, is an unforgettable experience. The sparrows do tend to mess on the tablecloth when trying to pinch some sugar, but for an evening meal the rooftop restaurant of the Hotel Danielli cannot be beaten, looking across, from just beyond St Mark's Square to the island of San Georgio, with all the evening life on the waterways, gondoliers plying their trade, vaporettos dashing about across to the Lido and up the Grand Canal, and the little motor launch regularly plying across the waterway from St Mark's and The Doge's Palace to the Cipriani. Occasionally, too a liner will sweep majestically past to its moorings near the station. Such memories live with one forever.

Probably one of our best adventure holidays was to Iceland and Greenland. We spent a week on the east coast of Greenland at Angmassaluk, in the one hotel. We would watch small icebergs floating in and beaching with the tide, and walked up to a glacier melt lake half a mile or so inland from the town, the banks a mass of 'spring' arctic flowers. We decided to have a quick dip in the lake, very cold though a beautiful sunny day. We had no costumes but there was no one about except some locals fishing on the other side of the lake. Later we walked round and were intrigued that the Inuit family with their two children packed up and hurried off before we had a chance to greet them. We realised, however, when we got to the picnic spot, that with the sun behind them the view of our bathe must have been clear indeed! Who were these weird Europeans? Not the sort of people they wanted their children to meet, surely! In Iceland we did a tour which crossed the central wilderness of the island. Again we bathed, in volcanic hot springs. The colours of the rock formations, the superb waterfalls such as the Gullfos, and the active volcano of Hekla visible at that time again were impressed on one's memory.

An early visit to the USA was aided by my stepbrother, Tom. He had gone to New York and was a radiotherapist at the Mount Sinai Hospital in that city. He had boasted that in the States he could save in a year more than I earned, and when he had suggested that prior to my visit to the World Psychiatric Association meeting in Mexico City, where I was speaking on 'the Psychosexual Clinic', we might go on a vacation, he paying all the travel costs, I jumped at the offer without guilt! I was wanting to visit a district general hospital unit in New York and meet a colleague who worked there with whom I had corresponded, and determined therefore to visit him before meeting my stepbrother, and the two of us would then fly off wherever he chose.

I left my hotel in Central New York and got the metro to the nearest stop to the hospital, in Harlem, and walked to the hospital where I was greeted amiably. My colleague enquired where I'd been staying and, on learning I had travelled by metro and on foot into Harlem, threw a fit. On my departure he insisted on putting me into a cab and sending me back direct. No white man walked around Harlem alone, even in the daytime, I was firmly told! Innocent abroad!

Tom and I flew to Puerto Rico and spent a few days exploring San Juan and hired a car to drive round the island. We then went on, with a brief stopover in Port-au-Prince, Haiti, to Jamaica, staying in Ocho Rios, where the hotel beach was swept with a broom every morning before breakfast, and similarly toured the island in a hire car visiting Kingstown, the rain forest and doctors' bay, the blue lagoon and the limestone falls. The next stop was Merida on the Yucatan peninsula of Mexico where again we were able to hire a car and deposit it eventually in Mexico City. We visited the Mayan Sites of Chichen Itze and Uxhmal and then drove round the Gulf of Mexico to Villahermosa and Veracruz, up on to the alta plana, past the active volcano of Popocatepetl, through Pueblo into Aztec territory, finishing in the capital itself. Here, Tom left me and I joined the conference where I met, by arrangement, my old buddy Ian Martin again.

Ian and I both liked travel and conferencing and had met at Netley Hospital in the Army. We went to a number of conferences, sharing a twin-room (for price convenience I hasten to add) and indeed I once jocularly introduced him as a speaker at a meeting I was chairing as 'a friend with whom I had slept in more countries than with my wife'. The audience appreciated the joke but I was not sure that Ian had been amused! However, it had some truth. We had been to conferences in Honolulu, Vienna, Kyoto and Athens together, and at that stage Shirley, because of young children and her teaching commitment, had missed out rather. I promised when she retired to take her to the next one that came up. It proved to be Glasgow.

One conference leads to another. In Kyoto one of our party, a young Taiwanese doctor called Mina Hong, was present. She proved to be married to the ano-rectal specialist at Taipei General Hospital and, as I was speaking on the treatment of impotence and frigidity, she put me in touch with a doctor who ran an equivalent clinic in Taipei. The following year I received an invitation to be guest speaker at the international conference on Neuropsychiatry in Taipei. My Chinese colleague was speaking on 'Shen Kuei', an interesting ejaculatory disorder found in South-East Asia particularly.

My interest in languages led me to try to learn to speak some Chinese before I went, and I sought out a Chinese-speaking Malaysian postgraduate student at York University, Kitken Loke, who undertook to teach me the rudiments. She also translated the first paragraph of my talk for me so that I had it off pat when I went. The local Professor of Psychiatry who introduced me said that sadly I would be giving my talk in English. When I stood up to speak and launched into 'fluent' Mandarin Chinese, it brought the house down! At the banquet at the end of the conference I was guest of honour and it became clear they were trying to get me tipsy. Apart from dropping a sea cucumber halfway from the dish to my plate onto the cloth, while using a pair of chopsticks, I did not disgrace myself, however. The Chinese race do not hold their liquor as well as Europeans, and the ano-rectal surgeon and myself had to assist the professor of psychiatry from Kaohsiung University to his car! Mina Hong kindly took a few days off and acted as my guide to take me round the local places of interest, including the mausoleum of Chiang Kai-shek, and the fabulous Taiwan National Museum, and the Hongs had me to dinner at their apartment in the city.

At another conference, in Jerusalem, under the auspices of the international group of Medicine, Law & Ethics, I was invited to return three years later, to the next conference in Tel Aviv and chair a symposium on gender disorders. This led to a fruitful contact, out of which a book came to be published, and to my wife and myself having two further visits to the country.

The Society of Clinical Psychiatrists also spread its wings in the early eighties by hosting their annual conference outside of England on alternate years. We went to Guernsey and to Ireland and to Gibraltar, where we were royally entertained by the local medical societies. Our most ambitious visit, however, was a study tour of China in 1989 with a mixed party of psychiatrists and their

The committee of the Society of Clinical Psychiatrists in Gibraltar

partners. There were social activities as well as visits to hospitals, and we had a Chinese guide to assist us. Memorable moments were a visit to a commune village where we were entertained by the nursery school children with a beautiful song, and my wife and a child psychiatrist led them with a rendering of 'The wheels on the bus', causing such chaos that it probably took the local teachers some time to restore order to their rather over-regimented brood. We visited an orphanage and children's hospital in Shanghai and were very impressed by the imaginative approach of staff with relatively low funding. We saw an elderly people's home, where handicapped children were looked after during the day to the mutual benefit of both while their parents were out at work. We went to the Bethune Memorial Hospital in Shijaozhuang, which was off the normal tourist route. The treatments used and the knowledge of the local doctors were up to date and impressive. The cleanliness of the building, however, was terrible!

On the first morning, we were woken by the sound of Victor Sylvester dance music in the town square which we overlooked. We looked out to see the square busy with the elderly doing their exercises, but the younger were ballroom dancing! Our lady child psychiatrist who had gone out to watch was swept up by a local Fred Astaire and as the crowd separated to watch, he whisked her round in a quickstep!

The delegation at the Bethune Memorial Hospital in Shijaozhuang, China

There was an excellent indoor food market. Using my smattering of Chinese, Shirley and I decided to buy some pears which we saw. I looked up the word for pears and said in my best *Beijing de hua,* 'Can I have four pears, please?' I got the wrong classifier (the collective noun for fruit – as we might say a 'slice' of bread or a 'flock' of birds) and the girl serving, without thinking, corrected me. Then she was embarrassed and her colleagues laughed. We gathered a little crowd who followed us round to see what else these odd English would get up to. Everyone was incredibly friendly. After seeing the terracotta warriors, the Great Wall and other sites and sights, we finished up in Hong Kong where we had a meeting hosted by the Hong Kong Psychiatric Association, and a trip by hydrofoil down to Macao for a day tour and to see the casino.

My wife and I were able to make one more trip to the Near East early in the 1990s, with an adventure holiday group, and visited Jordan, Syria and Israel. I had a meeting in Israel, but the rest was pure holiday. We flew to Amman and drove down to the Red Sea via Petra, staying a few nights in each. We returned to Amman, and hired a car and driver to take us to Syria where we were to stay in Damascus, and Palmyra. Our driver seemed a little nervous going into Syria. As we waited at Customs a polite and handsome Syrian spoke to my wife and suggested very politely that it was not the custom to stand in the queue, but better if she sat with the ladies. 'The older men,' he said, 'are liable to be agitated if a woman joins the queue. Your husband can take your passport.'

We had been warned not to take anything into Syria that would suggest we were also to visit Israel since they were technically still at war, so we left a case at the hotel in Amman to pick up on our return. We then realised that this contained the address of our Damascus hotel! Our driver took us to a cab rank in central Damascus and dumped us there. The Syrian cab drivers were clamouring for the fare but as we didn't know where to go we opted for the British chargé d'affaires, who proved to be out to lunch. Eventually we decided to phone the travel agent in London to check the address! All this with minimal Arabic. We were to discover that it was not possible for an individual to make an overseas call without booking, but were directed to a travel agent over the road where they could make a call for us. Luckily the London travel agent was able to give us the address, which turned out to be just round the corner. We arrived and were welcomed and after that the trip was delightful. We explored the Souk, visited the home of Judas, where Paul stayed, in the street called straight, and dined on pork washed down with a fine wine in a local restaurant! A car was to take us across the desert to Palmyra. The ruins by moonlight were an incredibly beautiful sight. Shirley having the tomato salad at lunch proved a grave error which gave her, luckily only for about four hours, an acute attack of desert diarrhoea!

Eventually we returned to Amman and the following day took a bus to the Allenby Bridge for the crossing of the Jordan into Israel. At the border

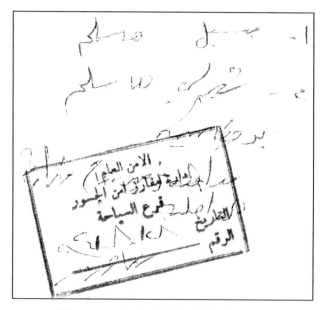

Visa to anywhere! Allenby Bridge document

checkpoint we were at first told that our documents were not in order as we did not have a visa. The customs officer was, however, very kind and spoke some French, and rang personally to Amman to clear us, giving us a written and stamped pass in his own hand, and off we went, through the new country of free Palestine and on into Israel proper and to Jerusalem. On the way back four days later our Israeli taxi driver did not wish to drive through Jericho and took us instead over some part of no man's land to the north of the Dead Sea, depositing us at the checkpoint on the Israeli side but missing the Palestinian checkpoint. We had to walk back to this to get our papers stamped before returning once more over the Allenby Bridge to Amman and thence home.

CHAPTER 10

In the long run

MY SPORTS CAREER has been moderate – no real high spots but personally satisfying. After I went off into Army Service I never again played cricket, lacrosse or rugger, nor did I do cross-country running thereafter. I continued to play squash and tennis throughout my life and still do at minor club level, and I have also taken up golf – and play badly. My main loves, however, have always been, as practical, fives and croquet. Minor sports, but the one-eyed man is king in the land of the blind, and better to be a reasonably good exponent of a minor sport than a nonentity in a popular one perhaps!

In my student days I entered a number of regional and national rugby fives tournaments though never won anything. There was a very strong contingent of old Sedberghians floating about on the fives scene at that time, Rodney Dodds, Giles Shaw, Gerald Vinestock, the two Smith brothers, Duncan and Jonathan, and John Guthrie, to mention a few, all getting half blues or winning major national events. I was foolish not to have played regularly at Cambridge. However, at that time there was no national or regional Winchester fives tournament, and in the seventies when I had a little more time again I began to look at the possibility of organising one.

The first stage was to do a survey of where there were Winchester-style courts available and to this end I circulated all the schools which I could trace, and universities, to get a base. The majority of schools had the Rugby or Eton-style courts, and a number had irregular and virtually unclassifiable ball courts of varying shapes and sizes. Rossall School had six Winchester-style courts with no back wall. Bootham School in York had a square buttress on both side walls near the back, and no back wall. A number of schools had lost their fives courts over the years, and some had even, sacrilegiously, converted Winchester courts into Rugby ones! The Catholic Schools also had a number of ball courts more in the style of the handball games of Ireland, the USA and Europe. It was not until some five years ago that attempts were made to have some joint competitions of these various styles, and the Rossall courts have been used and come into their own.

The survey of Winchester courts identified some forty courts in use or usable. Apart from two in the Channel Isles, a few private ones, and one in Nepal, we identified four schools who had enough courts (four or more) to mount a reasonable tournament, these being Winchester College itself, Sedbergh, Malvern and Bradfield. I decided to rotate the tournament through these four schools, with the permission of the headmaster and master in charge of fives, and we held our first national Winchester Fives doubles tournament in 1982 with a good entry of some sixteen pairs. I continued to play competitively until I was 60. The tournament became popular and the quality of play very high. Two figures of great significance in the fives world, Tom Woods and David Barnes, were greatly supportive and presented trophies. For a while we produced a newsletter and did our own thing, but in due course we became a sub-group of the bigger Rugby Fives Association and under their sponsorship.

We also started a women's national Winchester Fives Tournament with trophies for both double and singles games. This was first held at Bradfield in 1988. Four female players have dominated the scene but new ones are now coming along. For many years Paula Smith and Denise Hall-Wilton won, with my daughter Melanie, who was Secretary of Reading University Fives Club (who played on the Bradfield courts), coming third. Melanie has now won a number of singles and doubles trophies in both the Rugby and Winchester games.

My other, and continuing, love has been croquet. I learned my skills at Cambridge, honed them at Bart's and after some years in the wilderness re-entered the scene by joining the Nottingham Club in 1967 when working in Doncaster. Association croquet is a complex game, rather like snooker on a lawn with the tactics of chess thrown in! It has a national body, plays test matches with Australia and New Zealand, and has local and national

York Croquet Club

tournaments and competitions through the summer season. It has a handicap system rather similar to that of golf, the stroke handicap more or less matching in the skill sense. The lawn is 35x28 yards in size. My best handicap has been five, but at the time of writing is beginning to creep up and is now eight. *Sic transit gloria mundi!*

When we moved to York in 1970, clearly Nottingham was too far. The nearest club was Hull, which I joined. There was an abortive move to get a club going in Harrogate but this failed after a couple of years. Some fifteen years ago I decided to start a club in York and gathered together a nucleus of six enthusiasts, did some advertising, and eventually we persuaded Benningbrough Hall to allow us to develop the walled garden into a croquet lawn, good enough for match play. Sadly this venue (National Trust) did not prove very satisfactory and after a couple of seasons we were able to persuade York Council to rent us a redundant bowling green, (happily not a crown green!). Eventually we moved to the present site on Scarcroft Road where there is a joint bowls and croquet association with two lawns, and have won the local league and the Northern League on occasions. For a few years I was chairman and Shirley social secretary, with a thriving club of some thirty members. My son has taken up the game and is now an occasional player in Dublin.

During the years that the family were still at home, and we had acquired Shirley's father's caravan for keeps, we took off with the three children on some splendid vacations. Since the whole family seemed to have taken to Geography as part of their A level equipment, these holidays were of some practical value as well as generally broadening one's horizons. After a year or two of visiting Scotland, Wales and the Lake District with the touring van, named Katie, our first trip abroad was to Brittany and Normandy. We finished up in Trinité sur Mer after a short stay in Lille, or to be more exact Cysoing, where we made again the acquaintance of the Descatoire family, José now married with four children; the parents still in Cysoing in the old house but with a bungalow beautifully furnished for their retirement in the grounds; Edith, sadly somewhat in disgrace as a consequence of a divorce, not in evidence! But what a change in Cysoing, and indeed France, since 1947, now prosperous, flourishing and rebuilt. Madame Rejkewaerts took us over the Belgian border for a drive. 'Les glaces sont trop mieux dans la Belge.' We also visited Paris, where all the girls' dolls, which had come with us of course, had to be taken to see the fountains!

A couple of years later we headed for Norway. We took the car ferry from Newcastle over to Bergen, and set off via the Hardanger Fjord en route for Oslo. We camped a few nights later on the shores of the fjord, had a bathe in icy cold water the following morning, and headed for the local hotel for a *smørbrød* breakfast. We were seated, by the waiter, and invited to go up to the serving table to pick what we wished. At that moment, however, a party of Germans from a coach came in, and we decided to wait till the crush had gone.

Wrong! When they had left off from milling round the serving table there was nothing left. And I mean nothing. It was as if locusts or termites had come through. The hotel were embarrassed and we were given some eggs, cornflakes and coffee, and not asked to pay.

I have to say we saw a similar occurrence in a Paris hotel a few years ago, with Americans, one person carrying off about twelve pats of butter and four glasses of orange, just for himself. We watched. Not that I'm racist. The Americans are an interesting collection and certainly not one race. The white settlers who have dominated North America for I suppose some 300 years, now rule the earth, though know little of what goes on beyond their shores. Only a small percentage travel abroad or have passports, and few learn a second language, except perhaps Spanish. What is outwith their shores is a museum and it is up to those who inhabit it to learn English. Secondly there are the freed African slaves, still somewhat second-class citizens, either appearing threatening, as in parts of New York, or stereotyped as in the South, as the Al Johnson 'coal black mammy'.

'But,' I asked the friend with whom we were staying in Santa Barbara, 'what of the native Americans who used to own the place?' He smiled. 'Oh, yeah. We gotten some of them – in the reservations.' It intrigued me in 1988 when we did our 'American tour' that while the South African Bantustans had received so much criticism, and rightly so, the distinction between Bantustan and a reservation was somewhat subtle. When I got to know a young Navajo woman (Yes! But more anon), she told me that education in the reservation was on the whole poor. But if you lived in the reservation you got a state grant. If you left the reservation to live elsewhere, why, you lost your state grant so couldn't afford to get educated anyway. However, two events had brought them into the money, courtesy of some slick lawyers. Firstly, although alcohol was controlled in the reservation, gambling was not and they had opened a casino. Secondly, they had found oil under some reservation land. The State Government had quickly stepped in and suggested that the locals only owned the land to a depth of so many feet and didn't own the oil rights. This was challenged in the federal courts, and they won. And about time! The history of white dealings with Native Americans only some six generations back, such as the Long March, has been appalling, but no worse than the Australian Aborigines, the Inuit and a number of racial minority groups around the world. Look at the books of Kings and Samuel 1 and 2 in the Old Testament to learn about racial cleansing!

But how did I meet Shawnee Vega? Well, our American tour was thuswise. We stayed first with an old school friend of Shirley's on the East Coast near Santa Barbara and did a tour round the Sierras, taking in San Francisco, Yosemite, then Death Valley and Las Vegas, before leaving them and hiring a car ourselves to drive across to the Grand Canyon and up eventually to Denver where we met other friends, and went with them to New Orleans. Finally we flew to New York for a few days before returning home. After leaving Grand Canyon we stopped off in the Navajo Nation at Cameron for lunch. A local Native American in Grand Canyon had said the goods and petrol in the reservations didn't attract a purchase tax and would be cheaper. At the stationer's in Cameron, being as how I was interested in languages, I thought I'd get a *Teach Yourself Navajo* for interest: and they hadn't one. Well, in Cardiff you'd certainly find a *Teach Yourself Welsh* and there are more people who speak Navajo than Welsh. So when we got to New York I went to the main bookshop, the equivalent to Foyle's, and asked to be taken to their American Indian language section. They hadn't one! Indeed the language section as a whole was extremely thin – Spanish and German basically. So when we got back to the UK the bit was between my teeth! The next time I was in London I went to Foyle's, and demanded to be taken to **their** American Indian language section. The Norwegian assistant replied, 'I'm sorry – ve haf not got one.'

'But you are Foyle's!' I expostulated. 'If not you – who?'

'Haf you tried the Third World Bookshop on Charing Cross Road?'

'But America is not a Third World country.'

'No – but perhaps the American Indians are.'

Wise words from one so young.

I visited Charing Cross Road. No luck but this was now a crusade, though not the way King Richard did it in Constantinople! I had bought in Cameron a monthly magazine called *The Navajan*. I wrote to the editor asking why there was this problem and what to do! He published my letter! Within a few weeks, three ladies had written to me; two who had been to the Native American Studies degree course at the University of Colorado sent me a book on the Navajan language. One was Shawnee Vega, and I finished up having a five-year-long correspondence with her. I think Shirley felt that at some 4,000 miles distant I was pretty safe!

But to return to caravanning after that long digression, we headed for Oslo on our trip with the children, and returned over some hair-raising passes, and through long tunnels through the mountains via Vik and the Sogne Fjord. The Jaguar and the caravan performed beautifully. We reached Bergen again after a long steep zigzag descent and took the ferry back to Newcastle upon Tyne. We drove back to Crayke. Twelve miles from home the bolt on the towing mechanism on the caravan sheared through and the caravan slewed off the road to the left. The weight of the Jaguar held us and we stopped and were able to get it sorted out with no damage done. If that had happened the day before we would, I guess, have all been over the cliff and my memoirs would at this point have ceased!

We made two other major caravan trips before the teenagers decided to do their own thing. One summer we decided to follow the River Rhine from its mouth, in effect Rotterdam, up to its source on the Rhine glacier and finished our outward journey at Interlaken. We took in Liechtenstein whose borders embrace the Rhine Valley upstream from Berne and where we found a campsite up on the hillside above Vaduz, (and nearly burned out the clutch, this time in a Rover. It finally burned out some three weeks after we got back! There must in my youth or childhood have been 'something I did good' to misquote *The Sound of Music*) and were there for the Swiss National Holiday. We could see across the valley all the firework parties that evening.

The final trip was to Spain, back to a Jaguar again, this time an XJS. We drove through France and over the Pyrennes, taking in Andorra and exploring this tiny republic 'en route'. We finished up north of Barcelona on the Costa Brava where we were very hot but had superb snorkelling. The long drive back, however, was tedious and I think decided us all that with five almost adults – well four; Shirley **was** adult – that would be the last.

So the 'children' grew up. Let us get up to date. Melanie went to Reading for her BA degree, went to London and became a Chartered Surveyor with Gerald Eves. Eventually she became enamoured of a vet from Devon, another story, and they now live happily ever after in Devon and have two children called Toby and Jessica, who at the time of writing are aged 5½ and 3. Fiona went to New College Durham, got her B.Ed degree, taught in Grimsby and Thirsk, and in due course married her first love, Andrew. They have three children. Matthew is now sixteen and heading for A levels and I would guess a sports degree in due course; Benjamin is twelve and now in the senior school at Easingwold, and Daniel aged six is at Crayke School, the village church school at which Shirley is a governor. Fiona has gone back to part-time teaching. Michael, at the time of writing in his fortieth year, a frightening thought, is still single and seems to enjoy European ladies. After working in Spain and in Germany, (and learning to speak Spanish well enough to be best man to his school buddy John Torlesse at the latter's wedding in Barcelona and to give his speech in Spanish) he spent a period working in Bath in an architect's office and he is now a partner in an architectural business in Dublin.

Shirley became the teacher in charge of a nursery in York and stayed on until 1991. By then education was in the throes of political correctness. She took early retirement! I too was nearing fifty-five and getting a little frustrated with the way psychiatry was going in the NHS. I was no longer what I considered a consultant should be, the head of a team, being consulted as a specialist in my craft of which I had a quarter of a century of experience. I was but a cog in a management-supported wheel. I didn't like it. In the spring of 1988 I was approached, head-hunted I suppose one would now call it, by a private company that was establishing private hospitals for psychiatric illness, an offshoot of the Priory Group and run by John Hughes. During the summer there were negotiations. I knew that on my fifty-fifth birthday, 7 February 1989, I could retire from the NHS with a pension that would be 37/80ths of my salary. In August 1988, I was offered the post of Medical Director. The hospital was yet to be built, and due to open in March of 1989 in Harrogate, the company to be called Cygnet Health Care. I would be paid a retainer from the autumn and would be in on the development and staff recruitment. I went home and discussed this with Shirley. We agonised over it for some thirty seconds. I accepted.

I put in my intention to retire from the NHS to the managers, as of 7 February, (to give me the extra added pensionable year) and began to wind down my commitments. I had a research project ongoing which was of interest to me. I had attended a meeting a couple of years before in London under the auspices of Rosemary Steele, the guru in the UK on this subject, on 'Kirlian Aura Photography'. In essence this was a way of displaying on a photographic 'positive' – i.e. print paper – the electro-magnetic field around biologically living matter: the so-called 'aura' of some alternative medicine and other therapists. The medical interest lay in the fact that a hand print taken by means of this Kirlian machine showed changes which seemed to be associated with body malfunction. This had been taken up by those interested in acupuncture, in Chinese Medicine, and in the 'meridians' used in that area. Changes had been noted in cancer, for example, and in the field of abnormal psychology where stress and anxiety particularly showed obvious changes in the print. I was interested in some work that had been published on these prints in schizophrenia and depression, and on serial prints of people under treatment for anxiety states, where it was suggested that progress could be monitored through Kirlian prints.

The first question was how valid were these results, and what was the level of test/retest reliability. In other words, if you took a print of someone's palm, and did it again the next day, would it be reliably similar? Also, what would be the effect of everyday items on print variability, such as having to hurry because one was late, having had some strong coffee, smoked a couple of cigarettes, or drunk alcohol reasonably recently before the print was taken. These were the sorts of things that could alter such things as adrenalin output, or perhaps other transmitted agents in the body and which might influence the electro-magnetic field or indeed the conductivity through the skin. If these were important, then they would need to be monitored before other more interesting changes could be verified.

The initial step was to get used to the machine and collect up as many volunteers as would be prepared to have their palm print taken, and receive a copy, to get a bank of normals. Secondly, some volunteers would be needed to do some serial prints over time, and be prepared to smoke, drink coffee or tea or whatever and have their print taken before and after. Thirdly, we could start taking prints of outpatients who volunteered similarly with various psychological problems, anxiety, mood change and stress, to see if a pattern emerged. At a later stage it might be possible to do the same with a group of in-patients with more serious psychotic illnesses, and test them before and after treatment. For example what effect might electroplexy have? I acquired through a grant the necessary equipment, in particular the Kirlian camera which was quite expensive, and a room that could be used as a photographic dark room, and began to collect up volunteers.

At a later stage it occurred to me that it might be possible to utilise this technique in the monitoring of impotence and frigidity, and collected up a small number of volunteers who were prepared to try this possibility with me. Sadly, in one sense, my move to take up the Medical Director post put a stop to Kirlian research since in my new job I had neither time nor facilities, so I was only able to present preliminary findings to the research committee.

CHAPTER 11

Musing on the muses

ALL WORK AND NO PLAY is said to make Jack a dull boy. As the children grow and become independent, leave home, marry, there is a sense of bereavement and loss, which I guess most people feel. We had a sizeable garden which could occupy us in suitable weather. Shirley, through her superior knowledge, was in charge of flower beds and I cut grass, dug a little, and cut hedges – until I fell off the stepladder on to a concrete path and broke a rib, after which we got 'a good man'!!

We both liked to travel; we both liked music; Shirley liked to swim; I liked to play squash, and we both played tennis. We joined the local club. We also occasionally played nine holes round our local golf club. We increasingly went out to the theatre, to concerts and to dinners, and we began to play bridge more frequently with our friends. My main hobby, however, increasingly became writing. Some of this was work-related, some simply for pleasure. The book published in 1975 by Butterworth's on *Psychiatric Illness in Adolescence* had sold only moderately, being rather specialist. On the other hand *Psychiatry made Simple* published by Heinemann's in 1982 sold well. In between times, however, I had published two other books, which related to the marital and sexual counselling with which I was becoming increasingly involved. *Sexual Disorder* was published by Butterworth/Heinemann (as they now are) in 1978, and concerned itself with the diagnosis and treatment of such problems as impotency, frigidity, ejaculatory disorders and vaginismus, with suitable helpful diagrams to explain the 'sensate focus' method of treatment.

My mother, when I went into psychiatry, had not been over keen. 'Why didn't you go in to a more respectable speciality, like say gynaecology'? But when I became a consultant she was pleased, and when I had my first book published it lay on her table casually, so that when her friends came to coffee she could say, equally casually, 'Oh yes, my son wrote this.' So, when my book *Sexual Disorders* came out I gave her a copy. Curiously, it did not appear on the coffee table. Indeed, it was in her bookshelf back to front! I looked in it one day and found that some of the admittedly rather explicit diagrams had been cut out. This book was translated into Spanish and sold well in South America.

The other book, for copyright reasons partly, was published by C. S. Thomas in the United States under the title *Psychosexual Disorders – a Review* and was commissioned by them. It covered in the first half much the same ground as had *Sexual Disorders* but the second half of the book was devoted to what once upon a time might have been called sexual deviancy, and to gender problems. Sexual behavioural anomalies or minority pursuits, call these things what you will collectively to be politically correct, was a mish-mash of conditions which themselves were only important if they were causing distress to the individual.

Homosexuality was perhaps the largest group. Prior to 1967 male homosexual acts had been illegal, and courts often referred individuals apprehended for such behaviour, on conviction, to psychiatrists as a better, more enlightened (!) alternative to prison. A strange form of enlightenment but better than theretofore. After 1967 homosexual acts between two consenting adults in private ceased to be illegal, the law ceased to have much interest therefore, and only those homosexual people who were distressed by their condition tended to attend. Why would a happy homosexually orientated individual want to see a doctor? — except of course that such people are just as likely to get appendicitis, pneumonia, schizophrenia or boils as the rest of humanity but **more** likely to get depressive reactions. Why? Because with Jews and Gypsies, they are historically one of the most persecuted groups in Western society, largely due to bigots who quote out of context passages from the Bible or Koran where homosexual acts appear to have been disapproved of under Jewish law two thousand years ago.

Indeed, much evidence suggests that homosexuality is innately determined, genetically in a large percentage. You don't catch it, any more than those with a homosexual orientation are going to catch heterosexuality. But they not infrequently need counselling, as do all persecuted minorities. They harm no one any more than redheads, who are of course also statistically deviant, being outwith the blonde-brunette continuum, who are the norm. Perhaps, since redheadedness is (erroneously) associated with a fiery temper, they should all either be compulsorily shaved or dyed black! Or imprisoned if they get too fond of each other!

Apart from sexual orientation, there were of course a small number of people troubled by 'perverted practices', those whose sexual orientation was such that they were attracted to minors. (Miners is all right!). Paedophilia is, at the time of writing, one of the latest witch-hunts, along with downloading pornographic pictures of children. Not that one approves, but witch-hunts are very dangerous too. Then there are those only able to be aroused by fetishist objects or situations, and those with really excessive libido.

Gender is different from sex. Gender is the concept, in this context, of masculinity or femininity, maleness or femaleness, but not sex drive or orientation. Nor is it what is now known in colleges of higher education as 'Gender Studies', which is more to do with the current vogue of women feeling they have been oppressed, that is, a sort of sociology course. No, gender is the concept within oneself of **being** masculine or feminine, despite one's anatomy.

It is as if brain gender identity is at variance with bodily gender identity. 'I am a man locked in a woman's body' or vice-versa. Difficult to understand, the 'in-betweens'. It manifests itself in milder forms in the inner need to identify, in clothing, habits or lifestyle, with what is perceived to be the other gender's persona – i.e. cross-dressing in the transvestite individual, or, in the more all-enveloping form, trans-sexualism, in the conviction that one **is** the other gender, and the desire, increasingly practical with modern surgery, to 'change sex', which actually means to make the body more like the body of the desired gender and less like the one that one is stuck with. These problems are still pretty taboo, open to mockery by the ignorant even more than homosexuality, and very distressing to some individuals who have this in-betweenness, though to those who come to terms with it, it can be a source of much inner satisfaction and knowledge. Not many (about 1 per cent of the population in fact) have the privilege of being able in some degree to be in both camps (no pun intended!). Counselling is directed towards developing one's own self respect – 'I am what I am.' I coined the expression 'bigendered' to contrast with 'bisexual'.

I had got the writing bug – I suppose it was in my mother's genes; and my great-grandfather's. It is also in my son. I wrote articles for journals, researched topics for presentation as learned papers, and tried my hand at novel writing. To date I have not been able to get anyone to publish a work of fiction, though I did, at a publisher's suggestion, write a couple of rather steamy specialist novelettes for a specific cross-gender readership. They were little love stories – boy wants to be girl – gets accepted as such – lives happily ever after! – but a bit naughty! The first was published under a nom-de-plume – the second should have been but worryingly appeared in print with my real name! Rather soberingly they made me more money than *Psychiatry Made Simple* but I ran out of ideas!

When Clifton Hospital in York closed in the early 1990s I felt that a history of the hospital ought to be written. It would have been sad had the place, in its day one of the finer county mental hospitals, innovative in its treatments and one of the earliest to use electroplexy and to set up industrial therapy units, sunk without trace. It had served the community for a century. No one else seemed interested so I took on the task with the help of Shirley, and of the archivist from the Borthwick Institute, who was working on the hospital archival material. This book, called *Clifton Hospital: an era* was published in 1996 by Wildflower Press.

I also became involved in editing a number of books. The first had been the proceedings of the Second National Conference on Psychosexual Disorders held in York, and mentioned previously. After I became a trustee for the Beaumont Trust, because of my increasing work with gender dysphoria, this body decided to publish a book on transvestism. I edited the publication, again by Wildflower Press, and wrote the chapter on the medico-psychiatric input into the subject. This ran to a second edition.

Whilst I was a member of the Royal College of Psychiatrists' Journal committee in the nineties, I was asked to produce a book in their monograph series, published by the Gaskell Press, on psychosexual disorders, and to commission the authors who would contribute, and coordinate the editing. This came out some five years ago. Finally (so far) I edited a book for the Society of Clinical Psychiatrists produced to combine the 25th anniversary of the society with the millennium and was a collection of chapters from individual authors well known in the psychiatric world on topics of their expertise and choosing, ranging over matters of current import and thoughts on where psychiatry might be going in the years ahead. This was published by the SCP and printed in Derby by El Peco Press. At the moment, having had time on my hands for a year or so, I have a novel *Just Polly* and a book with a religious theme seeking publishers, the latter called *The Deity for Doubters*. My first novel *Gretel* never found a publisher. I must redo it one day.

One topic that has never seen the light cropped up some fifteen years ago when one lunch-time, as one would, I was idly reading through the Vagrancy Act of 1744 (well, why not?) Paragraph 19 caught my eye. *Nothing heretofore said shall in any way remove the rights of Dutton of Dutton or his heirs in perpetuity* – or words to that effect.

'What an odd thing to find in an Act of Parliament,' says I. Detective work was required. Now it is fairly easy to work back in time concerning Acts of Parliament, since the present act will detail what it is replacing and what has been repealed. This in turn can then be looked up too. It is much more difficult to do the same thing forwards, because one does not know if and when the Act one is reading has been replaced.

Dutton of Dutton went back to the thirteenth century, and King John. Vagrants in those days, like strolling players and minstrels, were, if they got into trouble, not particularly distinguished from the mentally ill, or as they were called, the 'furiously and dangerously mad'. Vagabonds and the like needed to be licensed to leave their registered parish if they wished to entertain 'abroad'. Now the Dutton family lived near Chester, on the Welsh borderlands. The Welsh chose to besiege the City of Chester. Down the road the Duttons were having a knees-up at a local fayre and the crowds had gathered. The Duttons received a message that Chester was having a problem. 'Come on, lads' he no doubt cried to the assembled mob, 'let's go and sort out the Welsh' – or something similar in Chaucerian English! 'Hurrah!' they no doubt all cried, and off they went. 'This will be a good wheeze.' They succeeded, and the King was duly grateful.

'You, and your heirs in perpetuity', he announced 'shall have the right to license vagrants and strolling minstrels in the county palatinate of Chester, for ever and ever. And can charge them a farthing a time for your trouble.'

Now a quarter of an old penny in those days was a tidy sum. They minted half-farthings and third-of-a-farthings up until Queen Victoria's time. That was before inflation!

So there it was. If you weren't licensed you were whipped, and returned to your parish into their responsible care. This right had been held by the Duttons and their descendants for 800 years! When I was at a meeting in Chester, I decided to go and see Dutton Hall, on the edge of Dutton Village. I found the Home Farm to the Hall but where was the Hall? I could see a workshop up a drive with people working in it, probably part of the farm. I walked up to ask directions.

'Well, it's here,' said the man, 'or was. You can see the foundations.'

'What happened to it?'

'They took it away.'

'Took it away?' It sounded a strange way to put it.

'Yes, the Dewar family took it away!'

'How and when?'

'In the 1930s. They were the whisky family. Lived in Sussex, I believe. Mrs Dewar wanted to build a new east wing on their mansion, and when she saw it was for sale, she rang her husband and said, "I've found a perfect east wing for our house!" So they took it down, stone by stone, loaded it on to fifteen steam lorries and off they went south! And rebuilt it down there as it was.'

An extraordinary tale! The next time I had the opportunity and was up in London, I took a train to East Grinstead and with my camera approached an imposing building, now a prep school. I had written in advance and had permission to see and examine the 'East Wing', a beautiful and restored Elizabethan manor tacked on to the other main building, beautifully beamed inside with a splendid fireplace. So that was Dutton Hall. Who has the rights to license is uncertain; perhaps it is held by the heirs, the Kilmoney family, or the Dukes of Hamilton.

The other great love which Shirley and I shared was music. Curiously there did not seem to be much of an inherited factor here. My Aunt Ethel had achieved an examination in singing with the Northern College of Music, and sang with the Philharmonic Choir, along with her fiancé, in Sheffield, but that was about it. Funnily enough my early inspiration perhaps came from my prep school, Moorlands, in Leeds, where the music master persuaded our primitive choir to sing 'Hark how the trumpet's voice' from Berlioz's *Faust*, for our end-of-term concert. We had a piano at home and I found I could 'vamp' out a tune and harmonise it in a simple way. Sedbergh was a very musical school where I sang in the choir and learned the piano but I never became proficient in sight reading. In later years I started to learn the clarinet, and the 'guitarrre-zither', picked up from a junk shop. At Cambridge I sang with the Granta Singers and briefly learned to play the chanter. At Bart's I sang in the

Rahere Choir. Then there was a long gap. Shirley too had sung in her school choir, and learned the piano. At Cambridge she sang with the university choir under the baton of Boris Ord. Then she too entered the musical wilderness. However, what we did do was to become increasingly involved in attending classical music concerts and opera, and collecting tapes, and then CDs came in, and amassing a large collection of classical symphonies, concertos, and indeed various other examples of musical expression, including Frank Sinatra and the music of an American Indian Pow-Wow, courtesy of Shawnee Vega!

York was rich in musical opportunity with the Barbican Centre, the two theatres, the Minster, the two concert halls at York University, Ampleforth Abbey, the Harrogate concert halls, and Leeds, where the Grand Theatre & Opera House hosted the English Opera North amongst others, and Leeds Town Hall which had a superb Victorian concert hall. Then there was Harewood House where the Earl, patron of English Opera North, hosted a series of chamber concerts each year for those on his list – which we were. We were 'Friends' of English Opera North and got as a consequence early booking opportunities. York had the Bach Choir, the Minster Choir, the Philharmonic. You name it they had it. We joined the Easingwold Singers. We also took the opportunity when abroad to go to concerts or opera and were lucky enough to attend both in Vienna, and opera in Paris, ballet in Tallin and in Riga and concerts in St Petersburg and Venice. In Beijing we went to the circus!

I had got the Gilbert & Sullivan 'bug' at Sedbergh when acting in *Pirates* and continued it at St John's College, Cambridge where Shirley joined us. We took the opportunity wherever it presented to see any opera of the thirteen collaborations Sullivan had with W. S. Gilbert, only managing a performance of their **very** first collaboration, *Thespis*, a few years ago by an amateur group. It is rarely done. The Gilbert & Sullivan Society hosts a competitive festival over a three-week period in Buxton each year at the Opera House there, and most of the operas are performed.

Sullivan, however, was a prolific composer in the Victorian era and wrote far more than simply comic operettas. He achieved considerable fame in his day for his oratorios, presented at the Leeds Festivals. He was trained and in the choir at the Chapel Royal, a skilled organist and conductor, studying music on a scholarship won to the Leipzig Conservatoire. His serious works written in the late nineteenth century pre-dated Brahms and Tchaikovsky. He won the Mendelssohn scholarship, and his early music shows this composer's influence. He was knighted by Queen Victoria, principally following his grand opera production of *Ivanhoe*, revived in Edinburgh in its centenary year. His piece for his Leipzig finals, *The Tempest* was presented and caused immediate acclaim in Britain. He wrote two ballets, the best known being *The Enchanted Isle* – (*L'isle enchantê*) and a symphony (*The Irish*), a cello concerto recently recorded by Julian Lloyd Weber, and numerous religious choral walks, a song cycle, hymns, including 'Onward Christian Soldiers', and a number of operettas with librettists other than Gilbert, such as *Haddon Hall, The Beauty Stone* and *The Emerald Isle*. The latter, a rather silly story and not currently politically correct, nevertheless has two superb melodies in it. Sullivan died in 1901 before it could be completed. A young composer, Edward German, finished it for him and it was performed successfully, posthumously, in London. His oratorios were perhaps typically Victorian and have been through a period when such music was out of fashion. Happily, it is experiencing some revival, and recordings are now available of *The Light of the World, The Martyr of Antioch* and *The Prodigal Son* among others; and two *Te Deums* and a piece, *In Memoriam* to remember his father's death.

From the above paragraphs, the reader will note me to be a Sullivanophile. Indeed, I have recordings of all the extant music of Sullivan which is an interesting collection. There is a Sullivan Society which exists to promote and have performed Sullivan's more serious music. It produces a magazine, and on alternate years mounts a weekend meeting at which at least one major work is performed. The conference moves around and has taken us to Edinburgh; to the Gaiety Theatre, Douglas in the Isle of Man, Cheltenham and Nottingham. It is an intriguing mix of a group: enthusiasts, people with high musical knowledge, a few eccentrics – and Shirley and myself!

What do we do ourselves these days, apart from listen? We sing in the local Easingwold Singers, play the piano, and I have spurts of interest in the clarinet. My son, who learned the violin, and I played some impromptu duets occasionally before he went overseas, and that was memorable, at least for us!

An interesting aspect of life has been the joining of 'clubs'. This is a little out of fashion except in certain London circles but even for a 'provincial' has provided a useful place to stay, quiet and more exclusive than an hotel, and a good place to dine. I first joined the United Sports Club, situated in Whitehall Court, when I was a student at Cambridge and representing the university at lacrosse and on the judo team. It shared premises for a while with the National Liberal Club, and had a very fine dining area. However, with the decrease in interest in men's clubs, it merged in the late sixties with the Golfers Club, and after a while this club moved to premises shared with the St James Club, at St James Street off Piccadilly. In the seventies this too closed. In the meantime I had been invited to join the Authors Club (merged with the Arts Club, and with very attractive premises including a pleasant garden). They had an interesting programme of dining events but no sleeping facilities. They did, however, have arrangements for overnight stays at the Lansdowne Club just off Berkeley Square (the Authors Club being on Dover Street), which again had a fine art deco dining room, squash courts, and its own swimming pool with poolside bar. I remained a member here until retirement at 65 when the cost became rather a pointless luxury. I was in any case a member and Fellow of the

Royal Society of Medicine, in effect a London Club, with excellent sleeping and dining facilities, and was also a member of the Royal College of Surgeons with similar facilities, the former on Wimpole Street and the latter in a fine building in Lincoln's Inn Fields, so there was no shortage of places for my wife and me to stay. At one time there was a club in York, The York Club of which I was also a member, but the premises ceased to be available some ten years ago.

CHAPTER 12

God wot

WHEN CONSIDERING WHICH 'special subject' chapters one should include in autobiographical memoirs, important aspects of one's life, be they hobbies, triumphs or crises, then for Shirley and myself, religion must deserve a special place. Not that we are in any sense 'over pious', but religion, philosophy, one's personal ethical concepts, must play an important part, even if one were an atheist. Shirley and I were both baptised into the Church of England and this formed the basis of our upbringing, both Sedbergh and Guildford High School for Girls (a church schools company) having this ethos as their base. As a child I was taken regularly to church, St Chad's, Far Headingley in Leeds, with my father and mother. We usually walked the mile or more from home, past the filter beds and through a little wood as a short cut. When my father died, at 51, it was in St Chad's churchyard that he was interred.

At Sedbergh there was a strong protestant ethic. The headmaster, Bruce-Lockhart, was a Presbyterian from Scotland. There were no games on a Sunday; we went for a walk. The Presbyterian boys were admitted to their church and learned their catechism. We had a course of talks from a Father from the Community of the Resurrection from Mirfield, near Leeds. We were confirmed by the Bishop of Bradford. Sedbergh put religious faith high on its agenda, and the atmosphere, somewhat monastic and within the fells and beautiful dales, lent itself to this. It made a big impression. The school prayer went

> *Make this school as a field that the Lord hath blessed, that whatsoever is pure and holy and of good report may here forever flourish and abound. Enlarge it with a wider usefulness, and exalt it in the love and reverence of all its members, as an instrument of thy glory.*

One learned to pray.

At Cambridge and Bart's I was a regular church attender, and involved in choirs that sang church music. I went through a 'high church' phase, Anglo-Catholic one might say, but for a few years after qualifying, largely for practical reasons, I tended to lapse. Then when the children arrived we became more involved, as a family, again. This we have continued to do over the years, but have not felt committed to a particular sectarian creed. Like many Protestants we tend to believe what we believe. The importance is a belief in a creative force, and some sort of personal connection with the deity, through the concepts delivered by Jesus of Nazareth but surely indeed by other prophets throughout the world and down the ages. We attend York Minster at times, and Ampleforth Abbey, but mostly our local church of St Cuthbert in Crayke, where in due course we have become increasingly involved in the choir, and on the parochial church council, as in Shirley's case lay chairman and myself as clerk.

However, it has been the history and philosophy of religion that has increasingly with me become a hobby, if that is the right word. By inclination I am now, after opportunities to see people from many parts of the world at prayer, a pluralist. That is to say I believe that God has revealed his truth in diverse ways and at diverse times in history to diverse peoples, and that one particular revelation in time to a particular nation is unlikely to be the sum total of God's relationship with mankind. Most people adopt the religious beliefs of their parents and those of influence with them in their formative years. That is fine. If we choose to believe it to be the best way, that is fine too. But assuming there to be one God, then all who pray to God will be heard. His name will vary from country to country – Jehovah, God, Allah, Brahma or Vishnu, Duw, Dieu – Lord, Father, Athair, Pater – what's in a name?

As to prophets, how do we define a prophet, or a saint come to that? Is a prophet someone who has a gift of prophecy and is able to interpret revelations from God? What has happened to prophets since say Malachi some 400 years BC? The Jewish Old Testament prophets will be well known to many of us, Isaiah, Jeremiah, Elijah and Elisha. Jews and Moslems and many Christians will see Jesus as a prophet, and John the Baptist also. We could call Wesley and Fox prophets; surely Mohammed would qualify as a prophet by any definition; Krishna? Gautama Buddha? Joseph Smith of the Church of the Latter Day Saints? Billy Graham?

Most religions seem to believe in higher beings, God's messengers, such as the angels of Christianity, Islam and Judaism. Gabriel, Uriel, Michael and others are named. The Hindu religion uses the word 'deva' but recognises beings higher than humanity who serve God. Does God manifest Himself on earth? Moses seemed to think so. Christians believe Jesus to have been a manifestation of God on earth in human form and call Him the 'Son of God'. Hindus believe Krishna to have been a manifestation of God on earth in human form. Are both true? Is neither true? We shall only **know** if and when we reach Heaven. Until then we use faith and belief. Why would God not manifest Himself more than once in different ages of time?

My travels I believe have given me insights into religious practice which many never see. It is ignorance that causes prejudice. Jerusalem I suppose is unique at least to the religions of 'the book', i.e. the Jewish Testament, accepted by Jews, Christians and Moslems alike. It is the Holy City for Judaism, the site of the Great Temple. For Christians it is where Jesus preached, ate the last supper, was tried and subjected to crucifixion, and 'rose again'. For Moslems in addition it is a place visited by Mohammed and where he was taken up to Heaven on a visit, or in a vision, from the dome of the rock, a beautiful mosque on the Temple Mount.

Israel, Palestine, Syria, Jordan contain a mass of religious sites and experiences. In Jerusalem we visited the Church of the Holy Sepulchre, whose different Christian sects own different bits and vie with each other, the whole being overseen by a Moslem to avoid further controversy! The Copts possess a chapel on the roof. The Protestants have gone a few hundred yards up the Damascus road, believing that Golgotha was sited there, and also the rock tomb, which certainly best matches the New Testament description and is known as the Garden Tomb. Take your choice. Then in the Armenian part of the city is a superb monastic library. On the Mount of Olives is Gethsemene, and a chapel whence Mary is said to have been bodily assumed. Down in the Kidron Valley is a beautiful very old church where Mary was said to be buried and near Ephesus in Turkey is St Mary's house where she lived out her last days in the care of St John, and died. Take your choice. There is another legend that Mary travelled with Jesus after he survived the crucifixion, on his way to the Euphrates Valley and thence to Kashmir. Mary died and was buried somewhere on this route, and Jesus's tomb is located near Srinagar. Well . . .

Jerusalem also has numerous Jewish historic sites, the Wailing Wall which is all that remains of the temple, being a traditional place of prayer and pilgrimage. Where the temple stood is now one of Islam's most holy sites, the beautiful octagonal mosque of the Dome of the Rock, and another mosque, the blue mosque also on the plateau. One can (depending on the political situation) drive the few miles to Bethlehem and see the basilica over the alleged site of Jesus's birth in its crypt. One can drive down the road to Jericho and turning right bathe in the Dead Sea, see the caves of Qumran, drive to the spectacular fortress of Masada, and, beyond, the supposed site of Sodom. One can then drive north again, up the Jordan Valley to the Sea of Galilee, or Lake Genesseret, and to the attractive town of Tiberias. Further north on the shores of the lake is Capernaum, the site of Paul's house, and the site of the sermon of the Beatitudes. Turning left one comes eventually to Nazareth and Joseph's house, on to the sea at Caesarea and the remains of Roman occupation, and at Haifa the site of the head church of the Baha'i religion. And so back down the coast and beyond Tel Aviv to Joppa. It brings the Bible, both Old and New Testaments, alive. The mediaeval buildings, over decorated and over touristy, do not for me produce an atmosphere. But Capernaum, when the crowds have gone, is beautiful, and on my first trip, when we sailed across the lake and landed here, it was most evocative. This is where Jesus preached and it is real.

On our trip to Jordan we were fortunate in arriving at the main mosque, where the King of Jordan worshipped, not long before it closed to visitors. Shirley, having donned a blue robe and head covering, and I, were shown round personally by the guide, including the Royal Apartments and the crypt where their synod was held, and the utterly beautiful central place of worship in the mosque, with its superb chandeliers. But it was when we were in Turkey in Selchuk, near Ephesus, that we saw more what Islam was about. There was a mosque on the edge of the town near the Temple of Diana, with a kind elderly custodian who spoke a little English and showed us round, and gave me a Moslem catechism in English. It was a place of peace and reminded me of a Franciscan church.

Islam accepts the Bible as the word of God, and Jesus as a prophet, but Mohammed as the last of the great prophets and the one who received from God through the angel Gabriel the definitive word. To obey the law is important, to give alms, to make a trip to Mecca on pilgrimage, and to love God: not too complicated and as a creed very successful.

The incredible basilica in Istanbul, at one time an orthodox Christian cathedral, then a mosque, now a museum, goes back to the seventh century, the Hagia Sophia. The building of such a dome so far back in time without modern building techniques was amazing. Same God: different people with different ideas. In Tokyo I went to a Shinto service. People in a holy building; a priest taking the service; prayers, to God. In Taiwan at a Confucian/Taoist shrine I shared a prayer with a friend who worshipped there, a peaceful place for personal prayer. In Neasden at the beautiful Hindu temple we shared in their service.

In Rhodes and other Greek islands there were a vast number of little wayside chapels, mostly nicely maintained; but the face of orthodoxy we saw best in Russia. We had a holiday which gave us three days in Moscow where I was able to get to Moscow University, and three in St Petersburg with a week's sailing through the inland waterways between the two, sleeping on board and stopping off at various places en route. We attended two services, one in St Basil's Cathedral, and one in a monastery that we visited. The interiors were dark, the priests largely within the sanctuary of the church, the congregation out in the nave, standing: chanting, incense, pomp and majesty, but all praying to God. A different ritual, a different style, but the object the same: worship and entreaty. The same can be found in York in English, in a small chapel in the Groves belonging to the Celtic Orthodox Church, a non-chalcedonian denomination similar to Coptic worship, and presided over by their Bishop, Bishop Stephen. In Thailand and in particular Bangkok, I experienced Buddhist worship in a temple with monks, a priest in charge, worshippers, incense, music and prayer. Different from Orthodox Christianity of the near East and Russia, but the key items were the same – and there was prayer and worship.

For many Christians, Rome is the central pivotal spot of Christianity. The Pope of Rome and the Vatican oversaw Western Christendom, until the reformation and Henry VIII's break with Rome, in unity. Since the

The author at Moscow University

reformation, the church in England, and the Lutherans in Northern Europe and
Switzerland led the way in what became a fragmentation of religious practice
through a host of non-conformist and defecting groups. Not that this was the
first schism for Christianity. At the major councils of the church over the
centuries, those who could not agree with change broke away. The Nestorians
left at the council of Ephesus, the Copts at the Council of Chalcedon, both
over arguments about the nature of Christ, and the major schism, between
Orthodoxy and Roman Catholicism, in the tenth century over the nature of
the Trinity (the 'filioque' insertion) but more pragmatically over the sacking of
Constantinople, the then centre of orthodoxy, by the Romanite Crusaders. The
Coptic Pope remains in Egypt, the Syriac Pope remains in the Near East and
the Armenians do their own thing. The fourth to the seventh centuries were
times when Christian doctrine was being formalised, and argued over, and the

nature of Christ (man or God, or both, and if both how conjoined; consubstantial and co-eternal in the Trinity, or was it a Duality, and how did this fit a monotheistic creed, if at all?) were questions that occupied intelligent minds, who were not often fully in agreement!

The resurrection, and the doctrine of atonement are the key elements that divide Christians from Jews on the one hand, and Muslims on the other. There are valid arguments on both sides. The atonement derives out of the Jewish entrenched ideas on sacrifice. God required sacrifice to atone for sin. People didn't like to sacrifice themselves so someone else, for example a prisoner taken in war, or a child, or better still as civilisation matured, a lamb, first-born and without blemish, was sacrificed to God (who liked the sweet savour) by the priests at the Temple. So if God gave His 'only begotten Son' to come to earth and be the greatest possible sacrifice, by humanity killing him, and then being forgiven, what could be greater? Then the resurrection to prove the reality of everlasting life.

The contrary view looks carefully at what is known from the New Testament and other contemporary writings, such as Josephus. Jesus was condemned to crucifixion following an agreement between Herod, and Pilate. The Roman soldiers carried it out. There were supporters amongst the hierarchy and within the Roman army indeed. What then happened? Jesus was taken along the Via Dolorosa route, which Shirley and I traced on one of our Jerusalem visits, and which forms the basis of the Catholic service of the 'Stations of the Cross', to Calvary. He was nailed to a wooden cross through hands and feet (or more likely wrists and ankles. The others might tear out), and along with two others was set up for public view at Calvary, somewhere outside the pre-Roman City Wall. This was said to be at the third hour (9 a.m.). Then at the ninth hour (3 p.m.) he was given something to drink. Shortly after, he was considered to be dead. This was a Friday (i.e. before the Jewish Sabbath, which would start at sundown around 6 p.m.). It was necessary to get people down and out of the way before the Sabbath started. The two criminals had their legs broken to speed things up. This was the custom. It was not done to Jesus (why not?). Instead, one of the soldiers stuck his lance into Jesus's side, which bled. (Dead bodies do not bleed because the circulation has stopped). In addition, 'water', presumably lymph collecting from hanging in that position for six hours, came out. How far therefore did the spear go in?

So, friends got permission from Pilate to have Jesus's body removed. Pilate expressed surprise that he was already dead (people usually lasted longer), but agreed. So friends took the body to a tomb, carved out of rock, and a very large quantity of spices and liniments was taken too. This would be no doubt getting on for 6 p.m. on Friday. He was not of course buried in the sense of being covered with earth. He was laid on a slab covered with linen cloth in a room hewn out of the rock. It is well described in the Gospels.

What then? Saturday was the Sabbath. The disciples, and initially the women (Mary for one) went there at sunrise on Sunday. This was some thirty-six hours (not three days) after Jesus had been placed there. And they found him gone. One account says two men (? angels) spoke to them. There was no sign of the guard of soldiers. Where were they? Another says Jesus himself spoke to Mary; then a day or two later Jesus turns up at a meeting of the disciples, and later Thomas is shown the wounds by Jesus. Healing by then? Jesus is around and heading for Galilee and is seen for some six weeks and then is 'taken up'.

Sceptics of the resurrection story usually take the line 'not true'; 'faked'; 'soldiers bribed' etc. But a more possible option is that Jesus survived with the aid of good friends, some powerful narcotic in the drink and vigorous resuscitation in the tomb. Else why was Jesus 'dead' so quickly and suddenly, why did the soldier not break his legs, why did the blood flow, and so on? In other words, resurrection = resuscitation. Well, it depends on faith. The Christian will believe there was death i.e. the heart stopped, and a miracle later occurred preventing the otherwise inevitable brain deterioration which occurs normally within five to ten minutes at most but not it seems causing the wounds to heal. Does it matter? Well, the doctrine of the atonement would ring hollow if the event were simply resuscitation – and the 'proof' of the resurrection of the body would take a blow. But if Jesus were simply a prophet, with a God-given gift to heal and cause people to commit themselves again to godliness, it would not affect belief in God. We would be no different from Moslems or Jews in that belief; that Jesus was simply a very holy man. Faith in the resurrection of humanity at the last is common to most religions. But we believe largely because that is what we have been taught since childhood.

When I was a child, I attended for a while a group called The Crusaders, a sort of Children's Sunday School held on a Sunday afternoon, in Headingley. We were placed in small groups of which there were about five. Much to my surprise, since I didn't go all that often, I turned up one day to be presented with a Bible for my group being the one that had won the good attendance prize. I still have it, but certainly didn't deserve it!

There are other, more fringe groups in Christianity. One of these is the Mormon faith. We went to a Mormon service a year or two ago out of interest. The Church of the Latter Day Saints, as it is properly called, believes that in the United States, a hundred and fifty or so years ago, Joseph Smith, a prophet, had revealed to him through an angel, new insights into Christianity, and a history of the lost tribe of Israel who had crossed the sea to America. These writings were revealed through the prophet Moroni on golden tablets which were taken after Joseph Smith had received the translation, and disappeared again.

The Mormon church was a big church and was packed. The whole family, granny, children and babies were there. The young men acting as ushers were in smart suits; the choir was good. It was a little 'happy clappy', as we conservative Anglicans would say: a couple of people standing up and making public confession; readings from the Old and New Testaments and of course from the Book of Mormon. It was a fairly typical non-conformist service otherwise, but with a great sense of community spirit which impressed us. The service lasted over two hours and most people stayed through.

I have twice visited a spiritualist church. The first was out of curiosity when accidentally I walked into a session with a medium. I was, during the course of the meeting, addressed and told that the medium could see someone dressed like a monk with a beard, behind my shoulder. This was whilst I was recovering from hepatitis. At the time this 'vision' made no significant impact on me. The second was a normal non-conformist style service again, the main difference in belief from mainstream Christianity being the belief in communion with the spirit world.

After Shirley and I retired, in 1999, we sought a common interest to 'grab' us: post retirement bonding! Fortuitously we saw a paper pinned up in the church about courses in religious studies for mature students, part-time, organised by St John's College, York. We both finished up enrolling for an MA degree in theology! Because we both had degrees or post-graduate university diplomas, we were required to do only one year of the preliminary course (not having a BA Theology) and two further years, the final year being devoted to the dissertation.

Most of our formal work, lectures, discussion and tutorials were held, for our modules, at Ampleforth Abbey, who were involved as one of the colleges providing input for the degree. This was helpful as it was only twenty minutes away from where we lived. The course proved most interesting and the site, amongst the monastic buildings looking over a North Yorkshire valley, delightful. For the final dissertation year Shirley chose to do an in-depth study of aspects of the life of St Cuthbert, particularly as our own church site in Crayke had been given to Cuthbert in the seventh century as a resting place between Northumbria and York, on condition that he established a monastery and hospitium, (St Mary de Pratis) there. His mortal remains also had resided in Crayke for a while many years later after the monks had had to evacuate Lindisfarne, due to the Danish invasions, before eventually reaching his final resting place in Durham. Crayke Church is now dedicated to St Cuthbert.

For my dissertation I decided to research 'the non-chalcedonian orthodox churches, and their role in Britain today'. Well, I would, wouldn't I? I reckoned by the time it was presented I'd probably know more about it than the examiners! The non-chalcedonian churches, sometimes misnamed as mono-physite, were the churches founded by St Mark, and held the see of Alexandria. They were one of the first patriarchates to break with Rome and the other Orthodox Churches, in the sixth century, over the dogmatic issues of the nature of Christ.

Crayke Church

The reason I chose this topic turned on a chance meeting in the 'gents' of one of the Halls of a London livery company, where I had noted that the Master's chaplain who said grace was wearing a garb that was not Anglican nor Catholic, nor indeed Jewish, and I wondered from what branch of the faith he came. As we were getting ready to leave I found myself standing next to this prelate, as males are wont to have to do, at the urinals. Since Leo Abse's Act was some thirty years since, I was bold enough to address him and ask whence his robes derived. He proved to be of Coptic persuasion, and in particular the English Orthodox Church. He told me that in York there was a Bishop Stephen who led what was now called the Celtic Orthodox Church, now in schism with them, and that the English Orthodox under the leadership of Abba Seraphim of Glastonbury had recently formed a union with the Coptic Church in England whose leader was the Coptic Pope in Egypt. I was intrigued and resolved to explore it further, and it seemed to be a good potential topic for a little research dissertation. I spent the year visiting various places of worship: Armenian, Syriac and Ethiopian, in Britain. I met Bishop Stephen in York, who was initially ordained through the Syriac patriarchate which in Europe was based on a monastery in France. I had considerable help from him in preparing the background to my dissertation. I attended a number of services at the chapel in York. I contacted the monastery in France, and visited and interviewed Abba

Seraphim, also very helpful, at his monastic home in south-east London. We both obtained our MA (Theology) degrees, I in 2003 – of which more anon – and Shirley, who had had to take a term out, in the spring of 2004.

Crayke has another Saint, and those of you who regularly read your bumper book of saints at a weekend will know him – St Echa of Crayke. Not a lot is known of him. His Saint's Day is 5 May. To those who feel that invocation of the saints, to intercede for one in times of trouble, is a reasonable idea, Echa would clearly be the choice for a local! I like to feel I have developed a local interest, a mini cult, in this long forgotten saint. I have an oil painting of an old bearded man sitting reading, in my loft, which I inherited from my aunt. I imagine St Echa might have looked like that, sitting on the hillside at Crayke, looking out over towards York and the old Minster, across the Forest of Galtres. In the last year I have felt his help. I believe perhaps he was the vision behind me in the spiritualist church.

During our theology course, we discussed belief, and the evidence for the existence of God as outlined by St Thomas Aquinas, and others such as Augustine of Hippo, who have tried to sort out this issue in the light of their own experience. There are really two aspects. The first is God, the creator of the universe. That the universe is a creation is I suppose self–evident; how is another matter. But the early fathers looked to the orderliness of nature, the knowledge we have of beauty, of joy, of kindness, and indeed the laws of physics, that all go to suggest an intelligence, a 'mind' of some sort, and a creative force that has set up, or controls, universal truths of this sort.

It is a very big step from that to a personal God, who has created life on earth, created man, given mankind a soul, taken a personal interest in all mankind and has entered the earth's space in human form somehow to help them. In this area, human experience, insights formed by revelation, which is a personal awareness, and learning of the experiences of others, are more likely to produce a conviction, than simply being told, or reading books. Intrinsically improbable, it is personal revelation that is going to convince or convert.

Both Shirley and I had a sound grounding in Anglican Christian faith. One goes through phases of stronger or weaker faith in life, of doubting and ignoring, and returning probably in times of need, when there is a comfort in the belief of the power of prayer. Often, however, religion can simply become a social experience. My personal revelations, if they are strong enough to be called that, are probably only four or five in a lifetime, and the cynic could explain them away no doubt quite easily in other ways. But the interesting thing is the power of these little experiences which remain vivid and convincing years or decades later, even through times of doubt and disbelief. I suppose the first that I recall was some twenty-five years ago. I had been playing squash and was sitting in the changing room alone prior to having a shower. I

Shirley Haslam, MA, 2004 (Theology, Leeds)

became aware that I was travelling (not with a body) at an incredibly fast speed up through the sky and after a short time found myself going along a few feet above the ground in what looked like a very verdant green rainforest, along a path. I perceived it as Heaven; then I seemed to come down again and 'woke up' to find myself on the floor of the changing room having, I suppose, had a brief period of unconsciousness for no obvious reason. A very odd but vivid experience, and very pleasant.

The next followed the death of an old friend, Ingrid Flute, who died in a hospital in Hull from the after-effects of a ruptured aorta. A day or so later, I was not thinking of her or anything in particular. It was a sunny day. Across the sky appeared a vision of Ingrid's face, smiling down at me, filling the sky. The vision was huge but in proportion, like wide-screen cinema. It lasted only a few seconds and disappeared but it seemed very real and most odd.

The third was the day after my mother's death. Her body had gone to the undertaker's morgue. I was clearing out a drawer in her dining room. It was

Michael Haslam, MA, 2003 (Theology, Leeds)

dusk. I knew there was a presence on the stairs. This was frightening and I felt unable to go and look or go upstairs. I left the house. That experience and my sense of anxiety never occurred again in the house.

The fourth was a strange experience. I knew my mother had a cat, grey, with a little collar. I had seen pictures and drawings of her when she was a child. I was in the churchyard tending mother's grave a few months after her death when an identical cat walked up and started rubbing itself and purring against the newly-set gravestone. I stroked it, and it eventually walked away. It was almost as if I felt mother was somewhere there in this cat and was showing her approval. Daft? Yes. But . . .

For a couple of years after mother's death I still grieved at times. I felt guilt, and loss, as one often does in bereavement. I used to pray for her, and for my father who had died when half her age, in 1946. I visualised mother as she had been in her last years, frail and fragile. But one evening after prayer, I saw them, not as I had been regularly visualising her, but standing with my father, both smartly dressed and looking as if they were perhaps in their twenties, smiling at me. I had never visualised them like this before, and it seemed to give me great comfort as if, at last, they were there and together.

Well, what does one make of all that? Wish fulfilment? Coincidence? Me going a bit potty? Or some sort of demonstration which renews or strengthens faith in something 'beyond'. These sorts of experiences perhaps persuade the individual who experiences them but not usually others, who will tend to offer banal explanations. One does not usually talk of them. One tends to be embarrassed. It is easier to write them down.

CHAPTER 13

Blessed is the womb that bare thee
(Luke, 11: 27)

THESE MEMOIRS WOULD not be complete without a chapter devoted principally to my mother. As I said at her funeral oration, I had known her all my life. What an immense influence she had. But in this chapter I will look more at her last twenty years or so, when she lived just across the road from us in Crayke in a seventeenth-century cottage and where she died in 2002 in her 103rd year, on 26 October.

Mother was born in the nineteenth century and spanned therefore three centuries. She was brought up in a middle-class family in a middle-class part of Sheffield, on Rustlings Road opposite Endcliffe Woods and the Park. It was her father's second marriage to a much younger woman, and the children of his first marriage, about the same age, did not approve! Her father was an invalid, having broken a leg, and was bedridden for the last two years of his life, Mother spending much time sitting with him and helping him. She missed some schooling as a consequence. She was proud of the one famous ancestor, Sir Richard Arkwright. He had in his early days been a barber and wigmaker but working in the woollen spinning trade, invented a machine much more efficient for the running of looms which became known as the 'Spinning Jenny', and he made a fortune out of it. He had developed the factory village at Cromford in 1790, well before Titus Salt, and was a philanthropist. He built Willersby Castle, became High Sheriff and was knighted by George III.

Most of mother's early friends and relations had been in Sheffield and we often went there to visit. I had Uncle Edgar, mother's youngest brother as one godfather, the one who gave me a bugle (at my request!) as a confirmation present. My other godfather was Frank Rayner, a good friend of my parents who lived in Harrow and who entertained me at the Changing of the Guard on my first trip to London. My godmother, Auntie Queenie, and her husband Keeble Hawson, were also old tennis friends and lived in Sheffield. Keeble Hawson was a solicitor in Sheffield (Keeble Hawson, Steele & Carr) and into local politics. He became Lord Mayor of Sheffield and I was invited both to his inaugural party in the Town Hall, and also through some other friends, the Walshes, to the Master Cutler's Ball, along with Mother and the Hawsons' children, Neville and Ruth. Mother had, however, lived in Leeds since 1930 when my father obtained the post of Company Secretary at Thomas Burnley & Sons, run by the Shelton family in Gomersall, (and now demolished).

Mother in her prime

After my stepfather's death, the house at Westfield was much too large.
Mother had some close friends, the Wades, the husband being an MP in the
Liberal Party, in those days, but later elevated to the House of Lords and
becoming Lord Wade in the process. They had four children, the eldest being
Helen who was my friend and nearest to my age. I used to attend their annual
teenage dance with her at Allerton Grange and later in Horsforth. At any event,
the Wades too had a big house in West Park and their family too had flown
the nest. They decided to convert it into three flats, and asked mother if she
would like to take the ground floor flat at a fairly low fixed rent. It was a
mutually pleasant arrangement. The Wades also had a holiday house near
Pateley Bridge in Nidderdale where they spent a fair bit of time. So Mother
moved out of Westfield and into a pleasant flat with Lucie Hopps, her second
husband's first wife's mother, whom she nursed until her death a year or two
later.

We, at this time, were still in Doncaster. Mother had learned to drive in her
fifties, much to the amazement of her younger brother, and had driven my

stepfather around when he was not well. Now, she drove around elderly ladies from the Yorkshire Home, some younger than her! She drove over to Tickhill to stay with us from time to time and she and Shirley's mother and father would come with us to Whitby and Sandsend when the children were still in their early teens, and later, after Shirley's father died, the two grannies would join us.

Mother would sometimes regale the children with life in the early 1900s. She told of a time, I think it was her grandmother's ninetieth birthday, when the whole family hired a horse and carriage to take them on a day's picnic outing to Roche Abbey, some fifteen miles away towards Tickhill. Endcliffe Congregational Church had been involved in the outing which was reported in the local papers at the time. The trip included the Reverend T.W. Holmes who was a nephew of Elizabeth Oldfield (the granny), Mrs Howarth (another niece), and a Mrs Garnett, the latter's daughter. The groom got a little pickled during the day and they had a rather riotous drive home! In those days, horse-drawn trams passed their house on Rustlings Road. There were virtually no cars but many horse-drawn carriages and vehicles of all sorts. No radio, no TV, no aeroplanes, but there were steam trains, canals and turnpike roads, oil lamps, and gas in the posher homes. Domestic electricity was coming in. Country districts still used wells for their water. There were no washing machines, cooking was done on the kitchen range, and hot water came from the back boiler, heated up by the kitchen fire. What immense changes Mother had seen in her lifetime.

We got to know her better again when we moved to York in 1970 and the children would regularly go over, one at a time, to stay with her for a few days, and take walks to the Hollies, a park about half a mile away, where there were swings and a nice grassy area to play; or up to the 'Golden Acre', a park near Bramhope, in her car. But when mother reached 80, and was not so active, the Wades decided to sell the Leeds house. Mother needed to think what to do. As luck would have it, a cottage had become vacant just opposite us in Crayke which we bought, and on a cold December day in 1982 (when she was 83) she moved in.

It was a nice little cottage, though the frontage direct onto the main street had been 'modernised' in Victorian times with bigger windows and more light inside, but with the loss of the proper Yorkshire sash windows, which still remained at the back. Before our own modernisation it had had an outside down-the-garden double-seater lavatory and only one cold tap in the house, serving a kitchen sink. Heating and cooking on the living room range provided hot water from a back boiler, which could be tapped off and was filled with a bucket. We converted the single bedroom over the kitchen into a toilet and bathroom, put proper plumbing into the kitchen, and replaced the old living room range with a proper fireplace. The resultant cottage had two bedrooms, a large dining room and small lobby, kitchen and utility room. I built a patio for her and developed the back garden so there was a nice area to sit, and repaired the bricked garden room adjacent to the old toilets. It was not as spacious as had been her flat in Leeds, but was near to us, and she, though in her eighties, was still sprightly. She had sold her car finally a few months before.

She soon got involved in her main love, bridge, in a ladies four that met in each others' houses fortnightly. She would come over to us at weekends, and we were over at her house sometime every day. Her two stepchildren, Tom and Stella, had kept in touch, but Tom was now settled as a consultant radiotherapist in Calgary in Western Canada, and Stella, married with two children, was in Edinburgh. Mother would go up once or twice a year to stay with them, Stella's husband Rob being a vet in Edinburgh. So Mother lived happily ever after. She came with us for family holidays and babysat for us, and I would take her into York for tea at Betty's.

In 1994, when Mother was ninety-five, it just so happened that Shirley and I had been married thirty-five years and my daughter Fiona had been married ten years; a triple celebration. We decided to have a big family party and hire a boat on the river for a champagne supper. The plan was to invite all our old friends that we could find – you know, the sort who were in address books from one's childhood or teenage years – and have a grand reunion. Mother, and each of the three children, were allocated ten spaces and Shirley and I forty between us, which filled the boat. It would start at St George's Staithe, sail up to Poppleton, then downstream to the Archbishop's Palace at Bishopthorpe, and back to King's Staithe, taking three hours and serving a buffet supper. The night was fine, though a little windy. It was more difficult for Shirley to have her really old friends, as they tended to be in the south and married, but she collected up Sheila, an old college friend who had married David, an RAF officer who had linked his hobby on leaving with a job as Education Officer of the new York Railway Museum. When they first married, Sheila had had to sleep in a bedroom with model trains running right round the room on trellises! Now he had a gauge 1 steam layout in the garden. Later, David Jenkinson was to run a publishing business specialising in such titles as *The Livery of the London Midland & Scottish Railway 1934–1947* – of great interest to the enthusiast!

Mother at her age had difficulty filling her ten places with really old friends since most were deceased. Bunny Wade managed it, and Ida Dodge, a school friend from Sheffield, still full of vigour and a year older than Mother. Her oldest school friend, Ethel Goddard, now from Constantine Bay in Cornwall, was too frail to make the journey. Mother had as a teenager collected in an autograph album little poems and drawings and paintings, as was the fashion. All these old friends had been contributors. There were also a couple of old friends from Leeds, and the ATS girl who had been billeted on us in the war,

Mother on her 100th

Kathleen Graham, now living in Dinnington. But there were the offspring of some of these, who had also been my childhood friends: my two male cousins, Hedley and Robert Oldfield, and Shirley's cousins, Chester and Harvey White, the former, in general practice in Cambridge, who had rowed for the Oxford boat, and the latter who had played racquets and Royal tennis for Oxford and was now a surgeon in London.

Of my old school friends there were Roger Moat, now in business in Grantham, Christopher Davy, running the Leeds Metal Spinning Company, Anthony Baker, my oldest friend going back to when he was born (and I was one!), now married to Sarah, after leaving his father's firm (a steel works, Rodley Cranes, an offshoot of the Baker-Bessamer (Baker his grandfather) firm in Rotherham pre-nationalisation, and now somehow a chairman of a hospital trust, Donald Adams, the prosecuting solicitor for Sheffield, Mavis Hardcastle my first love at the age of five and now married to Peter Harper and working as a physiotherapist, and Hilary Lockett, my second love, at ten, who had married an old Sedberghian. (He was sadly to die a couple of weeks after the party.) Also there were Graham Burgess, then headmaster of a prep school in Hurworth-on-Tees and Edward Vickerman, also a prep school headmaster, whom Shirley called 'Cupid', which always made him blush, since he had first introduced us at Cambridge in 1953! And many more, 'whose names are forgotten and it is as if they had never been born.'

After the children were scattered abroad, Mother and I established a habit of going to her favourite spot, the Lake District, for an early autumn long weekend whilst Shirley did a 'relative tour' in the Surrey-Kent area. Mother and I went to stay at the Old England for some years during her nineties. We would go on one of the lakes. It was lovely to see her at ninety-five being helped off the steamer. I would lift her down off the gang-plank and off to have a coffee at the little café. One year we went on Windermere in one of the old Swallows & Amazon-style steam yachts, on others a trip round Derwentwater, on Ullswater to Pooley Bridge and back, and on Coniston to Brantwood, these being the four lakes which had commercial craft. In the car we would go for lunch at the Lodore Swiss Hotel in Borrowdale, and down to Grange-over-Sands to the hotel we had stayed at during the war, one summer holiday, when the East Coast was closed.

Sadly, although remaining physically strong, Mother started to develop a loss of memory, of Alzheimer type, in her later nineties and became increasingly dependent. The last time we went to the Old England she got muddled in the night and locked herself, accidentally, in her room. I found an hotel at Lakeside at the bottom end of Windermere which had rooms on the ground floor for disabled, with an adjoining room with connecting door. Mother needed to get up to the loo at night and needed to be guided, and helped to some extent with dressing. But we had two years at this hotel, the second being in her hundredth year, and I remember on the last morning we sat out in the garden overlooking the lake, with a little band playing in the sunshine, while we sipped cocktails and admired yachts out in the bay. She was really happy on that morning. It was the last time she was ever to see the Lakes.

Mother's eyes had been giving her trouble. One eye had become very sore; she had been put on some drops for the infection but in fact it turned out to be a glaucoma which had blown up acutely, and she lost the sight in that eye. The pressure in the other eye was also raised and she started on drops to reduce this pressure. It was only partially successful. The eye specialist whom she saw seemed reluctant to operate, due to her age, but the field of vision had deteriorated and he voiced the opinion that she might go blind within a couple of years, but only if she lived that long! She was ninety-six at the time. I sought another opinion from Mr Percival in Scarborough. He said that there was also a cataract, and it would be possible to do both procedures, under local anaesthetic, at the same time, a procedure known as a phacotrabeculectomy. Mother agreed and in the meantime was put on some tablets to reduce the alarmingly high pressure. This worked but made her dizzy so that in getting up to go to the loo she overbalanced and fell against the side of the bath, causing a Colles fracture to her left wrist. This was set and put in plaster, but when she went for her operation for her eye in a Scarborough nursing home some two weeks later, she had only really the use of one arm.

The operation was initially a remarkable success. Mother had to keep the eye covered for two days, and stay in bed. I stayed over at the nursing home. She needed full nursing care. When the bandages were taken off she was happily amazed. She could see beautifully out of the good eye and could see me clearly. The following day she was allowed up to go to the loo. I was waiting outside. She called from the loo, 'Everything has gone black. I can't see at all.'

Luckily Mr Percival was in the nursing home. He came straight up. The globe of the eye had lost its pressure because the intra-ocular fluid had leaked out.

'We'll take her down to theatre and refill the globe. This can occasionally happen. It should be all right.'

Mother was remarkably calm and helpful in theatre. Again the procedure was carried out under a local anaesthetic and she returned an hour later with vision restored. We all relaxed and Mother was very happy.

Two days later the same thing happened.

'Obviously the aperture we made for the release of fluid has been a little too large. But to restitch it with your mother conscious would be very difficult for her. We shall have to risk an anaesthetic.'

Mother was off to theatre yet again. I waited anxiously. It took a while and she was asleep on returning. However, the operation itself had been a success. She would need the bandages on again for a couple of days. So, no vision, and a 'pot' on her left forearm! When Mother came round she was rather confused, tried to get out of bed, needed twenty-four-hour 'specialing', and had to be fed. Poor old thing! What a state to be landed in at ninety-six. She remained in hospital for a week. The vision was really very good, all things considered. There was some tunnel vision, but she could see to read large print. She was, however, a little paranoid, a bit suspicious of people. Was the food poisoned? Were people trying to get rid of her?

We decided that she would come to stay with us and we would convert the dining room into a downstairs bedroom for the time being, it being next to the downstairs cloakroom toilet.

'Shall we drive round the marine drive before we set off home?'

Mother thought that would be nice. It would be a sight of the sea now her eye was improved. Unfortunately she was a little too agitated to appreciate it.

The journey home took about an hour. By halfway she was beginning to say, 'Where are you taking me? This isn't the way home. Are you taking me to a home?' She needed constant reassurance. At last we got home. She recognised the village, and her relief was visible.

We had a difficult few weeks. The confusion gradually subsided, but she would see shapes and lights which she misinterpreted (illusions) often as people in the room, a phenomenon which is not uncommon. She was better with a not too dim light left on. Her wrist healed well and the plaster came off. A return visit to the eye surgeon showed a successful result. Her vision when fixed on a spot was quite good in the one eye. The other was irremediably blind. The good eye had reduced peripheral vision, but she could see to read. Indeed, when sitting in our lounge by the window, she noticed that her bedroom window was a few inches open, across the road some forty yards away! But she would not know if someone were sitting in the room diagonally to her on the 'blind side'.

When she was ready to go home, we arranged an 'intercom' in the bedroom so that at night we could hear if she were all right, and she could speak to us in our bedroom if she needed help. This worked well for some months, but in due course someone needed to sleep in the house with her. Shirley and I did a rota for four nights of the week and had a nursing auxiliary for the other three. In the meantime, we would make regular trips to various places for afternoon tea; she would come over to us at weekends for the two days as a rule, and we would play bridge, Mother and I taking on Shirley and whoever to make up a four. It was sad to see her skills slipping. She could still play a good hand, but her calling began to be erratic and she preferred to play with me. We would go up to Darlington to have lunch with Ian Martin, and some bridge, and have Neville Webster from Harrogate, the son of one of Mother's old friends in Leeds, Margaret Webster. Joyce Cox would also come over, the daughter of another old friend. We discovered that Elizabeth Morley, who had as a student lived with Mother for a while after my father died, and was an old girl of York College, also lived nearby, and she too came to see us.

There came a time when Mother could no longer play bridge, but could still play Scrabble®, so we changed to that. By the following year that too became impossible and we reverted to dominoes, which she played almost until her death. As she became more confused there needed to be increasing home care which became twenty-four-hour care in due course. We were very fortunate in that the local mental handicap hospital at Easingwold had closed a few years before and there were a number of women who had worked there as nurses or assistants, and had experience of looking after confused individuals, who had been organised by a more entrepreneurial member of their group into a carers' team. These people were a godsend to us and we were able to allow Mother to stay in her own home, so much nicer and secure-making for those becoming confused, until the end. Sadly in the last few months Mother became difficult, sometimes rather aggressive, and took a dislike to Shirley, who indeed was the one who did the most caring for her, doing her washing, changing, and cleaning for her much of the time. It upset me when Mother expressed these feelings.

After someone's death it is common for those who are bereaved and grieving to feel guilt. Sometimes I got cross with her. I could shout. Sometimes when we had been out for a lovely afternoon tea, we could get back only for her to say, 'This is not my house', and refuse to go in. Then I had to manhandle her in, usually with her shouting abuse at me! On another occasion she decided the dining chairs were not hers and tried to throw them out into the road. But through it all she could, at times, be the same old lovely Mother. She was now only five months off one hundred and three years old! We would talk of things she did as a child, or I would read to her some of the poems or short stories she had written, or talk of her holiday in Venice. Once, when I had got cross with her, she wept and said, 'All I ever wanted was for you to be happy.' It still brings tears to my eyes as I write this. I felt so awful. It was all so sad.

In September, Shirley felt we should have a break and booked us a week in Madeira. The carers also felt the task was increasingly difficult and we arranged for mother to go for a week's break into the local hospice. On the day we were to go I took her down in the car and we went in, with her case, to the waiting area. I stayed a little while and had a cup of tea and then kissed her and got up to leave. She didn't really know what was happening. My daughter Fiona was going to go regularly to visit, and other friends. But she looked so little and frail, and pitiful really, as I left. I was not going to see her for a week. I had been with her every day and most often nights as well, for two years. I went away feeling dreadful.

The holiday in Madeira was lovely. Shirley and I had a week without hassle to relax. We had some lovely meals in little bistros by the waterside and in the old town. I rang on alternate days and was told all was well. We got back on the Sunday lunchtime and I went down at teatime to collect her, having not had a chance to see Fiona beforehand. I arrived at the little hospital and went in to her room. Her cheek was severely bruised and she had a black eye. Her speech was difficult to understand. She had just been incontinent and was being 'cleaned up'. She looked terrible. 'Would you like her to stay one more night and you could come down tomorrow?'

'No, thank you. We'll manage.'

'She's not walking without assistance.'

'I can carry her.'

I picked her frail little body up and carried her out and to the car. I doubt she weighed six stone. The nurse opened the car door for me and I sat Mother gently in the car, and put the seat belt on. We drove back to her house. I lifted her out and carried her in to the house and sat her in her armchair.

'Are we home?'

'Yes.'

'Thank God.'

'Don't worry, we won't leave you again. We're home now too.'

Shirley came over from our house.

'We'll get you upstairs and into bed, then I'll stay with you.'

I carried her upstairs and we got her undressed and into a warm bed. I gave her a drink. She did not seem to be able to swallow it too well and only had a few sips. It was now 20 October. I stayed the night and tried to give her as much fluid as I could. The following day I pieced together what had happened.

Mother had initially been put in a single room, but was not being 'specialed'. The floor had a mat but was not a carpeted floor. She was told to ring the bell if she needed anything. No doubt in the night when she woke wanting the loo she would have thought she was at home and would expect the commode to be at her bedside. In getting out she fell and I believe had fractured her maxilla. It must have been very painful. She was moved to a dormitory room the following night and had cot sides, but when she needed the loo and tried to get out and found she couldn't, she became disturbed and started shouting, and woke everyone up. At some stage a doctor was called and she was in due course put on a sedative, in fact haloperidol, a small dose, but it is a strong acting anti-psychotic drug. One of its side effects is to give muscle stiffness, and this can affect the tongue and swallowing muscles in those especially sensitive, such as the elderly. We knew her to be highly sensitive to thioridazine, a not too dissimilar drug but milder, that she had had for a short time after her eye operation. I believed her to have developed side effects, affecting her swallowing, from the drug Then a couple of days later, for whatever reason, she had got diarrhoea and became incontinent. And that was how I had found her. We also discovered she had developed a bedsore on her bottom and her heel.

I got the haloperidol antidote and tried to get her to take some, but it didn't taste very nice and she refused it. We got some iced lollies and these she was able to suck to moisten her mouth and tongue. She was very dry from dehydration. It was clear that the lack of fluid and the loose bowels would cause her kidneys to pack up before very long. Intravenous fluids seemed impractical, and at $102\frac{3}{4}$ perhaps over heroic. She would have pulled the tube out.

We had a very tender week. I stayed two of the nights, including the 25 October. I slept that night beside her on the double bed and held her hand. She was refusing everything by mouth though her speech was a little improved, but her pulse was rapid. She was aware I was there and would squeeze my hand. She was grateful for her mouth being regularly wetted.

On the morning of 26 October the nurse took over for a while and I popped down into town. She died whilst I was out.

I had not felt grief like this. It was painful. Perhaps the nearest was when I had seen Michael off in the ambulance on his way to Great Ormond Street when he was ten, and I wondered if I'd ever see him again. I knew I wouldn't see Mother alive again. Friends said, 'You did all you could. Not many sons would have been so attentive. She had a good life. She was 102' – and so on. But I only felt grief and guilt; guilt at the times I'd got cross with her; guilt that we'd gone away to Madeira and left her, and what had happened.

The funeral was beautiful. Would that Mother was able to know we cared. The church was full. The bell ringer (Peter Hepworth late of Crayke Castle) tolled the bell the day of her death, one toll for each year of her life, as was the tradition in the village. One hundred and two tollings of the bell. Not only was Mother the oldest resident, but the oldest lady ever to have lived and died in Crayke since records began. As the funeral cortege entered the church the organist played part of Sullivan's *In Memoriam*.

Mother had had a splendid party at our home for her hundredth birthday and made a little speech of thanks. All her old friends (those who survived) and their offspring, had been there. Virtually all of them also came to her funeral. We had her favourite hymns, including 'O love, that will not let me go'. Then we sang 'Just a song at twilight', her favourite song, which was one she used to sing to me as a child to lull me to sleep nearly sixty-five years before:

Once, in the dear dead days beyond recall
When on the earth the mists began to fall
Out of the dreams that rose in happy throng
Low to our hearts, love sang an old sweet song
And in the dusk, where fell the firelight gleam
Softly it wove itself into our dream.

Still we shall hear it, at the close of day.
Just a song at twilight,
When the lights are low
And the flickering shadows
Softly come and go.
Though the heart be weary
And the day be long
Still to us at twilight
Comes love's sweet song
Love's old sweet song.

Michael read one of her poems.

A whisper is blown by the breeze
A whisper that summer is near
A message from over the seas
A message that brings good cheer
How many sad hearts will rejoice . . .

I gave an address. It was hard but I made it through. Though sad, it was about a celebration of a wonderful life. I finished by quoting the last verse of her first published poem, when she was thirteen. A doll had fallen in the fire, and been rescued:

So now you look old, and your life has ended
But if you're good, I'll have you mended.

Sadly we could not do that for Mother.

Then we left the church, and followed the coffin to the graveside – just the family. A prayer was said, the coffin lowered and earth cast upon it. I remembered standing beside Shirley at the burial of her parents, some years before, in Stillington Churchyard.

So that was the end. That was that. We turned away. But memories were left, and perhaps God had received her. Perhaps she was reunited with her parents, and Gerald my father, and her brothers. Perhaps so.

CHAPTER 14

Private side

THE EARLY 1980S were a strange time in medicine, and indeed around the age of fifty is a strange time for humans too. A lot of things are happening. Children are growing up and leaving home. Marriages often go through dodgy patches. People realise they are not immortal. They wonder if they can still be attractive. They wonder what lies ahead. What is life all about? Is it just for the moment we live? It is called the 'mid-life crisis'! At the same time mortgages are getting paid off, salaries are increasing with seniority, and school fees no longer need to be paid.

I needed new challenges, perhaps a new environment. I sought this, I suppose, looking back with the gift of hindsight, in two ways. The first was in private practice. At this time I had a ten-session per week contract (a session was three and a half hours) and took rooms at the Retreat, a private hospital, one half-day session per fortnight initially, later moving to the Purey Cost Hospital in York, and finally to rooms with a consortium of colleagues on a weekly basis at St Mary's in consulting rooms.

The second new challenge seemed to be in getting slightly over-involved with the delights of somewhat younger women. This sport, middle-aged married men and single ladies in their twenties to early thirties, is, sadly (I say this as a seventy-year-old who now ought to know better) mutually enjoyable and a challenge to both parties. But as an infidelity it is letting down the prime object of one's affections, back home – and is DANGEROUS! Most seventy-year-olds will tell you this. But men of fifty and girls of twenty-five don't listen. One meets people at work, at hobbies or sport, or whatever. The mid-life crisis is proving something, and often disaster can follow. I was as unwise as most. The only comfort is a statistical one. 40 per cent of us at any given time are 'at it'.

My mother, having experienced a similar burst of activity from my father (who then died at fifty-one!) would say that men were much worse than women in this respect. I would point out to her that, ignoring homosexuals, it takes one of each so, if 50 per cent of men were at it, 50 per cent of women must be at it too. Or maybe 50 per cent of males were mildly at it, and 75 per cent of women weren't, leaving the 25 per cent of women who were at it, at it twice as often as the 50 per cent of men, by getting through twice as many. Mother never could get the logic of that!

Anyhow, one adjusts. As Shirley says, 'It is important to be able to move the goal posts.' But loyalty is tested indeed.

Early in the 1980s the British Society of Medical & Dental Hypnotists set up an examination for a certificate of competence which I decided to sit, having learned a little of the art previously in Newcastle. This proved a help in private practice. There was not a lot of time for this kind of relative luxury in the NHS, but I used it to induce relaxation in anxiety management with some success. I also discovered a course was being run in York by the Esalen massage therapy organisation to learn massage techniques and thought this could be a useful skill to teach, particularly in couples who had an impotence/frigidity type of problem who were working through the sensate focus routines, and in those who wanted an alternative treatment for stress management. The course was interesting and quite fun, being held in the early evening at an alternative medicine centre in the town. I introduced it with a few patients at Clifton Hospital, but it was not a very practical treatment for me to carry out and was soon taken over by physiotherapists. Anyway, I got my certificates of competence.

In August 1988, after my two-year contract with Cygnet Health Care, to set up a unit which was to be called the Harrogate Clinic, had been signed, I spent a month in the United States on vacation, with Shirley, and in September we began the process of interviewing staff and working out with the team as it built up all the management matters that starting a new unit demanded; publicity; notifying general practitioners; working out what would be needed in the way of equipment, and so on. We recruited a second consultant, Dr Hollingsworth, who would be deputy medical director, and in turn would have a two-year contract. We also recruited a number of visiting consultants who would have admission rights when we opened, and the senior nursing staff. Meanwhile the conversion of and extension to what had been a large town house to create two wards of some twenty beds each, in private rooms, and to create an outpatient suite and office accommodation, had begun. It was quite an exciting challenge and required a new set of skills. I began to wind down my new patient caseload and in particular the clinic for marital and sexual problems, since it seemed unlikely that I would or could be replaced when I left. This would leave a considerable void, as we took referrals from a very wide catchment area and were nationally known. A number of GPs protested at the probable closure, but the administrator anticipated transferring my two sessions at this clinic to a special interest alcohol clinic.

We started to take patients as of 1 March 1989. Dr Hollingsworth and I would take it in turns to provide consultant cover at night. A local GP practice would provide general medical cover. An anaesthetist was coming in, three mornings a week as required, to administer anaesthetics for electroplexy. We had an opening ceremony where a plaque was unveiled by my old friend, and now MP for Pudsey, Giles Shaw. He and I and the chairman made little speeches. Drinks and canapés were served. Then we sat down to await customers!

Admissions soon began to come in, largely from visiting consultants in Leeds and Bradford who liked our facilities. I ran my clinic in York and started a fortnightly clinic in Middlesbrough, and Dr Hollingsworth did similarly in the Skipton-Airedale region. Financially it was a success for me. I had my NHS pension, having taken early retirement in February 1989, the medical director's salary, and what I could make out of the private practice. I enjoyed the first year. It was noticeable, however, that some stresses were developing between the medical staff and the senior nursing and administrative staff, fuelled we felt by the company administration. It became clear that Dr Hollingsworth and I were seen as stopgaps, not having a large in-patient private clientele, until two Leeds consultants could be persuaded to join the team. This was disappointing and indeed, before the two years were up, Dr Hollingsworth resigned. My contract was not renewed since Cygnet Health Care decided that now the clinic was up and running, formal medical directors were not needed. I continued to base myself at the clinic as a visiting consultant but decided to look elsewhere for additional income to make up the loss of the director salary in 1991.

One opportunity arose from a private obesity clinic which operated in York. At that time they were expanding into Northallerton and other towns. They were looking for medical staff, and since there is a sizeable (no pun intended) psychological element to weight control, I applied, and obtained a two-session contract in York and a session in Northallerton, while continuing part-time private practice in York and Harrogate. We tended to use appetite suppressants, very acceptable and problem-free to clients, but increasingly frowned on because of their potential to be habit-forming. However, it was quite fun to do and we rarely had vacant spaces in the referral waiting list.

Meanwhile I continued my hobby of writing, and was on the committee of York Medical Society with the hopes of being president in a few years time. I was invited in due course to be president of Harrogate Medical Society on which committee I had also served. We had an interesting programme in my year, with some psychiatric input. We had a visit to Gibraltar with the Society of Clinical Psychiatrists, of which society I had now become chairman, and a trip to China also with the SCP. I produced a book on the history of Clifton Hospital. All in all I was still fully occupying my time! We had between us, until Shirley retired from teaching, the highest income ever, with the lowest outgoings, reaching £100,000 in one year. I drove around in my Jaguar XJS. Life was good!

The China trip ended with a meeting in Hong Kong, and a symposium on alcoholism. An interesting speaker from Mainland China spoke on alcohol problems in minority groups within China, where the dominant racial group is Han. He believed that this was due to the lack of prestige and self-esteem which such communities felt in the presence of a ruling group from whom they may feel excluded. I was reminded of the Inuit (Eskimo) people under Danish rule in Greenland when we visited Angmassalak and where boredom was another factor, and lack of opportunity for advancement. There was always a drunken group in the town square in an evening. An Australian doctor at the meeting described similar problems amongst the aboriginal people there, and of course drink was a problem amongst native American people after the White Settlers created reservations and was why alcohol was not saleable in most reservation territory. It is all to do with disenfranchisement.

In 1994, another challenge came my way when I was 'head-hunted' for a post back in the NHS as medical director of a health service trust in South Durham. I was interviewed at an hotel north of Middlesbrough and in due course offered the post, which was a part-time (twenty hours a week), administrative and with no direct clinical commitment. I would be a member of the Trust Board and would represent medical interests and medical planning in the district.

The post was based at Sedgefield in Winterton Hospital, and covered what would have been the B-Group Management Team in pre-trust days, i.e. the non-acute and community hospital work. The major part was psychiatry, Winterton being one of the larger Victorian-built county mental hospitals which were gradually being run down with a view to providing community and general hospital-based care in a more modern environment. All good trendy stuff, and it was my main role to steer this concept through. I travelled up to Sedgefield three days a week and the rest of the time did my private practice, giving up the Obesity Clinic in the process.

In addition to the big psychiatric hospital, I covered elderly people's accommodation in Bishop Auckland, Community Centres in Newton Aycliffe, and others; a mental handicap unit; psycho geriatric beds; childcare in community paediatrics; and an orthopaedic long-stay unit. Finally at the world's end, or so it seemed on my first visit in a mist, at the far end of Tow Law, a lonely town on the edge of the wilderness before the high hills towards the Scottish Border, I covered a unit behind a high fence where some fifteen difficult-to-place young people with various types of learning disability lived in what was whimsically called 'Care in the Community'.

The mental handicap hospitals had been the first to go in the headlong rush to community care. Of course the hospitals had been communities, institutional admittedly, but people who are vulnerable often like to live in a more secure, safe and familiar environment. I have lived in various institutions at different times in my life – boarding school; an army barracks. Monks live in institutions, and prisons are institutions. I have by and large enjoyed my experiences of such community living, and for people without family ties it provides companion-ship. The mental handicap hospital had social centres, often their own school, a swimming pool, and a caring environment. The 'community', however, by which we mean that place outside the walls, is not by and large caring, may be hostile, lacks understanding of the frail, and is often rejecting. The 'community care' for fifteen people in a hostel cannot provide anything like the variety of facilities of the 'institution', and the community by and large doesn't really want to know – 'not in my back yard'.

There was quite a lot of travelling, therefore, to get round my catchment area, and also a lot of meetings. I was expected to be at the various medical staff meetings, to be involved in recruiting and interviewing new staff, and in troubleshooting. I was also expected to be at the various administrative meetings: with the chief executive; with the Board, and at occasional 'day-away' meetings – a sort of exercise in bonding for Board members when various topics to do with policy might be debated in an environment (usually a nice local hotel) which was free from the usual routine tasks, pleasant, and where friendliness could develop. (And a waste of money!). All this in three days a week did not make for a quiet life, but it was an exciting new interest and I enjoyed it.

During my four-year commitment we had not one, not two, but three reorganisations. Winterton did more or less close, but the new facility in Bishop Auckland did not materialise and indeed the acute short-stay psychiatric facility was eventually taken over by Darlington. The reorganisations involved in the first place competitive tendering, an exercise supposed to create competition and improve efficiency but in reality creating chaos and bad feeling. Subsequently in another reorganisation competitive tendering was scrapped. Then we had the merger! This was initially with South Durham to create a unified psychiatric service which included the psychiatric unit at Darlington Memorial Hospital. Later it was to include psychiatric services in North Durham too. In other words back to how we had been twenty years before. One wonders how much all these unproductive changes have cost to complete the circle, or even square it. If only the government would mind its own business!

Another committee was the hygiene committee. It was an area where 'us old stagers' who could remember Dettol, Lysol and scrubbing up in theatre, got hot under the collar. When I was a houseman working with Gordon Bailey in Harrogate, if one of his patients had got a post-operative wound infection, there would have been all hell on. Matron would have seen it as a personal affront. The sister on the ward would have held an enquiry. Heads could roll! Indeed, it very rarely happened. Nurses did the cleaning and the sister saw to it that they did. Bathrooms and bedpans were spotless; floors were washed with disinfectant; sheets and patients' bed attire were changed; patients were washed, and bed curtains were taken down and washed regularly. There was no dust and no germs on patients, nurses or doctors.

Where did it all go wrong? I am being anecdotal, but our local hospital, quite good as scales of goodness go, looks and is dirty, and has more post-operative wound infections than hot dinners. Who was the idiot who scrapped the matron and has he yet been hanged?

Where did it go wrong? The ethos changed. Matrons and sisters were abolished or lost their power. Nurses no longer saw menial tasks such as cleaning, washing and bedpan hygiene as their job. They were too busy having meetings and being barefoot doctors – the 'nursing process'. Outside cleaners were brought in but it was not the same. The sixties saw the rise of COHSE and an anarchic attitude prevailed amongst juniors. Casual clothes were worn. Doctors relied too much on the view that antibiotics would cure it all. Visitors were allowed in at all hours and spread any infection going around the place. And hospitals became overcrowded as beds were dismantled, wards and hospitals closed, the population increased and instead of running at the accepted safe norm of 80 per cent bed occupancy, efficiency demanded that 95 per cent bed occupancy, or sometimes even over 100 per cent bed occupancy (people sent on leave) prevailed. Management got into the hands of lay administrators instead of doctors and nurses, and these people were interested in efficiency, which usually meant increasing the numbers of admin staff, but had little knowledge of medical and nursing concerns.

Have I said enough? It's a bee in my bonnet. What can be done about it at this stage is a difficult one. The ethos needs restoring. Staff loyalties need to be redeveloped. Nurses and doctors must define their roles. Sisters and matrons with power must be re-employed. Basic hygiene must be retaught. Less whistle-blowing and telling tales behind people's backs, and more help if something or somebody fails, rather than suspensions, enquiries, and other money-wasting pieces of nonsense. It works in much of the rest of Europe. It ought to work here.

One area that was impressive was that of some of the day and hostel care for the elderly and those with learning disability. It was remarkable how well an adolescent with Down's Syndrome could be brought on, and integrate with society if given a chance. It was equally remarkable how the atmosphere in a **good** home for the elderly with dementia of varying types could be improved by adequate, and adequately trained, staff who had **time** to devote to reminiscence therapy, as pioneered in Clifton York and other places in the seventies. Of course the bad ones were awful.

I have often meditated on the limits which people's brains impose on them. It applies as much to animals as to man. If there is a soul, or a conscious mind even, it can only express itself through the computer we call a brain. It is in there, but it can only communicate at the level of its brain development. Thus a hamster is a hamster. A guinea pig is a guinea pig. The guinea pig cannot learn hamster skills even if it is a clever guinea pig. A dog can bark and wag its tail and so on. It can be a very clever dog but it cannot talk. It does not have the equipment or the thought processes that could ever create this. Its computer is not as good. Our hamster was clever. He could open the cupboard door where the vegetables were kept and steal a sprout. How he learned to do this

was amazing. But he never shut the door afterwards. His brain could not allow
of this ever occurring to him. He could in his transparent rolling ball, tour the
house (downstairs). He could steer it, brake and accelerate. It was remarkable.
We would hear him coming from the kitchen, and he would seek us out. But
he couldn't be house-trained. He would **never** ever understand that concept,
nor the need. It is the same with the human brain. It is very clever but it cannot
perceive objects in the dark like a bat can. It cannot smell as well as a dog. We
cannot alter the capability of our genetically determined brain connections
except in a very limited fashion. Nor have we a lot of control, most of us, over
our emotions and our drives.

A fascinating area of study is what happens to all of this if the brain is
damaged for whatever reason. The part of the brain that is damaged no longer
functions properly. A common situation (for neurological reasons) is a failure
to be able to recall names of people or things. Try as he may, the post-stroke
victim may be unable to speak. Yet the part of the brain that is involved in
expletives, for some reason, a slightly different part from the rest of 'Brocas
area', and more in tune with emotive states, may remain intact. This may mean
that the victim can only communicate by uttering 'damn' or a lot worse, to the
concern of visitors in reply to any question asked. It is like the barking of a
dog. The victim may learn to say 'damn' in a variety of intonations, and people
close to him may be able to have some understanding of this. But unless he is
lucky and some skills return or are taken over by other bits of the brain, the
victim is stuck with it. He may still have full understanding of what is said to
him, but can only reply 'damn, damn, damn, damn'. Imagine how frustrating
this must be. He is trapped in his damaged brain, and cannot get out. The hen
is trapped in a hen brain. She cannot conceptualise beyond what a hen brain is
capable of.

If one thinks of the more extreme views of those who believe in
reincarnation, including non-human species, then the soul is trapped in its
brain. It can do nothing else. It is important therefore that we understand
the limitations of our fellows. People who are damaged, or born that way, are
trapped. But they still deserve love, and indeed more patience and understanding than most, not less; not ostracism; not turning away; not embarrassment; not fear. The same applies to our cousins the orang-utans, and other
apes.

So I continued in this role until my time came to leave Sedgefield and the
Trust for whom I worked. I continued a small amount of counselling and
psychotherapy for a year or so, but did not take on new work, and at 65 I
retired. I remained on a few committees, continued my chairmanship of the
Society of Clinical Psychiatrists and the Journal Committee of the Royal
College of Psychiatrists, and for a while as examiner for the Professional and
Linguistic Assessment Board, and I played an active role in the trustee

committee of the Gender Dysphoria Trust. But Shirley and I were seeking a new interest, a post-retirement bonding, and this we were to find in theology! But not yet.

CHAPTER 15

Alter ego

GENDER AWARENESS is a mental process, presumably brain derived. It is the inner conviction that identifies one as masculine or feminine rather than male or female. Probably at least 90 per cent of people have no incongruities in this, maleness matching the inner concept of masculinity and both conforming to the bodily configuration, penis in the male, vagina in the female. Most people with no experience in the field therefore find it hard to conceptualise what it might be like if these parameters are not entirely congruous.

What, however, do we mean by masculine or feminine conceptually? There are male and female stereotypes; there are male and female secondary sexual characteristics – voice change, breast development, body hair and so on. There have been research studies in recent years that have shown subtle brain differences between the sexes. There are certainly hormone differences. To what extent do these colour and mould inner awareness or patterns of behaviour? Statistically males appear to have better co-ordination skills and focussed attention. Females have better verbal fluency and skills of social interaction. In terms of natural selection this is not surprising. For millions of years, male humans have honed their hunting skills, females their skills of child-rearing and running the domestic side of life, in the village and tribe.

There is, however, a considerable overlap between the sexes – height, voice pitch, so-called maternal instinct, aggressiveness, and so on. People are less aware that there are many states of partial or total intersex, for a variety of reasons. Some 1 per cent of children are not always so easily slotted into male or female, at birth, by genital configuration, later hormone production, or chromosome analysis (the xx, xy, and more sophisticated genetic tests). There are in-betweens. In-betweens do not sit easily in our dichotomised society.

Just the same, with the inner awareness of masculinity/femininity, this in-betweenness can also occur. Big arguments rage as to how much is innate, genetic or totally derived 'in utero' on the one hand, and nurturally determined by early environmental influences on the other. Identification can be affected in two areas. One is that of sexual orientation: most men are attracted to women sexually; most women are attracted to men. But not all. 5 per cent or so – the figures vary – are not attracted to the 'opposite' sex, but are attracted to their own. Some people seem to be capable of being attracted to both. Are they lucky or unlucky? Homosexuality has been proscribed in Western society for thousands of years by religious groups and in civil law since Henry VIII in England. Probably few groups in society have been so persecuted, apart perhaps from Jews. Why? It may not be the inclination of 95 per cent of the population, but really it hurts no one. Should we persecute all the 5 per cent minorities? Red-heads, epileptics, diabetics, gypsies, croquet players, or long-distance cyclists?

Until 1967 when Leo Abse's bill went through Parliament, male homosexual behaviour was illegal, and penalties ludicrously severe. Oscar Wilde was a victim, but also very many others, often talented artistic and sensitive people. Where was the threat? People who are not so inclined do not suddenly change what is largely an innate predisposition, either way. The law, becoming a little more enlightened, in the pre-1967 years often offered the homosexual person who came before the courts, a compulsory treatment order as an alternative to a jail sentence. Often the offence would be importuning. Psychiatrists offered either analytical or behavioural therapy, the latter being usually aversion therapy. We had a unit in Newcastle in the sixties that took on such cases. We had slides of hunky men, and slides of saucy women. The patient was wired up to a shock box. A slide of the hunky man appeared on the screen. After a short interval the patient received an electric shock – unpleasant but not harmful. He could switch it off, and his reward was the disappearance of the hunky man and the appearance on the screen instead of a saucy lady. The patient was conditioned to prefer the lady to the man by this process. This was carried out by learned men, acting in the supposed best interests of the patient. Naive? Yes. Did it work? No, not for long. The patients learned what to say! And it got them off a prison sentence. Of course the doctor or psychologist carrying out the procedure saw both the hunky men and the saucy lady pictures without getting an electric shock. Very nice! Did it make them turned on by hunky men? No.

During 1967 there ceased to be any illegality in homosexual behaviour between consenting male adults in private, so the courts stopped sending us cases and we stopped doing the treatment, though aversion therapy was still used for alcoholics and compulsive gamblers. No homosexuals volunteered! But caution. The law is still an ass! Leo Abse's bill, as it came to be known, does not apply completely throughout the British Isles. For many years it has still been illegal in the forces, in the Merchant Navy, while on board ship; in Northern Ireland and the Isle of Man (recently changed); if one or both parties are under the age of consent, (and this, as women will well understand, was set originally at 21); if one party doesn't consent; if more than two people are present (it is then not in private); if in a place to which the public has access (this has led to some interesting test cases. In a car? In an hotel bedroom? In the back of a closed van and therefore not viewable, but parked in a hospital car park? In a male public toilet?) Convictions have been upheld in all these situations.

In fact, female homosexual behaviour has never been illegal unless it causes a breach of the peace. Queen Victoria didn't believe it existed! Should the homosexual act include sodomy (anal intercourse) it could in Henry VIII's day be a capital offence. In Victorian times this was reduced to life imprisonment, and now to a maximum of ten years, though of course legal now between consenting male adults in private. But caution! It is still illegal between a man and a woman whether in private or consenting or not. Beware the policeman hiding in the wardrobe!

That year I gave an amusing lecture to a meeting of the Leeds Law Society, on the legality and illegality of orifices and what could or could not be put in the three main ones (mouth, vagina and anus) and by whom, when and where. Of course penetration of any orifice by a human with a non-human (bestiality), even if the non-human says, 'go on, more, more' (or would if they could), is totally illegal. Ten years! A man was charged a few years ago for masturbating a consenting dolphin and I once had to do a report on a lady who, for money, had indulged with a male Dalmatian dog while the client watched. A friend of the client had subsequently tried to blackmail the 'lady', and the latter had reported this to the police. The blackmailer was cautioned. The voyeur had not committed any offence except aiding and abetting the commission of a felony, but the lady was 'done', under a Victorian Act, for bestiality.

However, watching people when they don't know and don't wish it, is an offence under the 'Peeping Tom' Act of seventeen hundred and something, still on the statute book. I had a patient who was cycling down the road and noticed a woman undressing in a lighted window. Being a normal male, he alighted from his bicycle and returned to get a better view. A man in a house opposite, who one might assume just happened to be bird watching through his binoculars, saw the man in the garden and rang the police. The cyclist was duly apprehended and taken to court. Was the woman in the window charged for indecent exposure? No. If it had been a female cyclist and a man undressing in the window, who would have been charged? Answers on a postcard. And they say it's a man's world!

But to return to gender, to masculinity and femininity. A proportion of individuals, again about 5 per cent, have some doubts about their gender orientation. At one extreme is the individual who has an inner conviction that they are in the wrong body, in the sense that they are a 'woman (in the mind or brain sense) trapped in a man's body' or vice-versa a 'female' who feels to be a man trapped in a woman's body. This is difficult, both for the 'sufferer' and others to explain and understand. How do they know what being a man or a woman is, what being masculine or feminine is, if they have the body of one and are raised appropriately to the body? The fact is that this sense of masculinity or femininity is strongly felt and sensed, and such people know they are 'not right'. They do not identify with others of their designated gender.

They do not feel comfortable with their bodies. They reject secondary sexual characteristics when they develop and they find that their interests in general much better match the other gender from the one in which they have been reared. They are the 'tom-boys' of the girls' class and the 'Nancy boys' or 'cissies' of the boys' class, but this is not homosexuality since they do not have sexual feelings for their 'own' sex (i.e. the sex in which they are being raised) as would the homosexual; rather they wish to be the opposite sex and identify with them. Such young people are very misunderstood and the butt of mockery or hostility.

What causes this gender mismatch? It does not seem to be environmentally determined. There is some evidence for subtle brain configurations making the male to female T.S. (transsexual person) have a more female-looking brain with scanning techniques, and vice-versa. There is some evidence for a maternal hormonal defect triggering femininity in otherwise male foetuses.

We did an interesting study in York, a research project eventually published in the *Journal of Clinical & Social Psychiatry*, and a gender specialist journal, whereby volunteers who were gender dysphoric were given a loading dose of a female hormone (oestrogen) and their pituitary hormones (luteinising hormone and follicle stimulating hormone) were measured at the start and after three, six and nine days. The typical female pattern is for a dip, a rise above normal, and then back to normal. The male shows a dip but no extra rise. 60 per cent of our volunteer group showed a female response pattern. A group of Leeds University male psychology students acted as a control group. Here only 10 per cent showed the female pattern (two students). What that showed about the test, or about the students' sexuality, history does not tell us!

At the other end of the scale from the T.S. is the individual who shows some ambivalence about gender orientation. The difference is between 'I'm a woman in a man's body' and 'I would prefer to be a woman; I think and feel like a woman, but I realise I'm not.' The conviction of the T.S. may be almost psychotic. The transvestite (T.V.) wants to identify with the femininity within him but is not pestering for 'sex-change' operations. He simply wants to adopt full-time or part-time, a female identity and 'act feminine'. This will usually express itself in clothes, and the various accoutrements, habits and mores of the 'other' gender. Sexual orientation is not affected, though for a male to female T.S. who is convinced he is a woman, who does he see as a sex object? Does the post-operative T.S. switch to liking men sexually, or become in effect a lesbian? An interesting conundrum (see Jan Morris's book of that title). There are all shades of conviction along this continuum. All that I have said applies of course to the female to male, in reverse, though females wear what they like without much opprobrium.

We discovered a number of people with gender problems in psychiatric outpatients, depressed by their situation, or wanting to explore its meaning.

When we started the clinic for marital and sexual problems we saw many more. In Newcastle, Professor Roth had written a research paper on gender dysphoria and we tended to have a number of referrals to the department. In the sixties this group of people were little understood by society, often confused with homosexual people, and a subject of mirth and merriment, or hostility, as happens to most minority groups in society. On the positive side, however, to straddle the gender divide can provide insights not given to mere mortals, and in some cultures, sadly not a lot, such people are revered and may be shamans.

My personal contact with gender doubts came I suppose from a colleague in Newcastle who had written what was at the time the definitive book on transvestism and who himself was fairly well along the transgender continuum and did indeed eventually have some modified surgery. It was this friend and colleague (now sadly deceased) whom I saw some years later in Thirsk as an outpatient during his/her transition phase, and with whom I lunched at one of the local hotels in both roles (him, not me, and not both at once!). Just occasionally I had thought my own gender identity to be a bit fragile, but events that with hindsight can take on a level of significance could also be interpreted as chance. I remembered being intrigued by a boy in a kilt when I was about six. I had also gone to some lengths to have one of my own to wear on Sundays at Sedbergh – but that was in my 'Scottish' phase'. I could remember at about eleven sometimes wishing I were a girl but at that time I identified a lot with the Hardcastle girls who were my frequent companions, and it was probably merely a whim. Up to going to university I had certainly been a boyish boy, playing rugger, competitive in sport, plenty of male friends, though I did prefer lacrosse and tennis and did not enjoy the macho beer-swilling, smoking and laddish behaviour that many males adopted.

During my early teens I had tried on female clothes occasionally and enjoyed the experience. A female cousin once dressed me up for fun and I found it a good game, which I was reluctant to finish. But then children often play dressing-up games and switch gender roles experimentally, yet do not continue the habit. I did tend to prefer female company, finding them more companionable and in tune with my thinking and behaviour, but was certainly not attracted sexually to boys and was probably a fairly typical quiet sensitive male.

The thing I noticed, and no doubt girlfriends did, too, was that I preferred the passive role in an erotic situation, to be seduced and not the seducer. That suited some girls well since they did not see me as threatening, but others thought me to be uninterested, and accused me on more than one occasion of being slow! So was I mixed up, or did I have the great gift of being able to understand a little better than most both sides of the coin? One might say that this would be a useful talent in one setting out on a psychiatric career, since empathy is the crucial area of successful psychotherapy. Trust, however, is another crucial factor in human relationships and this works both ways. The patient must be able to trust the therapist, but equally the doctor needs to be able to trust the patient, or real empathy cannot succeed. Dangerously, some women will mistake the 'feminine' empathy in a male for making a pass and this can be the cause of all sorts of subsequent problems. The psychoanalysts explain it through transference and counter-transference. Often it is more earthy than this.

But life moves on and we had moved, though the moving proved to be rather spread out. Eventually when I moved to York, for some three months I lived in the residency, commuting at weekends to Tickhill. I was well supervised! On one occasion I invited my secretary to tea, and was amused that the 'gauleiter', the lady who looked after the nurses' home and the welfare of its occupants, popped in not once but three times during her stay, the first time to check the towels had been changed, the second to bring the new laundry, and the third to see if we were all right for tea! I'm not sure whose honour she was saving, but it was no doubt most thoughtful of her!

Very quickly the house that was being built on the plot we had purchased in Crayke began to go up and I spent time at the weekends popping up to the site. Other activities were soon buried in the need for more practical action as the job developed, and increasingly I needed to drive over to Harrogate as the outpatient clinics built up. Eventually the house was ready and we moved in, not without some delays and hiccoughs, and the children started at their new schools in York.

Nevertheless, my interest in gender issues continued and over the years I had the opportunity through my contacts as a trustee of the Gender Trust to experiment a little myself in the other role, which I much enjoyed, with the aid of a friend I made through the Beaumont Society. So during the years that I was involved, I was able to develop an awareness to some extent of the experiences that women had been learning since childhood, and these insights were, I believe, valuable in my gender work, which increasingly developed as my interest became more widely recognised. Females found gender in-betweens interesting but men seemed to find them a threat and would ridicule if they realised. Gender difference is still a very deep-seated taboo. Still, I had tasted something which fascinated me. How does the other gender really feel? What are the differences in the way people behave to you? Do you think differently because of your brain and hormones, or because of conditioning through the environment? Probably both.

There is an organisation called the Beaumont Society whose 'raison d'être' is to provide support and promote social acceptance for people with gender transitions, and to host meetings and gatherings where like-minded people could get together in a secure environment and be 'themselves' for a while. Many such individuals felt alone and tended to be rejected by society and seen as freaks, and so stayed 'in the closet'; as many minority groups do.

Victoria

A friend and colleague whom I knew to have the same situation was the one in Newcastle whom I was later to be seeing in Thirsk. The Beaumont Society held its second annual dinner in London at the BBC Restaurant in the Aldwych. He was a member and asked if I would like to go. I could join them at the hotel where they were staying. Shirley and I over the years attended a number of such functions and had a lot of fun thereby. But the Aldwych dinner was a real eye-opener. Some two hundred people were there, many in very expensive outfits. RGs ('real girls') composed perhaps a quarter of the guests. A little known duo called 'Hinge & Bracket' had been hired for the cabaret and were hilarious. I thought they would go far! I thoroughly enjoyed myself and met a number of very pleasant people from all walks of life. We were to go quite regularly to the annual do for some years thereafter, which later moved out of London and became a 'weekend', taking over a hotel out of season for the two nights and combining it with their AGM. Other weekend dos developed in Weston Supermare, Nottingham, Rotherham and Scarborough.

Largely through these contacts I got to know and be known. For the members, discretion was very important. Everyone in the Beaumont Society (named after the Chevalier de Beaumont, a well-known gender-bender historically) had a 'femme' name and a number. Nothing otherwise was revealed about their 'other life' at all. I chose the pseudonym Victoria! I don't know why! Eventually my contacts led me to a useful professional involvement with a Dr Russell-Reid and other members of the Association of Marital and Sexual Therapists including Martin Cole of Birmingham, who slightly notoriously had introduced surrogate therapy from the States for premature ejaculation, impotence and frigidity sufferers, and produced many educational films for schools. Gender reassignment surgery was increasingly becoming practised as a technique, and increasingly in demand, and a section of my psychosexual clinic in York became devoted to the needs of transsexual and transvestite clients. I worked for a while with a Mr Eastwood, a surgeon in Leeds who would carry out such surgery, and later a Mr Royle and others in the London and South Coast areas, with whom Dr Russell-Reid liaised.

Reconstruction of the genitalia, male to female, had become fairly standard by the mid-seventies and early eighties. Castration was carried out and some of the penile tissue removed, the skin being inverted to create a vagina in the space between the rectum and bladder. Breast prosthesis could be carried out, the Adam's apple shaved off, vocal cords tightened, and electrolysis, and later laser therapy, used to remove beard growth. Give oestrogen 'replacement' therapy and 'Bob's your uncle'. Of course, there is more to passing as a female than that. There are mannerisms, the walk, getting up and sitting down, and so on. There is nothing that can be done about fat necks or broad shoulders or slim hips, but the change in skin texture and fatty deposition from hormone therapy is surprisingly good.

Successful female-to-male is less easy. The womb and vagina can be removed and a scrotal sac created, with a couple of 'ping-pong balls' inside, and mastectomy performed. But creating a functional penis is of only limited success. A tube through which urine can be passed is possible and increasingly effective but natural erection is not possible, and a prosthetic needs to be inserted. In both sexes the result is infertility and sterility, though orgasmic response may be retained. The individual looks much more like the real thing but is sadly not the real thing. Testosterone will cause the voice to deepen and create male body hair distribution.

We hosted in York in 1975 what was called the 'second national conference on psychosexual problems' and had a splendid dinner at the Merchant Adventurer's Hall on the final evening. Shirley and I were there as Dr & Mrs Haslam but many of the cross-gendered delegates chose to come in their, to them, natural role, cutting quite a dash! This conference led to a certain amount of international recognition and I began to be invited to speak at conferences worldwide on the subject.

Another organisation allied to the Beaumont Society was the Beaumont Trust, which had charitable status and was there to increase public understanding through education and publicity. I was invited to be a trustee of this group in my medical capacity and also to be adviser to the gender dysphoria group, which catered specifically for transsexuals. I attended their biennial London meetings and went on a number of occasions to speak at Trust gatherings in Manchester, Ghent, and to the equivalent American organisation in Provincetown.

Later I got to know a number of friends in this context, including Alice Purnell, the chairperson. Quite a number of 'RGs' were involved on the fringe of these groups. Some women, I think, felt the cross-gendered male to female to be interesting, less threatening than the macho male, and in tune more with their own psyches, and were welcomed. Apart from anything else, to be out in the town with an 'RG' gave a respectability to the cross-gendered person if 'read', and for the latter provided the sort of company with which the male-to-female felt most at ease. Knowing whom one could trust, however, was crucial, since, like homosexuality in the sixties and seventies, 'outing' could be very damaging to a professional career.

The Provincetown meeting was a fascinating experience. I hired a car and drove from Boston. The fishing port is very quaint and I was put up in a waterside self-catering hotel. Each morning of the conference delegates gathered for breakfast, usually outdoors, in one of the many cafés around the harbour. There were talks, lectures, seminars and advice panels on a range of related topics running right through the week. I gave my talk on gender rights in the UK in front of an audience of about one hundred, and also ran one of the symposia as chairperson.

Running parallel with all this there were various social activities laid on and one was a cruise out in the bay, whale-watching. A lot of delegates booked for this along with the general population. The most amusing part was to see that all the passengers born female and holidaying were wearing trousered garments, but one could spot the delegates. They were the only ones whale-watching in skirts! The whales came up close to the ship and we had a perfect view of them and they of us! On the final evening there was a dinner for all the lecturers, staff and organisers at a local hotel. Provincetown proved to be a town frequented by gays, and many of the premises were owned by gay couples. A very sad aspect was that the Aids epidemic was just hitting gays in the States and there had been quite a lot of deaths from people who had unwittingly contracted the disease.

A knowledge of how the other half lives is vital to successful transition. Such gatherings can therefore be very helpful to those transitioning, and can be reassuring to partners of the cross-gendered, who may feel very threatened. Women's magazines often have articles these days on cross-gender behaviour. Women react to partners with such interests in three ways:

1. Ugh – go away
2. Well, so long as I don't have anything to do with it, but I wish you wouldn't.
3. Oh, what fun. Can I join in? Let's do it properly!

I suppose lucky is the male 'tranny' whose partner is number three. At least the 'other woman' she is competing with is not a third party!

CHAPTER 16

Domum dulce domum

RETIREMENT IS A TIME for readjustment, as is marriage itself, and later, children leaving home. Husbands and wives need to get to know each other again a little more intensely. Husbands can be 'under wives' feet' and bored by not having a career any more. But it is a time to get things done that one has put off for years; a time when one **should** find more time!

One may, however, choose to seek new challenges, perhaps challenges that one can share. For Shirley and me, one of these was a theology course, as I have previously related. I also had three projects that I had promised myself to complete on retirement. The first was a stamp collection. My father had collected stamps and had a sizeable number of very early Victorian stamps, Penny Blacks, Penny Browns, and Twopenny Blues, and the strange half-size Half-penny Browns. Unfortunately they had been poorly mounted and some were damaged. I too had a collection that went back to the 1940s. My father had acquired a superb and massive loose-leaf album and we had started, in 1946 after his first illness, to transfer all the stamps into this new collection. Sadly by 1947 Father was dead, and the project was shelved for fifty years. It had to be completed. I owed it to Father to do so. It took me over a year and was finished and awaiting valuation in 2003.

The second task was to do up and rig two pond yachts. The first was a posh two-masted craft which had belonged to Mrs Hopps, and which I had inherited or acquired, I'm not sure which. The second, which my father had acquired during the war from a boy in Malham, who had carved it out of a tree trunk, had lost its mast. It was a single-masted yacht and needed quite a lot of restoration, as well as painting and rigging. They both looked very fine in their own ways when finished.

The third task was the railway. When the house in Crayke had been completed, we converted the loft into two rooms, adding a porthole window and two skylights; a Ramsay ladder gave access, and a partition created a bedroom for Michael when a teenager. The other half was the train room, with trellises round the walls and an extension to a fort, reached by a pontoon bridge. The layout was the O-gauge Hornby-based one that my father had bought and collected in the war years and before – six engines, with a clockwork one added and bought for £10 in a second-hand shop by myself a few years ago. When the children were young we had got it built, but because of mother's cellar flood only two engines would run. I had not the skill to restore the other four, but we were together building a signalling system and lighting various aspects of the layout. When the children left home it had been neglected and became very dusty.

There was a lot of work to be done, but, having joined the Hornby Model Railway Society, I came across someone who advertised that he would restore engines. I got in touch and within a couple of months all six were running well. These were 20-volt electric engines and there was a lot of rolling stock to go with them. The redoing of the signalling system has yet to be finished and remains a winter hobby. Our friend, David Jenkinson, now sadly deceased, who built **real** models, proper scale and built from scratch, would not have been impressed by my toy trains – but I was. It was a memorial to my father, as were the stamps.

Some ten years ago our house, built on a rather unstable clay hillside, and following a very dry couple of summers and a wet winter, began, at least the front lower quarter, to slide down the hill, and some worrying cracks began to develop. Eventually the house needed to be underpinned. Some ten years before that I had built a patio adjacent to the French windows leading from the lounge to the north-west, and had built some steps next to the very steep drive leading up to the house. The patio had to be dug up to do the underpinning. We had for some time felt that a conservatory leading off the French windows would make a great difference to the house. The foundations were half there with the concreting of the underpinning and simply needed extending out a further six feet. The conservatory could then simply be put on top. We were right. It was a very great asset to the house, and we breakfasted in there all the year round, retaining the small dining room for evening meals and entertaining.

Mother's house over the road also needed underpinning. Shirley suggested the large number of books which I had collected (hoarded) in our house and which were mostly in the front lounge and bedroom and loft had caused the house to sink through the earth. Maybe she was right. Anyhow it all got sorted out and increased the house value, no doubt.

The church and village were major interests for Shirley: that and the Conservative party, until the Major government. She was chairman of the Parish Council for a while and a candidate for the District Council. She was also on the Parochial Church Council and lay chairperson during an interregnum, a school governor of Crayke Primary School, and chairman of our local branch of the Conservative party for a few years. I remained as chairman of the Society of Clinical Psychiatry, as a trustee of the Gender Dysphoria Trust, and on the journal committee of the Royal College of Psychiatrists for some years.

In the sporting arena, Shirley swam regularly at the Ampleforth sports club, and we played a little tennis at the newly formed Crayke Tennis Club, and I played in the squash league at the Clifton Park Squash Club in York. We played social bridge with a number of friends, averaging about once a fortnight. But croquet was the main summer sport. However, as in squash, I was beginning to notice at 69 that my handicap was starting to go up, and my position on the league to go down! As Shirley would say, 'Anno Domini'!

Both Shirley and I have always loved little islands, and rarely a year has gone by without at least a week's holiday on one or other. I suppose our favourites are the smaller of the Channel Islands, Alderney, Herm and especially Sark, where we stay on Petit Sark at La Sablonnerie, run by the Perrées. Elizabeth's brother is a member of the island's Court of Pleas.

Herm is the smallest of the 'public access' islands. It has a very nice hotel, the odd farm, a cluster of houses and cottages, and a series of lovely beaches including the well-known Shell Beach. Alderney is big enough to have a quaint little town, its 'capital', St Anne's. It has an airport and harbour and had its own stamps at one time. It is the most northerly of the islands and nearest to France, and has been a fortified island since Napoleonic times. Many of the Napoleonic Forts are fine buildings and have been converted into dwellings or hotels. In the Second World War, when the Channel Isles were invaded, Hitler again fortified Alderney, this time sadly with extremely solid, extremely ugly, concrete which is virtually indestructible. But the island is quaint and the beaches superb. We took the whole family and rented Fort Clonque, a Napoleonic Fort on a small island attached to the 'mainland' at low tide, but an island at high tide, ideal for children and teenagers.

Alderney, and its satellites of Burhou, and Clonque, Herm and its satellite Jethou, Guernsey itself and its satellite Lihou, and Sark, with its satellite Breqchou, are all under the 'States of Guernsey' parliament, though Sark and Breqchou have a special status and to a large extent are independent. Jersey and its islands of Les Ecrehous and the Montiers have a separate parliament, the 'States of Jersey'. The language used in the parliaments is a Norman/French dialect, but hardly heard now among the 'natives' as a living language, English having swamped it out.

Sark is our favourite. There are no cars or aircraft allowed, though there are some tractors, and the 'taxis' are all horse-drawn carriages. The island is under Crown tenure to the Hathaway family, the Dame of Sark gaining fame by her handling of the German invaders in 1940. The island parliament, the Court of Pleas, is a feudal parliament, the tenants of original tenancies having a right to sit in the court, along with representatives of other residents, which are some 500 in number. The island village is quaint, there is a small harbour, and in contrast with Alderney and Herm, high cliffs. There are good beaches but not so easy of access. The southern end of the island is almost cut off from the rest by a very narrow and scary causeway, which leads to the other village of 'Petit Serque' where 'our' hotel is situated. Breqchou is a privately owned island just off Sark's west coast, and on it the Barclay brothers, who own the island and have a seat in the Sark parliament, have caused some controversy by building a vast castellated mansion and a heliport which some say breaches Sark's 'no over-flying' laws'. Second to Venice, Sark is where our flying carpet would take us.

But little islands and little countries continue to fascinate. We have been to Liechtenstein (where we honeymooned), San Marino and Monaco, Andorra and the independent theocracy of Vatican City. We have been to the Scilly Isles where we stayed on Tresco and visited the beautiful gardens. We took Shirley's and my mother on that holiday, my mother's first trip on a helicopter to celebrate her 90th birthday. Then we have holidayed briefly on Lindisfarne, spent caravan holidays with the children on Mull and on Skye, stayed on a number of Greek islands, and visited Gibraltar. We have holidayed on the Isle of Man and some eight years ago we had a week's holiday on Lundy Island in the Bristol Channel.

This is another quaint and anachronistic island, in theory outside British jurisdiction as being more than twelve miles off the coast, but England has claimed sovereignty. Some hundred years ago a man called Harman proclaimed himself ruler of Lundy and issued his own stamps. Then he issued coinage and the Crown stepped in and there followed an interesting legal battle which he lost. It still issues stamps, and is now owned by the National Trust, with a number of holiday properties managed by the Landmark Trust. Curiously there is a large Victorian church on the island with a peel of twelve bells, and bell-ringers go regularly to 'change ring' there. The island has one shop, one pub, one guest house and an 'island centre' where residents and visitors gather.

It is possible now to land by helicopter from the mainland. The normal route, however, is by boat, a cruise of some three hours from Bude or Bideford, or occasionally Clovelly, to the little harbour on the north side of the island. The ship can't disembark passengers if it is a northerly wind. My youngest daughter and husband had taken our cottage for the first two nights and we were changing over on the Monday morning. Yes, the wind was in the north. On the Tuesday we set sail, got to Lundy — northerly! They put us off at a jetty on the south side with a hectic cliff climb. A lovely few days. Day of departure: northerly! It had been a nice get-away-from-it-all few days. We had to climb down the cliff again and be ferried out to the ship in rubber dinghies!

In 2004, Shirley for reasons we shall see, visited Fair Isle with a friend, Valerie Black, and helped ring puffins. Where next? We shall see, but must get back to the Channel Isles one day. Perhaps the Azores and the Faroes ought to come first.

My other great love has always been Sedbergh School and most years since I left, some fifty or so years ago, I have been back for OS day, and to watch the 'Wilson Run', the big occasion in the spring term, the ten-mile cross-country fell run. For some years I went back with Graham Burgess, my best buddy when in my last couple of years at school. We missed a few due to National Service and early career years, but when children came along I would sometimes take one of them with me. When the school started inviting female partners, Shirley started to come with me.

The Housemaster, Ken Bishop, of Evans House and his wife Margaret, had become friends and we stayed with them on a number of occasions before they became too elderly for one to impose. He had been the new housemaster in Evans in my final year, when I had been head of house and an under officer in the School Corps, which Ken Bishop also ran, following his army service in the war. He had taught me French and German whilst a boy. I had in due course got on to the Old Sedberghian Club Committee which gave me much pleasure for many years, and Shirley and I became increasingly involved with staff, with Michael and Jennifer Thornley, Michael having been headmaster shortly after I left, and later secretary of the OS Club, and with the Baxters, headmaster in the early nineties, and the Hirsts, who remain head at the time of writing. For some years we stayed at a pleasant private hotel, The Thrang at Outhgill in the Mallerstang Valley, now sadly closed, and also at the Cross Keys Inn, a temperance hotel at Cautley, famed for the high waterfall of Cautley Spout, and its ham and egg teas in which boys and parents indulged, often after walking over the Howgill Fells to Calf and down past the spout to Cautley. Another pleasant hotel was the Barbon Inn at Barbon on the way to Kirkby Lonsdale.

When I watched the 'Ten' with Michael, or Graham, we would watch from Thrush Gill, ford the river Rawthey to reach 'Muddy Slide', and run back for the finish. The course of the run, starting in Sedbergh opposite Lupton House at 3 p.m. followed the Kirby Stephen road out of Sedbergh, bearing off on to 'Ten Mile Lane' and up onto the fell, running alongside the Howgill fells until it crossed the Rawthey again at a point a few hundred yards before Cautley. The course was triangular, the shape more or less isosceles, the second side being across the lower levels of Baugh Fell to Danny Bridge. Here the course crossed the river Clough and came up eventually onto the Garsdale Road and back to Sedbergh on what originally had been a grassed track, but in more modern times a tarmacked road, for the last two gruelling miles of the third side of the triangle. By bisecting the first side, and crossing to Muddy Slide which bisected the second side, one could reach the finish just before the runners, returning back on the Kirby Stephen Road – but you had to be quick. To use a car was infra dig but they were increasingly used in recent years. In later years Shirley and I would watch the start and get ourselves to Muddy Slide and back to watch the finish opposite the 'Grubber' gates. The record for the run was just under an hour and ten minutes.

I organised an Old Sedberghian dinner at the Merchant Taylors Hall in York, a pleasant occasion where also was held the York Cambridge Society dinners for some years. The Medical Society dinner was held at the Merchant Adventurers Hall. York is rich in beautiful medieval banqueting halls. A small one, where we held the Croquet Club annual dinner on occasions, was the Bedern Hall, also used by the Association of Freemen of England & Wales. I had been a Freeman of the City of London for many years and Shirley and I attended the dinners and the outings regularly. These, and the trips organised by the Livery Committee of the Society of Apothecaries, provided some very interesting gatherings, including a visit round Eton College and its library, a concert at Windsor Castle, the annual dinner at the Guildhall, and a regular trip to Twickenham for the Varsity Match. We also had receptions in many of the Guild & Livery Halls of the various companies, a trip on the river to view the ceremony of 'Swan Upping', and a visit to the College of Arms.

I had joined when at Cambridge, through being a member of the '16 Club', (the University Lacrosse Club), a London club called the 'United Sports Club' in Whitehall Court, which was a comfortable place to stay when up in London. The Royal College of Psychiatrists did not have 'lodgings', but I became a Fellow of the Royal Society of Medicine which had a 'domus medicus' on Wimpole Street, and could also hire rooms at the Royal College of Surgeons, of which I was a member. My son and I would go to the annual livery dinner at the Society of Apothecaries, and I took Shirley, my mother, Fiona, Michael and Melanie, in turn, to the Guildhall dinner, and to a tour and dinner in the Houses of Parliament, courtesy of the London Freemen.

Another organisation which developed in the seventies was the Association of Freemen of England & Wales. This body had been set up to bring together and support the guilds and liveries in the provincial towns and cities outwith London, who were struggling after the local government acts, but had existed since the twelfth century in England and Wales. A number of towns had guilds of freemen in addition to the trade guilds such as the Cordwainers, Merchant Adventurers, and many others. At the forefront were cities such as Newcastle upon Tyne, Coventry, York and Chester. Many had 'gone under'. The Association supported freemen's rights – e.g. to the strays in York, to grazing by the Beverley pasture Masters, and to property as in the Almshouses of Leicester. The Association arranged an annual weekend with a dinner and AGM and moved around the country. There was usually a church parade and procession on the Sunday morning from the Guildhall to the Guild Church, often led by a band and all dressed in their livery robes, a fine if slightly anachronistic sight. Some courts-leet were also members, and one AGM was held at Altrincham.

I had joined the Association when we came to live in York and this enabled us also to become involved in the York Guild of Freemen activities. In due course I was elected to the committee and became 'Warden of the North', a grand title which meant that I had to liaise with the various guilds in my area, and report to the two meetings of the committee per year. This provided some interesting trips, to Durham and Newcastle upon Tyne, Berwick-upon-Tweed, Alnwick and Carlisle, which at the time was dwindling through lack of new freemen. We tried to get Kendal going again, looked at Newbiggin, and at the fellmongers, but did not get anywhere. I also had contact with the Master Cutlers in Sheffield, and the Staplers Company in Leeds, though neither joined. The latter in medieval times had been concerned with the regulation of wool exports and imports from the continent.

Another minor hobby, I suppose, was genealogy. We had a Grant of Arms but that was relatively recent. We were not of those, like Pooh-Bah in *The Mikado*, who could trace his ancestry back 'to a protoplasmal primordial atomic module'! Shirley did best with her mother's side, the Dunstans, variously spelt, as were many names a couple of hundred years ago, as Dunstone or Dunstane. We were lucky at Martock in finding published parish records, and she was able to get back to the seventeenth century. I got my father's family back to the early 1800s and my mother's side, Oldfield and Barley, to a little earlier. No Earls or Dukes, only a couple of indiscreet liaisons and a great uncle who ran away to sea!

We played a little golf, initially on the Easingwold course and later at Gilling near Ampleforth. We dallied idly with computers but did not have the enthusiasm to get practised at it, though I did get given a second-hand set of computer hardware and learned the odd 'buzz' phrase such as 'download'. Not that we could do that as we couldn't make the printer work. Shirley had a word processor. Surely that was enough for a couple of pensioners!

We visited Venice once more, hopefully not for the last time, when sixty-nine. This time we were on a cruise ship, moored in Venice, and we slept on board. There were two cruises, the first went up to Burano, the lace island, and Murano, the glass island, and Torcello, and some of the islands of the northern archipelago. We saw the cemetery island for Venice, had a further day exploring Venice and then we set sail in the early morning mist, drifting over the water at sunrise and passing small islands, two of which had been in the past the men's and women's psychiatric hospitals, separated by a few hundred yards of water, another island where a monastery was now being developed into an hotel to rival the Cipriani, past the long line of the Lido eventually to moor at the attractive town at the southern end of the lagoon, Chioggio. In the shallows there were rows and rows of fishing nets and pots, and once looming out of the mist the bizarre sight of a caravan, sitting on an island not more than twice its own size, isolated in the middle of the lagoon! Finally, on the last day, we cruised back to Venice seeing the sun rise over St Georgio and the Santa Maria dello Salute, before being transported to the airport and home.

So, life went comfortably on, but it was to change and, when it did, friends were counted. Many colleagues supported me, including the Committee of the Society of Clinical Psychiatrists and members of the Committee of York Medical Society, of which I had hoped to become president. I would have liked to record the names of friends, and some former patients, who loyally stood by us in our difficult times. It would be invidious to name them, however. Easier to name those who didn't! But I won't! Some ladies whom I had known for many years offered help. I am very grateful for their kindness.

CHAPTER 17

How are the mighty fallen

MY PROFESSIONAL LIFE had been successful. In 1997, I was Medical Director of South Durham Health Trust, Chairman of the Society of Clinical Psychiatrists, had a double Fellowship, a Doctorate, and was a Freeman of London.

'Vain man! This very night . . .'

In the summer of 1997 a scandal blew up in Harrogate. A former colleague in his late seventies, suffering from cancer, and long retired, was confronted by a woman who was suing the Health Authority for not processing properly a complaint she claimed to have made some twenty years before. She was maybe hoping for some compensation. Where did this come from! Was she put up to it? Why had it taken so long (twenty years)? The health authority seemingly informed the police, and perhaps to cover their own backs, decided jointly to do a trawl. They advertised in the press; they set up a help line; they wrote to all his former female patients. Compensation was talked of. The MP, Phil Willis, got involved.

The name of the allegedly errant doctor was not at that stage published. It could have been any of three or four ex-staff. It could have been I. However, the public did not know and as part of this process a couple of women had come forward about me. Now, up until then I could say that in my career I had been remarkably complaint free. I had never had a complaint about my treatment. A woman who was a colleague whom I had seen in the seventies professionally had alleged unprofessional conduct but had withdrawn it, and in the early eighties a woman who had attended our psychosexual clinic had alleged I had been over familiar while examining her for vaginismus but had withdrawn the allegation. Finally, in 1983 just before I was due to take up my medical director post, another woman had alleged overfamiliar behaviour during interviews with her. This had been processed to the regional committee and I had met them informally, but the complaint had not been considered serious enough, I suppose, to pass on to the General Medical Council. I had, I think with hindsight, tended to have a flirtatious manner in my handling of females. Or maybe it was that I felt more at ease with females. Either way I was occasionally misread, and if this were unprofessional, then *mea culpa*. As I said to the administrator, at that time Peter Kennedy, 'Maybe I do sail a bit close to the wind. I must be careful not to give the wrong impression in future.' That

157

phrase he chose to write down and it has been quoted against me more than once! But I had heard no more of the last complaint and assumed it had been dealt with. At any event, three in a career in psychiatry of some twenty-five years was not bad; not unusual, but increasingly a problem as people have become more litigiously minded, and, mindful of compensation obtainable without proof, and, with anonymity assured, perhaps tempting.

When I heard of my colleague's predicament I was concerned for him. The massive activity going on behind one's back was completely unknown to me. The police had evidently interviewed all these people, taken statements, and trawled a very large number of people. It had been decided to set up an enquiry into how complaints had been handled a quarter of a century or so ago, by bodies that were no longer in existence, and my colleague was about to be charged with rapes and indecent assaults.

I learned all this during a discussion with my chief executive. There had apparently been an investigation of the three women mentioned above as well. (Whether they had come forward as a consequence of all the publicity, or been approached, I did not know). I was put on 'gardening leave' by the chief executive and later 'suspended on full pay pending enquiries' since the health authority decided to hear evidence from two of these three women (later a fourth popped up who had never made a complaint), even though the police had confirmed in writing that no criminal charges were to be processed. This was in 1997.

The enquiry was duly set up and held in York at an hotel, later in the year. It was inquisitorial rather than one being able to cross-question and hear witnesses' evidence. I sought legal advice, attended the enquiry, and made a statement, but on legal advice did not engage in discussions with the committee on the grounds that we felt the enquiry under the chairmanship of a Dr Manzoor had been set up improperly and was against 'natural justice'. Our impression was that the women were heard sympathetically. 'Poor dear, have a cup of tea. Don't worry, your names won't be mentioned. You'll have complete anonymity and probably be compensated.' Do I exaggerate? I don't think so. The material was passed to the General Medical Council who subsequently communicated with me. The enquiry report was leaked to the press, we never knew by whom, and the press had a field day. You can, dear reader, imagine the headlines. The consequence of all this was that in 1998 at a hearing of the South Durham management, I was dismissed from my post as Medical Director.

Had there been any complaints about my work or behaviour in my post of Medical Director? No. Were these allegations to do with any period of time I had been in employment? No. They were what came to be termed 'historical abuse cases' and dated back to some fifteen to twenty-five years before. So why was I dismissed without warning or any other of the procedures? 'Summarily'. Well, because of all the adverse publicity which would undermine my position.

But it was a private enquiry. Yes, but the findings had been leaked. Who leaked it? Well, the only people who knew were the people who held the enquiry so I was to be dismissed for matters irrelevant to my present post on the basis of unproven, non-criminal allegations on the grounds of publicity engendered by the very people who set it up? Yes. How about corporate bonding? Not one of the board has ever contacted me to sympathise from that day to now. We decided to take the Trust to an Industrial Tribunal, when my local appeal failed. This was held later in the year in Newcastle upon Tyne. The BMA assisted me. In the meantime the Trust had merged again into a total 'Durham Mental Health Trust', so my job as such was no longer there and I would have had to re-apply in competition with the Medical Director of North Durham, who was younger, when I was only some six months off compulsory retirement age. Anyhow, the tribunal sat and I won damages for improper dismissal but not wrongful dismissal – a somewhat pyrrhic victory. I received some £9,000 compensation. I decided to retire anyway at this stage, as in February 1999 I would be sixty-five.

So, I went on with my little bit of private practice, continued on my various committees, and waited to see what the General Medical Council might think of the allegations they had been sent. They move slowly and by January 1999 had not made any decision – at least not that had been communicated to me. So we settled down, I swallowed my pride, and we got on with life. As Galsworthy says in *Maid in Waiting*, 'Notoriety is not dispelled by legal innocence'!

26 January 1999 was my mother's hundredth birthday. We had arranged a nice party of old friends for her. On the Sunday a friend rang up.

'Have you seen the *Sunday Times*?

'No, why?'

'Well, there's an article in it about you and a colleague. I'll bring it over'.

The article was on the front page, next to Princess Diana. It was headed 'Psychiatrists accused of multiple rapes', and it was my picture, not my colleague's, underneath the caption. I was appalled. It didn't improve the party!

I saw my solicitor the following day.

'We should write to the *Sunday Times* and demand an apology and retraction, and compensation.'

This we did. The *Sunday Times* told us we could 'get lost'.

The question was whether to sue for libel, or just let it pass.

In the meantime, I had a routine letter from the General Medical Council pointing out that I would reach sixty-five on the 9 February. Did I wish to renew my membership? If so, fill in the form. There were a number of issues. The government had brought in a system of revalidation which meant that to stay on a register one had to show that one was up-to-date by continuing in work, attending courses and getting signed up. Many of my colleagues who were retiring saw no way of staying on the register, and without it they would not be able to prescribe or do their private practice. So there was no point. Secondly, I felt the establishment was letting me down. The leaked enquiry had been very damaging to my reputation and I had had no help. Indeed the opposite from my college, who had decided to remove my name as editor of a book on psychosexual disorders that I had worked on for them, and had dropped me from the Journal Committee. Hardly support. Indeed they were distancing themselves from one of their fellows, and a founder member. So much for 'fellowship'. I wondered what they thought the word meant. Finally the GMC itself had, I felt, been biased in their dealings with the enquiry. I wrote to them and said I no longer wished to belong to their club.

Amusingly, not long after, the GMC wrote to me (another department?) about elections to the Professional Conduct Committee. So I gathered the necessary number of doctors required to support my entering the ballot and did so. Where was the left hand that the right hand knew so little of?

Then we discovered that the Sunday Times had details of my case, only known to the GMC and the doctors involved in the complaint. How had they got it? Either the doctors had divulged to the paper information which was confidential and given to them in confidence by the patients, or the GMC itself had passed it on. If the first, then that was professional misconduct. If the latter then a head should roll at the GMC. We wrote the latter a solicitor's letter, requiring an explanation. They prevaricated. Then I got a letter from the GMC discussing the cases raised at the enquiry and referring these to their professional conduct committee. This must have been a third hand that did not know what either the left or right were doing. Then I got a letter from the Voting Committee to say I couldn't be in the ballot since only GMC members could be voted for, and I had discontinued my membership. Then I got a letter from the Disciplinary Committee saying they proposed to bring the enquiry matter before their committee at a hearing, but if I should choose to resign 'with honour' forthwith, they would not pursue the matter further. That was nice. They clearly did not know I was not a member anyway and hadn't been for three months. So I haven't heard from them since.

In the summer of 1999, I discovered that: 1) the article that the Sunday Times had published was on their website, and 2) a colleague in the gender scene, a doctor, had written to a sizeable number of my colleagues drawing attention to this article, in a clear attempt to defame me. We sued him for libel and won. We decided to go ahead with suing the Sunday Times.

What a lot goes on behind one's back these days. Perhaps it always did? The Sunday Times, sensibly from their point of view, set out to 'stitch me up' by finding more evidence of a compromising nature about me, if they could. Two of the three ladies changed their stories (coincidence?) and a fourth came on the scene. This lady had, as we discovered, made a complaint about a sexual indecency against her in the 1970s by my colleague. This did not get her anywhere and she was approached, through the woman who was leading the attack, aided by Phil Willis, MP for Harrogate, by the *Sunday Times*. Surprise, surprise, she made a complaint that I had indecently assaulted her in 1981 while she was a patient of mine. The complaint was that I had been overfamiliar during a treatment session; and again at a second and possibly a third (she was not sure) treatment session two weeks, and four weeks later. Had she complained at the time? No. Did she willingly attend and submit to the same treatment at the subsequent one or two sessions? Yes. Did she continue to see me as an outpatient for some months thereafter? Yes. Then she claimed that six months after this she had mentioned a concern to a social worker friend who had evidently explained the complaints mechanism.

In 1984 this woman had sought me out again to see me as an outpatient, and again **privately** as a paying patient in 1987, and had made no complaint on either of these subsequent occasions. Criminal intent? No. Non-consensual? Hardly since she had continued to attend. Beyond reasonable doubt guilty (over twenty years later)? Hardly. Found guilty? Yes. We continued our case against the newspaper.

Anyway, to continue the story chronologically, we heard no more until 2003. We had just returned from a trip to my daughter's and had arrived home quite late. We thought we'd have a lie in. A little before 7 a.m. there was a banging on our front door. Police! I was arrested and taken to York Police Station. After I'd gone, four policewomen arrived from another car, and proceeded to spend some hours searching the house from top to bottom, taking all my private patient notes away (of questionable legality), my computer, and various other items ('anything of a sexual nature'). We should be so lucky! We were amused by the removal of the computer. What they hoped to find who knows, but as we had had it only a few weeks and not even learned how to use it, good luck to them.

I was held in a cell in York, interviewed for most of the day and got home in the evening, 'bailed' to appear again a couple of weeks later. On that occasion, after more questioning, I was charged with a rape and four indecent assaults! The case was heard in the Magistrates' Court a week or two later, with full media coverage, of course: 'Disgraced psychiatrist' and all that kind of stuff. The Magistrates' Court in York simply passed the matter to the Crown Court, where I was listed to appear in November 2003.

My legal aid solicitor had acquired a barrister and a QC of some repute, and we met with the barrister on a number of occasions to plan how the defence would be managed. We did not meet the QC at that stage. Then, some six weeks before the case was due to be heard, the QC pulled out, the reason being given that another case was running too long and he would not be able to give proper time to my case. This was a major blow and my team had to find a replacement who was free at short notice.

Shirley and I had decided, because of all the publicity, that we would stay somewhere other than in Crayke during the trial. We had to be in Leeds early each day. Shirley acquired an out-of-season holiday bungalow in Knaresborough. This meant we would be out of the way, but I could get the train in to Leeds easily from Knaresborough. It was an interesting journey, walking through Knaresborough to the station in a misty dawn, seeing en route Horsforth and the bluebell woods in which I played as a child, and getting to know some of Leeds centre again after all those years.

The first two or three days of the trial were taken up with legal argument. Was I prejudiced by the length of time since the allegations? by the publicity consequent upon the enquiry and the libel action? by the fact that, two years before, the police had assured me that they were not contemplating prosecution? the possible actions of the newspaper, and the destruction of many notes which were not normally kept beyond twenty years from discharge? The judge decided that the trial must nevertheless go on. Much of the case seemed to be about whether treatments used in the eighties were or were not useful. Had I used these treatments simply in order to entice women? The arguments seemed to me absurd. We had published papers in journals, lectured at meetings, and been in communication with many others who used these methods at the time.

In the evenings in our hideaway we watched TV or I did some work on the case. As Shirley was to appear as one of the witnesses, she was not allowed to be in court until her evidence was taken. We went to a nice restaurant on Knaresborough Station, and a 'Chinese' by the river. At the weekends we went back home and tried to pretend things were normal.

The trial took a month. Goodness knows why! The issues were I felt straightforward. On the evidence, or lack of it, was there intent? No. Was there lack of consent? Hardly, since two patients had continued to see me and the third had said to her GP how much better the treatment was making her. Was it beyond reasonable doubt? How could it be with all that, and after a time lapse of fifteen to twenty years?

Eventually the QCs made their closing speeches and the judge summed up. The judge was the libel judge from London who in fact had been the judge at my pre-trial libel hearing. I did not feel he emphasised the points that I felt to be crucial. The jury were sent out and were out a day and a half. One of them was ill and was discharged, which left eleven. Eventually on the Friday morning they came back in.

'Count 1. Have you reached a verdict?'

'Yes.'

'What is your verdict?'

'Guilty.'

We went through all the counts. Count 5 was reached by a majority verdict, that is to say ten. All counts were 'guilty'. We were, I think it is fair to say, 'gobsmacked'. The judge looked a little surprised too. He decided he would give sentence on the following Tuesday. I was given unconditional bail until then.

With an irony perhaps only God could have devised, on the Monday I was due to receive my theology degree at Leeds University. So, we all got in the car and drove over to Leeds on Monday morning. I got my gown, had my photo taken and we had coffee and biscuits before we entered the Main Hall. We listened to the speeches, and in due course I took my turn, going up onto the rostrum and receiving my MA to the applause of the assembled company. We went out to lunch and tried to have a normal evening. I packed a case. I had been to the bank and building society in the afternoon to sort out what we would do with finances, since a custodial sentence was expected. I drove my car, which needed a repair job, down to the garage. I handed over insurance policies and papers to Shirley. And, eventually, we went to bed and tried to sleep.

On the Tuesday we were back in Leeds again. This time there was all the family, plus a posse of our friends. We met in a local hotel and marched down to the court. All the press photographers were there in another posse, flashing lights, videos, and in we went. We met our legal team. We embraced (the family; not the QC) and went into court. This time, instead of being behind my legal team in the well of the court, I was at the back, behind the bullet-proof glass screen. Two of my accusers and their group were in the visitors' gallery along with all my crowd. The judge came in and we all stood. After preliminaries, the judge addressed me.

I was sentenced to seven years for rape, three years for one indecent assault, and eighteen months for the others, to run concurrently.

That was it. I waved to my family and was led out by the rear court door, duly handcuffed, and down into the cells. Decline and fall.

CHAPTER 18

De profundis

AFTER A BRIEF MEETING with my legal team, who promised to start negotiating an appeal, I was given some sandwiches and an orange drink, and was left to wait some two hours. I was then put in a police van, all my belongings having been checked in and put in a sealed bag, and I and some six others left out of a rear exit and headed for Armley Jail. The jail was quite well known to me, as some ten years before I had visited prisoners from time to time to do psychiatric reports or to confirm Mental Health Act Orders. Little did I think then that I would be coming in, in a prisoner role.

The journey only took some fifteen minutes. After another hour's wait I was taken into reception, where I was to strip, be briefly examined, have a shower and put on my prison clothes. All my belongings apart from some toilet kit (no razor blade!), my watch and glasses were checked in, put in a bag, and were not to be seen again. The prison gear consisted of blue jeans, a blue and white striped shirt, army-style black shoes and boxer-style pale blue underpants. We also had a sweater, a tracksuit, a change of underwear, 'T' shirt, socks and two towels. The jeans were not the right size (too large) but we were not allowed belts. We were placed in a reception cell, shared, overnight and then placed on a wing in the big Victorian prison block the following day, where I was to share with a thirty-year old Moslem man from Kashmir, whose English was limited. He was a religious man and quite pleasant. Our cell had two bunk beds, a table, two chairs and two lockers. It had a stainless steel loo and washbasin in the cell, screened by a small walled-off area about three feet high. The view from the cell window was ironically out towards the Parkinson Building of Leeds University where I had received my degree two days before.

The prison was divided, in that an area was reserved for 'vulnerable prisoners', a large percentage of which were 'sex offenders', which I supposed I was, so I was on this wing. The main part of the prison, a Category B (prisons are categorised A: high security; B: secure; C: semi-secure; D: open) contained the bulk of the inmates, who looked down on the VPs, somehow believing that their offences e.g. 'grievous bodily harm' were more respectable than 'indecent assault'. This was made clear during exercise in the exercise yard which abutted onto part of the 'mains'. While walking round in circles (fifteen circles to the mile, I reckoned) one might be subjected to verbal abuse from the 'mains' windows, and we learned not to get within spitting distance of the inmates, which was an impressive ten feet with the wind behind them!

This phase of my stay serving Her Majesty lasted a month and I managed one visit, from Shirley, before I was told I was to be moved to Acklington, a Category C prison somewhere north of Morpeth in Northumberland and about one hundred miles, instead of forty, from Crayke.

What I found in Acklington turned out to be much more congenial. I was housed initially on H wing, a modern building on a site which had been an RAF base in the Second World War. I had a single cell, with its own lavatory and washbasin, a bed, chair, table, locker, television and electric kettle. After an induction week I found myself working in the tailors' shop as a machinist, an entirely new skill to learn, but quite interesting. It was warm, in a big ex-hangar, friendly, and with tea breaks! We worked from 8.30 a.m. to 11.30 a.m. and from 2 p.m. to 3.30 p.m. five days a week and received pay which worked out at about 25p per hour. Well, it's a living, and free board and lodging! I learned the mysteries of the five-thread overlocker and the Singer flatbed single-needle machines, and I assembled shirts.

H wing had four corridors, on two floors. In the central well were two pool tables, and in one wing table tennis and the other a table football game. The prison was in two parts, virtually separate from each other, and our side, the VP part, with some four hundred inmates, consisted of the H block, three blocks where most people shared a cell, (A, B and C), and a new block, J wing, which was a C+, semi-open, and for non-smokers, also single cell. I became quite skilled at pool!

There was a good library, a branch of Northumberland County Libraries, and a chapel and multi-faith centre served by a group of chaplains of various denominations and faiths. The gardens, however, were the highlight. They were marvellously well stocked and made a beautiful display from early spring onwards. Here we could walk at exercise times and enjoy the occasional sunny day. 2004 was mostly rain, however, until October when it became splendid.

One soon got into a routine. The rest of the 'inmates' were a good cross section of the population. There were the 'Jack the Lads', insecure, and so hunting in packs and wanting to throw their weight around, the odd bully, and a few who were clearly psychiatrically ill. There were the occasional priest, doctor, architect, businessman, even a lawyer, mostly middle-aged and serving 'historic abuse' convictions for things that they had done, or it was alleged they had done, often as much as twenty-five to thirty years before. What the value of a prison sentence was to them it was hard to see. Did society want this sort of revenge? Was it in some way meant to help society? It costs about £25,000 a year to keep someone in prison and the people who suffered more were their families who had to cope. Was it to prevent re-offending? Few were likely to in this group. And it all came from the taxpayer! If one hadn't 'offended' for twenty years it seemed a bit improbable that one would on the twenty-first! Or was it to do us good? No, it was revenge, pure and simple. Inmates were divided into 'deniers' and those who admitted and were prepared to accept their wrong-doing and address it in special courses usually run by young female psychologists and social workers. If one had an appeal pending then by definition one was a 'denier'. A not so subtle blackmail operated. There were three grades of privilege: 'standard' which applied to the majority, 'basic' which was the bottom and had no privileges (no TV, no association and 'banged up' twenty-three hours a day), and at the other end 'enhanced' (extra visits, some of one's own clothes and access to more open types of wing.) Well, deniers, however good their behaviour on the wing, couldn't go on the SOTP course and couldn't therefore become enhanced. People who offended in some way in the system could be given as a punishment a period of time on basics. Those who conformed, cleaned their cell, kept the rules, and went on courses became enhanced and enjoyed more visits, and could have more personal belongings, and more time out of the cell. They went to H3 and H4, or if non-smokers, perhaps J wing. Deniers might get to J wing, but not H3 and H4. Standard grade got three visits a month. Money was 'banked'. This might come from outside sources, such as family, or was earned through some work, or was part of the minimal allowance given to all. One's old-age pension or unemployment benefit if one qualified, had been stopped on entry into Her Majesty's jail. The accumulated bank was put into a 'canteen' account from which a certain amount per week was added. The canteen was run by Aromac and each week a list came round on which one wrote, from their catalogue, what one wished to purchase. The following week a pack arrived to be collected and signed for, hopefully containing what had been ordered. This would include stamps, groceries and toiletries, stationery and money allocated for making phone calls. These could not be sent in from outside.

In Category B prisons there was a limit on phone calls. In Category C it was limited only by one's cash. The phone was available at certain times, and one was allocated a pin number. One provided the wing officer with a list of numbers, names and addresses of those one might want to phone and each of these people was rung up to check that they were happy to be phoned, before the numbers were issued. One could then start phoning. The phone display showed how much cash was available. If one phoned an incorrect pin number, or a number that was not on the authorised list, then the call was rejected. It was not easy to get people who were out at work during the day to confirm their agreement to be phoned, and it took some time to confirm my son's number in Dublin!

Each week a menu was issued for the next week ahead, with a choice of four or five items which one ticked off and returned. The food was basic institutional food but quite nourishing.

Apart from the sex offenders' course, the prison ran a variety of educational courses and evening classes. Everyone under the retirement age was expected to work for the first three months, unless they had a doctor's certificate, in one of the workshops, mostly tailoring, but attaching plugs to wires, woodwork and gardening and laundry shops were also available. After three months one then had a choice of activities such as fairly basic education courses, but there were computer courses, and some GCSE and NVQ courses, the gardens, the wing orderly jobs, or serving in the prison officers' mess. I opted to do an NVQ in the tailors' shop to make it more interesting and qualified in a grade II course in 'performing manufacturing operations'. To be working was much better than being stuck in one's cell most of the day and had a reasonable social aspect to it.

One's mental and spiritual welfare was catered for by the multi-faith chaplains. I found our Sister Moira, the Roman Catholic chaplain, very helpful. Then there were various hospital visitors – Samaritans, 'Listeners' (inmates who'd done a counselling course), 'Pals', and so on. And, of course, the Ombudsman. Physical activities included a gym, to which I went twice a week with the remedial over-forties group and where I got fitter than I had been I guess since the age of twenty-one, apart perhaps from a couple of weeks that I spent at a TA camp in the early eighties, and I lost about a stone and a half and managed again to do press-ups and pull-ups, and eventually an upward circle! Once a week I played badminton and I walked a brisk mile in the gardens most days. There was football for the younger inmates.

So I settled down to my Acklington routine. One did as one was told and obeyed the rules and kept out of trouble. I moved after a while to a new wing where I had to share, but after some eight months got on to J wing which was the C/D or C+ non-smoking wing with single rooms, no locking of doors, and modern toilet and shower facilities. They had their own private garden, and a pleasant common room with a wide screen TV, pool, and table tennis. It was more like a hall of residence for mature students in a modern university, except, of course, for the perimeter fifteen-foot high metal fencing topped with razor wire.

Fine: but coming up in summer 2004 was the long awaited enquiry into 'how complaints were handled in the NHS', in particular with regard to my colleague and myself. This was chaired by a QC, Nigel Pleming, and followed another large trawl of ex-patients, one-quarter page advertising in the local press as far north as the *Northern Echo*, presumably because I had worked in Newcastle in 1964. Quite bizarre, and of course costing hundreds of thousands of pounds of health service money, which could be better spent, calling over a hundred witnesses, and lasting some six months; and of course taking place in the York Hilton Hotel – well it would, wouldn't it? – run by lawyers and administrators. One could predict the conclusions. 'The complaints procedures were found to be to some degree faulty. We recommend . . .' And it cost £3.2 million!

But of course they were looking at the workings of a health authority in the last century a quarter of a century ago, long since replaced by hospital trusts and a completely new administrative structure. Almost all those who had worked in it were retired, senile, or dead. New guidelines had been published and adopted years ago and following the first 'Manzoor' enquiry.

So what was it for? Our belief was that it was a whitewash, an attempt to blame managers and staff long gone, and to 'stitch up' more thoroughly the medical staff. The massive trawls and publicity, and the flawed inquisitorial structure of this quasi-judicial hearing which did not allow of cross-questioning did two things. It made all potential complainants aware that considerable compensation might be available to a complainer, regardless of the uncertain veracity or otherwise of what they said, and it ensured collusion of all such interested parties by allowing the women to sit in on the proceedings and have free legal support, while denying this to my colleague and myself. These women knew that the NHS had paid out £350,000 in compensation already after my colleague's trial. Furthermore, the chairman actually said he was not interested in the truth of allegations, but only in how such complaints were handled! He was interested in facts? Seemingly not.

There is a very fine distinction between 'truth' and 'a fact' which was somewhat lost on us. Furthermore, most of the 'complaints' were never actually made until the trawl, which came years (in some cases thirty years) after the alleged events complained of, and were mostly not made at the time. The time lapse made it virtually impossible to verify the truth of such complaints. Notes had been destroyed and the health authority no longer existed anyway. It was also virtually impossible to prove innocence. In fact the whole business seemed to many a farce and against 'natural justice'.

I was required to attend as a witness and in August found myself back in the Leeds Category B jail, 'banged up' for a while with a sufferer from schizophrenia and later a 'Jack the lad' who insisted on having the TV on twenty-four hours a day (literally) but with the sound turned low, whilst at the same time playing his stereo radio/cassette player full blast for some sixteen hours a day! I dubbed it my summer holiday in the lower Aire Valley. The day trip to York for the hearing was a blessed temporary respite, and the hotel produced for us a good sandwich lunch!

I had learned that one was required to take the oath and was therefore prepared for a dialogue.

'Chairman, before I take the oath, may I ask a question?'

'Certainly.'

'What is the purpose of this oath? I presume it is to undertake to tell the truth.'

'Of course.'

'So if one tells a lie, there is perhaps some sanction. Would this count as perjury?'

The Chairman began to bluster somewhat.

'If it is established subsequently that some of the witnesses have not told the truth, might they therefore be liable to proceedings being taken against them?' The Chairman knew what I was getting at. Could some of the witnesses who had testified against me be held responsible? The Chairman's reply was interesting.

'I am not prepared to continue this discussion any further. Are you prepared to take the oath?'

'I am perfectly happy on my part to undertake that what **I** say will be the truth.' I emphasised the word 'I' and the point I am sure was not lost on him. The Chairman appeared rather hostile during the three hours that I was questioned, but I liked to think that I made some points in my favour, as did my solicitor who was present. My wife was also allowed to be with me.

The report was due to be published sometime over the following year, so that continued to cast a slight cloud on the horizon. Also, the libel action against the *Sunday Times* remained to be heard, or settled out of court. I then awaited transfer back to Acklington, in all being in Leeds for four weeks. When I returned to Acklington I was housed for a while on the annexe of C wing, got back to my tailoring NVQ, and was in due course transferred back to J wing. My release date (on licence) was 14 June 2005, following upon our successful appeal to the High Court in May of that year, a matter which I must now relate.

Following my original conviction the barrister, who felt there to have been a miscarriage of justice, decided there were grounds for appeal against conviction. This he had set about preparing as it had to be in within twenty-eight days. This was duly considered by an appeal judge in Chambers, who agreed that a case had been made, and leave to appeal was granted. There is normally quite a wait for such appeals. It appeared that the QC dealing with the enquiry wished, however, to get on with this latter and was evidently able to pull strings, so my appeal was heard in May of 2004 on points of law and misdirection.

I won in part. The serious charge was quashed and my sentence reduced from seven to three years. This was important in that a sentence of four years attracts a two-thirds sentence served, and optional parole, whereas under four years is half-sentence served and out on licence for a further quarter. However, I protested, and do protest, that I have done nothing criminal. A criminal act requires intent, and a lack of consent, to an act of assault, beyond all reasonable doubt. In England innocence is assumed until guilt is proved. Not so now. An unsubstantiated and unsubstantiable accusation based on an event twenty to thirty years ago, with evidence to suggest that the act, to the extent it occurred at all, was consensual, is seemingly enough to convict. Reasonable doubt seems to have gone out of the window. I remain incensed by this travesty of justice. But the appeal court decided to let the 'minor' offences stand. The CCRC (the

Criminal Case Review Committee) took up the case with the Historic Abuse Panel and FACT (Falsely Accused Carers and Teachers), but there was a long queue and I would be released in all probability before it was considered. However, clearing my name was important to me. Our MP, Anne McIntosh, was helpful and supportive. Bishop Stephen of York was in touch, as was Peter Hamilton, our ex vicar, and Ian Hitchin, our current one. The Society of Clinical Psychiatrists went to great lengths to seek out new evidence and question the handling of the trial, and veracity of witnesses.

Not so the Royal College of Psychiatrists. They decided to remove my name from their List of Fellows before the appeal was heard, having already distanced themselves from me. I protested and got my solicitor to write but I did feel that they had rather lost the concept of 'fellowship' which used to mean supporting those in trouble. It was not, I concluded, (sour grapes?) an organisation actually worth belonging to. They had prejudged the issues and I had no opportunity to contest it.

The Royal College of Physicians and Surgeons of Glasgow were more polite but followed suit. The Royal Society of Medicine of which I was a fellow also discontinued my membership. Well, we wouldn't want a sniff of anything unseemly in these hallowed corridors, would we? I suppose honourable gentlemen always have resigned from their clubs over such issues, but before the appeal has been heard? A little over-hasty in my view.

How are the mighty fallen! So what was it actually like, being in jail for eighteen months? It may sound odd to say this, but by and large I enjoyed it! Of course, I missed my wife, and family and friends, and the freedom to go out to a meal and have a glass of wine, but allowing for the fact that I had to be in, 'banged up' as the slang went, the life, certainly at Acklington in Category C+ accommodation, was such that one could enjoy it. One could see why some young residents were happy to return: three meals a day, companionship, a warm room (usually) and bed, pool tables, a library, television, and security indeed from the nasty things of the outside. No worries, and enough money for one's personal needs, 'a burn'. It was fascinating and there were very few break-ins!

To me there was the interest in learning new skills. I did the NVQ and learned computer skills. I wrote quite a lot, and I read the classics which I had neglected in my youth (Dickens, Hardy, Jane Austen and the like), and most of all I studied humanity. Institutional living was no threat to us, as it was to some of the young ones. I had been at boarding school, halls of residence and the army. I was at ease with communal living. Nor were strange people any threat with my years of psychiatry, and my judo skills learned at Cambridge gave me a confidence (maybe misplaced after all these years, but it is how one presents oneself) that was not going to be intimidated by Jack the Lad. I was well equipped. But I was fortunate in being in the VP wing. The 'mains' were much rougher, I'm told, and bullying less easily controlled. There was some mob rule and cliques formed – a gangland culture. But the VP label did make one despised for some reason by the 'mains' and cat-calling was frequent towards 'sex offenders'. Yet this latter label could apply to anything from downloading pornography on a computer, to paedophilia, indecent assault and rape. Not all VPs were sex offenders anyway, and might be there due to age or infirmity.

What were the 'inmates' like? I was wont to say that the only difference between those 'inside' and those 'outside' was that the latter had yet to be caught. Indeed the inmates – 'convicts' – 'banged up' – were a cross-section of humanity, such as one might meet on any street in a city at any time. But this was an all-male society, apart from a few female prison officers and other staff. Indeed working in a male prison seemed a slightly strange job for a woman to take. It was interesting to be in an all-male society again for a while. Males, as many women might suspect, are in general an uncouth lot. They fart, spit, jostle each other, in fun or more aggressively at times. They swear. The f-word is very useful, rendering many adjectives, nouns and verbs otherwise redundant. The officers can be as bad! F . . . off! Get off your f . . . ing arse! f . . . ing get into f . . . ing work! etc. etc. The c-word is also frequent. The b-word is too mild to be of much use.

And yet – there is a camaraderie, and a sense of helping each other since we are all in the same boat. They can often be kind and sensitive to the problems of others. To my surprise 'gays' and 'trannies' were tolerated, at least on the VP wing, with tolerant amusement but no venom, and indeed liaisons between homosexual couples were not particularly discouraged as long as discreet. I dare say amongst younger ones the sexual outlet was masturbation, and this might be mutual at times, but I personally saw little of it and it is after all natural enough when deprived of the opposite sex. Pictures on the walls of cells were often of the pin-up type, some more lurid than others. But to my amusement, in one cell in which I was padded up with another inmate, he had four magazine pictures on the wall. One was a tasteful picture of an attractive young woman, full frontal and nude. The other three were rather weird pornographic portrayals of two lesbian females, bedecked in suspender belts, black stockings and high heels (!), who were performing singularly strange contortions in what was clearly a toilet. Well, each to their own. But the officer on his inspection round told my pad mate to take down the picture of the attractive nude, since it showed pubic hair and hardly visible genitalia, but he was allowed to retain the other three. The logic of this, I confess, passed me by!

One learned a degree of humility. The chapel and chaplains could have a big influence. I attended the Eucharistic Anglican and Free Church service on Sunday morning, and the Catholic Eucharistic Mass on Thursday evenings where I often read the lesson. It was also, being in prison, an opportunity to look at one's life, its strengths and weaknesses, what one had done for good, and what for bad. Why was I here? If this were part of God's will, then what was its purpose? What was I to learn?

Although I believed, and still believe, that I have committed no criminal act, I have not been 'banged up' by accident. A criminal act requires intent, a lack of consent by the other party, and to be for the jury 'beyond reasonable doubt'. How could an examination for vaginismus fulfil these three criteria? How could someone who had continued to see me without demur for some years after the 'offence', and had returned for more of the same on three occasions, say, twenty-five years later, that it was non-consensual, and be believed 'beyond reasonable doubt'? But I had been a flirt. I had perhaps become blasé and not over-concerned about the need for chaperones and the risk of false allegations. It couldn't happen to me? I had certainly broken God's sixth commandment as brought to the Jewish people some three thousand years ago by Moses, but so had a sizeable proportion of the population, and they weren't all in prison. Three years for overfamiliarity during an examination? Was this justice? Was I just the victim of a series of coincidences that had come together, and where it was convenient to 'stitch me up' to provide a report that would satisfy the public in their thirst for compensation, and scapegoats? My solicitor at the Manzoor enquiry said, 'Dr Haslam, you have been stitched up.'

But jail gave one some humility. It seemed best to be more honest and to try to eliminate sixth commandment problems! A simple incident in my early days illustrated this. An inmate, in his eighties and with a bad heart (what the hell was a judge doing committing him to jail? Where is humanity? Where is common sense?) had a dizzy turn in his cell and fell, striking his head. It required stitching and he was taken away to the medical centre for this to be carried out. Rather surprisingly he was returned to his cell early in the evening. I popped in to see if he was okay and saw that blood from when he had fallen was still on the floor and had not been cleaned up. He was not really in a fit state to be cleaning his cell, so I sat him down, got a bucket and mop and cleaned it for him. What a simple thing. But I was so moved by the effect of this that I went back to my cell and wept with a happy emotion. ''Tis better to give than to receive' working in simple reality. I hope it did him good at a practical level, but it certainly helped me at a time of stress of my own.

In the autumn of 2004 the libel action was settled out of court. The whole experience had cost me a lot of money. Much of my mother's inheritance had been eaten up. But we didn't go bankrupt. It was a very sobering experience.

And I wrote books: manuscripts — this one, two novels, a book about experience in prison called *Shrink in the Clink*, and a book on religion, *The Deity for Doubters*. So I used my time. Is this why God gave it to me?

It is my wife who has borne much of the brunt of all this, who had to become the decision-maker for a while, who had the worries. **We** were cocooned. We couldn't get out but nor could the world get in.

So Christmas passed. I had reached halfway in September 2004. I was due out on licence in June 2005, and would be on the 'sex offenders register', the first for a further nine months, the latter 'indefinitely'. Was I some kind of threat to women? How absurd! The allegations dated back a quarter of a century and I had had a whole, and successful, career since. But the law is the law, ass or not.

The enquiry report was to be published the following year, and bound to be adverse. This was the inevitable whitewash and sop to the masses. I sometimes thought myself a mixture of Clarke, Kennedy, and Clinton, not so exalted but equally prone to foolishness, though not criminality. Foolish by what standards? Honesty, I suppose. Why did Monica Lewinsky save a semen-stained dress for some years? Why did one of my accusers save a prescription I had issued, rather than cashing it, and then claim the indiscretion had been at a time she was a patient, when not till twenty years later did she choose to complain? Why is a cow? In fact the publication of the enquiry report was delayed (one wonders, in a paranoid way, if this were deliberate) until not long after I had been released on licence.

So the months went by. A second Christmas and New Year came and went, nicer than the first in its surroundings and relative freedom, but still 'inside'. The CCRC had a long waiting list of historic abuse cases to get through and were unlikely to investigate my case before I was 'out'. But in the New Year I could say, 'Well, fifteen more visits, five more jars of coffee to buy from the 'canteen', ten more sheet changes – and then I'll be out!'

Eventually the day came. 14 June 2005. Shirley came to pick me up in the car. It was an odd feeling. No ceremony. No band playing. No governor on the steps. The door opened and closed behind me. Well, we went to Druridge Bay and walked on the sand. We spent two nights in Warkworth to wind down, and perhaps avoid the press, then home for a few days, and to Whitby for a week in a beautiful old cottage overlooking the harbour.

Friends and relations were welcoming, apart from the Croquet Club! I was required to see my probation officer in York once a week. 'Licence' lasted nine months during which time I could not travel out of the UK. The CCRC appeal still seemed to be doing nothing. The main irritation and humiliation was being on the 'sex offenders register' which required me to report my residence and movements to the police for the rest of my life unless I won the appeal. But 'rules is rules'. And I couldn't go to the USA. Well, as Groucho Marx might have said, 'I wouldn't dream of visiting a country who didn't want me!'

The big issue, however, was the publication of the long-awaited report of the Health Enquiry. The press, of course, had a lovely excuse to have another go at us, the *Sunday Times* printing an article with the headline 'NHS allowed scores of rapes to occur' – or words to that effect. Quite untrue, but what can one do? The local press devoted a full page spread and ran the story for four days in a row. The report ran to a thousand pages and unsurprisingly thought that complaints had not been well handled, since it 'acquired' some fifty complaints that had never actually been made during the lifetime of that health authority. Words fail. But life goes on.

CHAPTER 19

Epilogue: I did it my way

MEMOIRS AND AUTOBIOGRAPHIES always have one fault. They cannot finish. As the last word is written, the writer is surely still alive, with however long still to go. Even if he dropped dead that day, he or she could not describe the funeral!

Prison ended. Life went on. One picked up the pieces, drifting into the sunset, together hopefully for a long time yet. Father reached 51 ¼, mother 102 ¾. Perhaps the average, 77, would give me six more years, twelve more holidays, six more birthday parties. Who knows?

How does one summarise a life? Mine has had its highs, its lows, its triumphs and humiliations, as do all lives. Frank Sinatra has always been a favourite of mine, from the time he took on the McCarthy absurdities in the USA. His song 'My Way' could be my theme tune!

There were times I'm sure you knew, when I bit off more than I could chew! But through it all . . . I ate it up and spat it out. The record shows I took the blows – but did it my way. And now, the end is near, I find it all so amusing. To think I did all that, and may I say, not in a shy way – oh no, oh not me, I did it my way.

Selfish? I don't think so. But it sums me up. If others do not like it, let them go their way. I will survive.

He has another – 'There was a girl in Denver . . . seems like only yesterday . . . I have been a rover.'

My girl in Denver was a pen pal and we never met – but let that go.

While in jail I read a lot about religion, not just Christian and Jewish, but Hindu, Moslem and to some extent other religions of the East and I read the book of Mormon. I am a pluralist by inclination. I believe if there is a creator of the universe who has a personal interest in creation and humanity, then it is unlikely that he/she only ever manifested on earth, to an obscure people with all the usual failings of humanity, in a small bit of the Middle East, to Moses for the Ten Commandments and to the Disciples in the shape of Jesus. Surely he/she would manifest too at other times and in other places and to other peoples. Why not? Krishna, Mohammed, Joseph Smith? Is it not arrogant of certain groups to think that they are the only ones with a clear view of the truth? And if God created us in his/her own image then God has a sense of humour and must wonder at the trivia of belief which separate humankind even to the level of war! I wrote while in jail a small religious treatise and set out what seem to me to be eternal truths of belief:

1. A creative force in the universe.
2. A personalised presence of a spirit in dwelling in a soul.
3. Belief in an afterlife.
4. Showing care and charity to all humanity.
5. All life should be held in respect.
6. That this creative force (God, Allah, Vishnu – the name doesn't matter) has spoken at different times and to different peoples of different creeds through the medium of prophetic souls.
7. The universality of prayer.
8. Loyalty and care to one's 'neighbours'.
9. Respect for all people's beliefs.
10. Helping the child, the needy, the old and the sick.

There could be more – but these are essentials and are common to all people's aspirations.

What has uplifted me? Such diverse and differing things. Glories of nature such as a fine sunset looking over from Herm to Guernsey; the back streets of Venice; high mountains; standing on Winder above Sedbergh looking across to the Lakeland Fells, rain and wind lashing one's face. Then there is music, such a range. Tchaikovsky's Fourth, Fifth and Sixth Symphonies; Rachmaninor's piano concertos; particular melodies: 'The Londonderry Air', 'Come away to the caves of Carrigclena' from Sullivan's *Emerald Isle*, Balf's 'I dreamed that I dwelt in marble halls', some of Sinatra's songs; Sullivan's orchestral piece *In Memoriam*, certain hymn tunes that are so evocative such as 'O Love, that will not let me go', 'Lord of all hopefulness', and many more. Poetry can be evocative too, for example, a poem by Timothy Birdsall, called 'Sedbergh Revisited', quoted amongst other verse in the appendix, where I have also included a poem by my mother, one by my son, and some of my own.

Life itself can provide a host of memories, some inspiring, some joyous and triumphant, and some humiliating and sad. It is strange how some, from sixty or seventy years ago, stick in one's mind while other events only yesterday are forgotten. Then there are moments of love, and of desire, too intimate perhaps to set down, too personal, but universally felt. Some of these items relate to particular people of significance in one's life, and their impact can be enormous.

My father died when I was just twelve. My memories of him are surprisingly few really. He showed me a field mouse in the garden, taught me how to skim a stone, showed me the air-raid siren on the roof of Thomas Burnley & Sons, and then was ill with a stroke, had forgotten how to play cribbage, called me John, and died.

Mother I knew for over sixty-five years and I have a host of memories: of her singing me to sleep with 'Just a Song at Twilight' and 'Go to sleep, my baby'; being proud of me over various school successes; being anxious when we were on holiday and the children were playing in the sea; teaching her to drive and her passing her test in her fifties; little holidays in the Lake District as she grew old. I was proud of her and everyone said what a good son I was, looking after her in her last years. But there is an overriding sense of sadness and guilt that in her last year there were times when I got so impatient and cross with her failing social awareness and her tendency to denigrate Shirley. 'I hate that woman,' she once said. And I shall never forget her reproach, 'And all I ever wanted was for you to be happy' nor the time I was swatting a fly that was bothering her and she said, 'Let it live.' Life was precious.

Shirley and I have had a wonderful marriage despite its problems. We are best buddies and have a lot in common. We had a wonderful wedding, a wonderful honeymoon. We have started the dancing at the Savoy and at the Café Real restaurant in Vaduz in Liechtenstein. We have been all over the world together, stood on the edge of the Grand Canyon watching the sunset, stood on the edge of the crater on Mount Vesuvius. We have cried together when our son was first ill; laughed together; been to concerts and opera in Leeds, travelled to Venice on the Orient Express and stayed at the Cipriani; seen the Falls at Niagara; bathed in glacier melt lakes in Greenland and hot springs in Iceland and the Dead Sea. We have watched with pleasure and pride the growth of our families and seen the girls wed. We have attended their degree ceremonies and shared in their successes.

I remember too Shirley's parents, kind, helpful and friendly, her father, Alfred, frail but standing firm at Fiona's wedding, her mother Eileen's first sign of Alzheimer's during our family holiday in Scotland. I remember the family holiday at Portmeirion – and Eileen's funeral.

The love which Shirley has shown in her loyalty, at times when I have let her down, and during my trial and prison sentence, is something for which I am and shall be eternally grateful. What would I have done? She didn't deserve all this. But we have had happy times even through it. There were good times when we stayed in one little holiday bungalow in Knaresborough through the trial, and ate of an evening sometimes at the little station restaurant, or the Chinese restaurant down by the river. Marriage is about sharing and friendship. Sexually we were as compatible as most, but that too is sharing, and it is companionship that becomes more important as the years go by. In 2009 we shall, hopefully, share our Golden Wedding.

The children produce another set of glorious memories and inevitably some sad ones. Fiona, now in her forties, was a sweet little girl. We lived in Tickhill when she first went to school at St Mary's in Doncaster. I used to drive her on my way to work and tell her stories about Brighteyes, who was I think a thrush, and about Willie Wasp, just as my mother had told me stories about Brighteyes when we would walk to Miss Davies's kindergarten in Leeds when I was that age. And in the evenings when I got home I would on occasions sing her to sleep with the same songs my mother used to sing me to sleep. Later, when all three were old enough, we would sledge in the winter on the steep sloping field opposite our house, and have summer holidays at Sandsend and once at Embleton on the Northumbrian Coast.

Fiona found a baby wild rabbit in a field at Crayke and as it was orphaned she brought it home and reared it, giving it milk (four-hourly) from a doll's feeding bottle, night and day, setting her alarm clock for the middle of the night to feed it then too. She was successful and it survived. We had intelligent hamsters, and guinea pigs, and once a gerbil that was eaten by the next-door cat. A guinea pig came on caravan holidays with us.

I remember Fiona getting confirmed at York Minster. The hymn was 'O Jesus, I have promised to serve thee to the end . . .'

Michael produces another set of memories. We got the trains running again after many years in a box. We explored the waterfalls on our Norwegian caravan holiday. At prep school he excelled at swimming, and later after the abortive term at Sedbergh (where he started learning the violin) he took up rowing back at St Peter's School – swam and played rugger, and rowed for the school. We went to watch him in an 'eight' at Roundhay Park, and on the river at Durham.

Many memories surround his illness: our fear and sadness when I watched Shirley and him drive off in an ambulance from our home, bound for Great Ormond Street; his guts at going back to school while still in a wheelchair; our joy when he first took some steps, at Sandsend later that autumn when we'd gone for a week's holiday: and his guts at telling me he could not go back to Sedbergh, knowing that I'd planned for him go there, and wanted to return to St Peter's. That illness was frightful but one positive thing was it matured him and gave him insights into suffering in other people, which I guess have stood him in good stead. As he grew older we have become good buddies. We go fell walking together, and play tennis and squash together, and he has been a great support during my fall from grace.

Melanie was a bright little girl, who could infuriate her brother at times by telling him, unasked, the answers to some school homework at which he was stuck. She got a bit bored with York College for Girls in her teens and got a Sixth Form Scholarship to St Peter's when they started taking girls. It was very good for her. She excelled at fives, and she became a good friend as she matured.

When Shirley's parents retired to Buckden we used to go up there for holidays to stay with them. I would take each of the children on a fell walk, one at a time, to suit their age and strength. Melanie and I (we called her Mo) walked once up into the deer park and the high ground over the river. It was springtime and some rams, no doubt frustrated, were in the field, kept separate from their lambing partners. When they saw us walking along, three of them charged us, heads down. I picked Melanie up and waited for them. Happily they stopped a few feet from us, looked slightly embarrassed, and started to crop the grass, letting us walk on! I remember Mo sledging; Mo on the beach at Sandsend, the three of them dressed identically in red and white stripey beach tunics, digging. Then she went to university and ran the Fives Club! I was very proud when she won the doubles cup in the Women's Fives Tournament that we set up in the eighties.

One big regret is that I was unable to see Shirley receive her degree in York Minster in 2004. Her Majesty required my presence elsewhere!

Well, 'to think I did all that – and now I've reached the final curtain.'

We have certainly travelled each and every byway. Which byways shall we return to before we get rowed across the Styx to oblivion or immortality? I must stand again on La Coupée between Sark and Petit Sark and watch a sunset over the islands. I must walk the back streets of Venice and drink coffee overlooking the Grand Canal. I must walk through Portmeirion and dine at the hotel; walk on the Heath in Surrey, and on the beach at Whitby. I must stand on the slopes of Winder on a fine day in a fresh wind and look down on the town and the school which formed so much of my character and life. I shall go back to the Cross Keys and breakfast looking across to the great water spout at Cautley, and read Tim Birdsall's poem; and weep. 'We are forgotten, but we still remember you.'

I have seen the glaciers of Greenland, the Canyon in Kawaii, Niagara, the Gullfoss, the Pyramids of Egypt; stood to receive my doctorate at the Senate House in Cambridge, and my Master's degree in theology in the Great Hall at Leeds University. I have taken my marriage vows (how easily they can be destroyed in a moment's foolishness) in the beautiful Priory Church of St Bartholomew the Great, West Smithfield; dined in the presence of the monarch; received the Freedom of the City of London; and looked out of a cell window in Leeds prison; been accused in the Crown Court of rape, been arrested and taken to a cell in York, and had my name erased from the List of Fellows in London and Glasgow.

Well, here I am still.

What shall be the hymns at my funeral?

> O love that will not let me go
> I rest my weary soul on thee
> I give thee back the life I owe
> That in thine ocean's depths its flow
> May richer, fuller, be.

and 'The day thou gavest, Lord, is ended'. And we'll have 'Lord of all hopefulness' perhaps too. I'd like Sullivan's *In Memoriam* playing as my coffin goes in. And perhaps Michael can read one of my poems, as he so movingly read one of my mother's at her funeral. Mother, unlike the doll of her poem, could not be 'mended' and at the last nor will I. What will be my epitaph? Well, I've written one:

> Have no sad thoughts for me;
> Smile – do not mourn for me:
> Just keep my memory
> Now I am gone.

That will do.

Appendix

A poem by Tim Birdsall

Sedbergh Revisited

Let me sit here in the sunlight. Let me rest awhile and sigh
Let me dream, and so remember how the years have hurried by;
Leave behind the city's squalor, all its mad disease and pain
Close my eyes, and feel my boyhood live within my heart again.
Let me stand again on Winder, in the magic summer breeze,
Feel once more the stones and heather; watch the bracken and the trees.
Let me see again the river, and the fields and walls and farms,
Sedbergh, let me feel you near me. Let me take you in my arms.
Here I lived and laughed and loved you when the world was fair and new
In your heart I lie forgotten; yet I still remember you.
Crook & Quaker, Dent & Dovecote, Lilymere and Wild Boar Fell
Calf, Killington and Cautley – I remember you so well.
There the rugger posts are standing, as they did so long ago,
And those ancient solemn buildings where the scholars come and go.
There the church and there the chapel in whose peace I learned to pray
Where the ghosts and hymns still linger in the shadows cool and grey
Where I hear my boyhood calling, calling to me soft and clear
With the beauty, with the freshness of a soul which is sincere.
Here I learned of truth and honour – grew to cherish and obey
All those fine ideals of goodness; which are gone from me today.
Here I dreamed my dreams of greatness; built my castles in the sky
Now that they are wrecked and ruined, let me rest awhile and sigh.
Let me call you, my companion, call you back to me and find
If you too are changed and different from the boys we left behind.
Laugh with me once more; remember all the happy things we knew.
Seek with me those golden memories which I buried here with you.
Are you there – and do you listen as I lightly call your name?
Will I know you still and love you, will your face be still the same?
Do you sigh with me in sorrow; do you brush away a tear
As you seek in vain those treasures, old and infinitely dear?
They are dim, and dark and dusty, for the years have passed them by
Here amid the evening sunlight, let us find them, you and I.
I remember other evenings in the summer, when we'd climb
On the slippery side of Winder, and would laugh away the time
Shout and sing in exultation with the fresh and fragrant breeze

Run and jump amongst the bracken, tousled hair and dirty knees
Flying limbs – and sparkling laughter, and our happy faces shone
We were happy: we were happy! We were young – and we are gone.
We are vanished and forgotten in the mists of many yeas
Dead the vital surging spirit; fled the hopes and dreams and fears
But the heart can yet remember as the gentle shadows fall
And softly in the stillness hear the voice of memory call
Calling, calling, in the sunshine, in the wind and in the rain
Come you back – come back to Sedbergh! Come and find your youth again.

A poem by my mother, Edna Beatrice Oldfield

Spring

A whisper is blown by the breeze,
A whisper that summer is near.
A message from over the seas,
A message that brings good cheer.
How many glad hearts will rejoice?
How many will long for its days?
Not a bird with silvery voice
Will forget to sing its praise.
For blossom of every hue
Will be dotted o'er landscapes green
While the stream with sparkles new
Through wood and field will gleam.
No heart should be dull or grey
For songsters will fill the air
With ditties both blithe and gay
And melodies rich and rare.

A poem by my son Michael

Have you got what you really want?

And you – who appointed you to judge?
Clamouring above the machinery of life;
Is your body above sin?
Your mind clear above the din.
You seek an end to this world of strife
        Of this world . . .
Imperfect as a shattered illusion:
        This world,
Veiled by its own delusion,
And yet, from your self-appointed pedestal
You denounce and scream,
Shattered now from your one perfect dream
        Evil systems in your eye

Your will to destroy
For them to die,
Then, mistake not who you force to death.

A selection of my poems

Stolen Night

Coy and shy: A new adventure
Trembling lips that dare to meet,
Fallen garments, carpet scattered
Lie unfolded at their feet.
First caresses hesitating
Each one for the other waits;
Taste of powder; smell of perfume
Mingle, as they seal their fates
Longing to possess each other
Arms entwined and close together
Hot excitement; sense of rapture
Trembling muscles wait for capture.
Downy hair, and warm sweet breath,
Beating heart – heaving breast,
Stronger love the two creating
By this first idyllic making.
Daylight comes now, slow and softly
Traffic's noise begins to mount
But for lovers, still and peaceful,
Only stolen night will count.

La Retourne

Il est mort, l'amour que j'ai eu
Cette fille, pas encore je la vois;
Cette bouche, que j'ai écrasé
Cette forme, que j'embrassais,
Il est allé – tout
Un jour, dans le soir,
Quand j'attendrai
Elle retournera
Donc, tout sera mieux
Tout sera beau; une réincarnation
Nous continuons, une immortalité, un éternité
L'amour se vive, maintenant.

Banged Up

A living death, with empty grave
And empty life, that goes from day to day

Pointless in its meaning.
Grieving for what is lost
Fearful for what may come;
Resigned; obedient to every whim
That regulations may dictate.

A pallid skin, on which sun rarely gazes
A pallid mind, on which moon's shifting phases
Have but little impact
Seen through thick barred windows;
Viewed through slitted doors
By guards who shout commands
Uncaring of one's fate.

Offence now has no meaning;
All are guilty and condemned;
Labelled inmate – convict – shamed.
Claimed innocence is denial
Of findings at the trial
By jury who with no concern
Return; to bring their verdict.

A dirty cell: a hell
Of linen stained by those
Who went before. Graffiti;
To record forgotten men
Whose life was put on hold so that society might feel
A sense of justice done –
Retribution – and vengeance now complete.

MTH – on his mother

Old Age

The thing I dread is to fall from bed
And land upon the floor.
But I know the carer will come through
She only sleeps next door.
But maybe she won't hear me –
Hear my frightened call;
And perhaps my leg is broken
If it were an awkward fall.
One feels so very vulnerable
When one gets old and frail.
I try my best to keep my health
But all to no avail.
My back's osteoporotic

My fingers shake and tremble
I tend to dribble at the mouth;
I conceal it and dissemble.
I used to be so smart and clean
When I was young and proud,
But now my jumper's in a mess
And if I'm with a crowd
Of friends; or kin; or helpers
Embarrassment must show.
My daughter feels ashamed of me –
Because I'm tired and slow.
I really am a broken reed.
I've lived too long, I know
The family don't like this talk
They speak of other things.
They remind me of the past,
The war; my school; my wedding ring.
But I really can't be bothered,
I do not see the need. I've even lost the
Will to feed – I wish that I could go.

Love's Old Sweet Song
(Just a song at twilight)

Once in the dear dead days beyond recall
When on the world the mists began to fall
Out of the dreams, that rose in happy throng
Low to our hearts, love sang an old sweet song
And in the dusk, where fell the firelight gleam
Softly it wove itself into our dream.

Just a song, at twilight
When the lights are low
And the flickering shadows
Softly come and go;
Though the heart be weary,
Sad the day and long,
Still to us at twilight
Comes love's old song;
Comes love's old, sweet song.

Even today we hear love's song of yore
Deep in our hearts it dwells for evermore
Footsteps may falter; weary grow the way
Still, we can hear it at the close of day.
So till the end, when life's dim shadows fall
Love will be found the sweetest song of all.

Index